SOUTHERN SIGNALS

Stories of innovation, challenge and triumph in Australia's communication history

PMG

SOUTHERN SIGNALS

Stories of innovation, challenge and triumph in Australia's communication history

HUGH TRANTER

Published by National Library of Australia Publishing
Canberra ACT 2600

ISBN: 9781922507563

The National Library of Australia acknowledges Australia's First Nations Peoples—the First Australians—as the Traditional Owners and Custodians of this land and gives respect to the Elders—past and present—and through them to all Australian Aboriginal and Torres Strait Islander people.

First Nations Peoples are advised this book contains depictions and names of deceased people. It contains content that may be considered culturally sensitive or distressing, including accounts of massacres perpetrated on First Nations Peoples.

Publisher: Lauren Smith
Managing editor: Amelia Hartney
Editor: John Mapps
Designer: Stan Lamond
Image coordinator: Jemma Posch
Printed in China by Everbest Printing Co. Ltd on FSC®-certified paper

Find out more about NLA Publishing at nla.gov.au/national-library-publishing.

Author note:

I acknowledge the Traditional Owners of the land on which I stand. I acknowledge the people of all the First Nations and pay my respects to Elders past and present.

This book was written on Gadigal Country and produced on Ngunnawal and Ngambri Country.

A catalogue record for this book is available from the National Library of Australia

Contents

Introduction

In 1746, a French monk and physicist, Jean-Antoine Nollet, decided to conduct an experiment. He assembled 700 fellow monks in a line, forming a human chain of about half a mile (800 metres). Promising vats of red wine to his nervous volunteers as a reward, he asked them all to pick up a long wire. Once they all had hold of the wire, he attached the end to a Leyden jar, a type of early battery. Along the line, monk after monk almost simultaneously received a jolt as the electricity ran through their bodies. Voila! Nollet had shown that an electric current can travel a long distance at high speed through a metal conductor.

Since early history, people have sought to communicate faster than their feet would carry them, or ship, carriage or horseback bear them. From relaying messages via smoke signals and beacons, to the sounding of horns or bells, people found ways to send messages some distance—but were always seeking ways to send messages further and more quickly.

By the mid-eighteenth century, humanity was on the cusp of great discoveries in communications, discoveries that would allow messages to travel around the world within hours, minutes, and then seconds. But these experiments were meaningless to the colony of New South Wales. When Governor Arthur Phillip wrote to London in 1788, pleading for more supplies for the struggling new penal settlement at Sydney Cove, it took almost two years for his request and London's response to complete the round trip of 24,000 kilometres by sea.

Those who arrived on Australian shores in 1788 and after soon learned of the importance of communications. Whether it was scratching with a pen, tapping on a telegraph transmitter or speaking through a telephone, they knew they needed communications to work across vast distances. They were quick to adapt new technologies. There was much information they needed—about government, weather, politics—and even more

The nineteenth and twentieth centuries saw an unprecedented level of global invention in communication technology. Here, three wireless telephone operators connect calls at a switchboard in Sydney in around 1930.

information they wanted—letters and messages from loved ones and news from faraway places.

This book tells the stories of new inventions in communication technology during key moments in Australia's history, including the use of wireless radio by Sir Douglas Mawson in Antarctica, the deadly business of being a signalman during World War I, the life-and-death communications of search and rescue, and the role of Australian receiver stations during the Moon landing of July 1969.

The book also examines more recent developments: the introduction of the internet in the 1990s, and the risks and challenges brought about by new waves of technology in the twenty-first century.

1

'The ships sail tomorrow'

Sending news to, from and around a big country

Dodging rotten tomatoes was an occupational hazard for eighteenth-century actors. In 1789, a London performer knew he or she could cop a piece of fruit in the face if the crowd was displeased. After a day's work, Londoners loved nothing better than to descend on the theatre. On 20 April 1789, a typically rowdy crowd arrived at the popular venue of the Royal Circus in St George's Fields (near Hanover Square in the heart of London), to watch a program that included 'a new dance (composed by Mr. Holland) called *The New Hollanders*. With an exact Representation of the Landing of the Convicts at Botany Bay'.[1]

The actors would have sought to extract the exotic and the satirical from what they knew of the first days of the penal settlement on the far side of the world. News of the safe arrival of the First Fleet at Botany Bay in January 1788 had come to London just over a month before. Newspapers were full of reports. Britain now knew that Commodore Arthur Phillip had guided 11 ships safely to Botany Bay, then relocated the settlement to Sydney Cove, disgorging over 750 of their exiled countrymen and women and 250 of their gaolers onto this faraway soil. Perhaps the writers of this theatrical skit had read reports that the going was hard, the Indigenous people avoided the new settlers, the soil was poor, some of the convicts were not suitable for hard work, and a convict had been executed for stealing food.

So how to grab the audience's attention? Dress the convicts in rags? Have them bemoan their lot as they step ashore? Cast the actors with villainous looks and sprinkle their dialogue with criminal flash talk? Fill the stage with strange trees and bushes? Dress actors up as kangaroos that hop across the stage? The imagination boggles. What we do know is, after a long and arduous voyage, Sydney Cove and Botany Bay had become a part of British consciousness. It had not been an easy journey.

Nine months earlier, on Monday 14 July 1788, four of the transport ships that had taken the convicts of the First Fleet to their place of exile in New South Wales departed Sydney Cove to return to England. These were the *Alexander*, *Prince of Wales*, *Borrowdale* and *Friendship*, under the

Following pages: Among the transports that would depart from Sydney Cove later that year, *Prince of Wales* and *Borrowdale* would return to the United Kingdom first.

command of Lieutenant John Shortland, Agent for Transports. Although three other transport ships, the *Charlotte, Scarborough* and *Lady Penrhyn,* had departed from Sydney Cove in May 1788, they were not sailing directly to England, heading first to China.

Watching the ships leave, the convicts and their gaolers must have felt Sydney Cove the loneliest place in the world. Their place of exile was a patchwork of raw clearings and half-built huts clinging to the shores—a long way from the familiar sights of bustling London and the picturesque villages of rural Britain.

It was now a year since they had sailed from Portsmouth in May 1787. Britain was 10,000 miles (16,000 kilometres) away as the crow flies. The

A view of the settlement at Sydney Cove on 20 August 1788, based on a sketch by Captain John Hunter, of the HMS *Sirius*.

colony was already short of food. Supplies had been ruined by weather and vermin; livestock had run away or died. To steal supplies brought a sentence of death. The very clothes on the backs of convict and marine alike were starting to rot away.

As bad as things were, they were going to get worse. It would be almost two years before any further help would come from England. The colony was on its knees, and help arrived only just in time.

Getting the message through

Sitting in his makeshift canvas-and-timber headquarters on the eastern bank of Sydney Cove, a worried Governor Phillip wrote his dispatches to the secretary of state, Lord Sydney, together with a range of other people in government. Phillip had overseen the painful process of settlement in an alien landscape, but as the *Prince of Wales, Borrowdale, Friendship* and *Alexander* prepared to leave, he knew he had to grasp the opportunity to call for help.[2] The stores brought with the First Fleet were meant to last at least two years, allowing time for crops to grow and the colony to become self-sufficient, but early crops had failed. He was also worried that the penal colony was not going to be a priority of the British Government; it was out of sight and out of mind. There were many precedents for settlements being abandoned, left to fend for themselves or evacuated. The nineteenth-century Australian historian G.B. Barton, in his book *History of NSW from the Records*, devoted a section—'Deserted Colonies'—to the subject.[3]

It was in a similar state of mind that Captain Watkin Tench of the marines also prepared a document to be taken with the transports. It was a hefty folder of papers, the manuscript for *A Narrative of the Expedition to Botany Bay*. He hoped the publisher he had had discussions with back in Britain, Debrett's, would receive and look favourably on his record of the fleet's journey to New Holland and the first days of the penal colony.

Following pages: The first published map of Sydney Cove, which appeared in July 1789, is attributed to former navy midshipman Francis Fowkes, transported for seven years for theft.

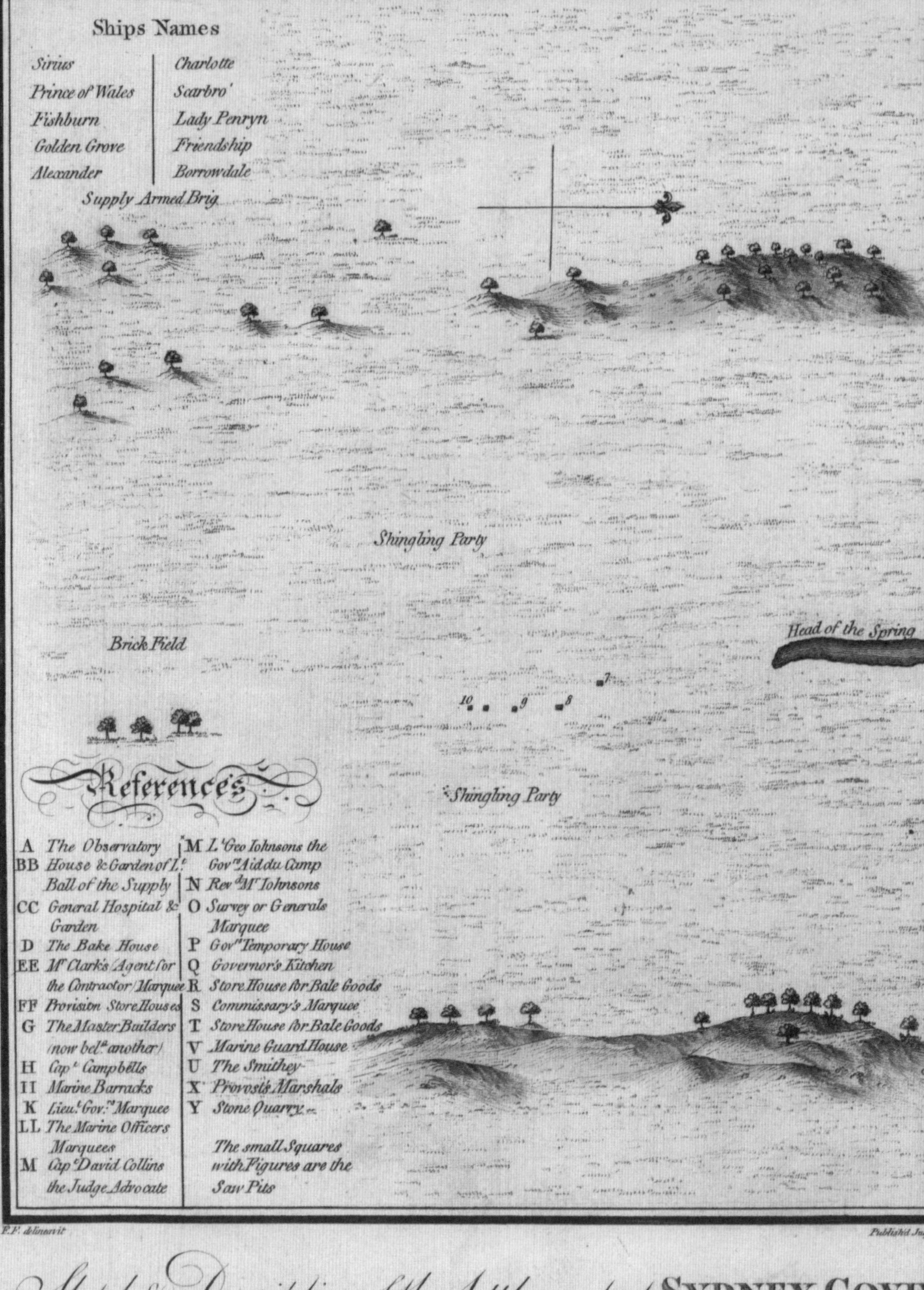
Ships Names
Sirius
Prince of Wales
Fishburn
Golden Grove
Alexander
Charlotte
Scarbro'
Lady Penryn
Friendship
Borrowdale
Supply Armed Brig
Shingling Party
Head of the Spring
Brick Field
7
10
9
8
Shingling Party
References
A The Observatory
BB House & Garden of Lt Ball of the Supply
CC General Hospital & Garden
D The Bake House
EE Mr Clark's (Agent for the Contractor) Marquee
FF Provision Store Houses
G The Master Builders (now belg another)
H Capt Campbells
II Marine Barracks
K Lieut Govrs Marquee
LL The Marine Officers Marquees
M Capt David Collins the Judge Advocate
M Lt Geo Iohnsons the Govrs Aid du Camp
N Revd Mr Iohnsons
O Survey or Generals Marquee
P Govrs Temporary House
Q Governor's Kitchen
R Store House for Bale Goods
S Commissary's Marquee
T Store House for Bale Goods
V Marine Guard House
U The Smithey
X Provost Marshals
Y Stone Quarry
The small Squares with Figures are the Saw Pits
F.F. delineavit
Publish'd Ja
Sketch & Description of the Settlement at SYDNEY COVE

Nº 258 High Holborn

Neele sculpt Strand

T JACKSON *in the* COUNTY *of* CUMBERLAND *taken*

The four ships that were about to depart became the custodians of a huge amount of material: numerous letters (official and unofficial), samples of flora, fauna and soil, drawings and artefacts. The period of the Enlightenment in Europe had led to European societies developing a rapacious appetite for artefacts from the world's civilisations.[4] Indigenous tools and weapons were highly prized, contributing to violent conflict between European colonisers and indigenous people.

When it came to the long-term future of the settlement, Phillip and Tench were both optimistic. With a world-class harbour and a healthy climate, they believed the settlement had great potential. Someone who did not share their view, and who had fallen out with Phillip, was the aloof and difficult commander of the marines, Major Robert Ross. In a letter to the British under-secretary of state, Lord Nepean, Ross wrote:

> *I do not scruple to pronounce that in the whole world there is not a worse country than what we have yet seen of this. All that is contiguous to us is so very barren and forbidding that it may with truth be said, here Nature is reversed.*[5]

Phillip knew Ross' views, and understood that both British public opinion and government decisions could be fickle. But he was bullish, and wrote to Lord Sydney:

> *nor do I doubt but that this country will prove the most valuable acquisition Great Britain ever made; at the same time no country offers less assistance to the first settlers than this does.*[6]

Phillip ended his letter by apologising for its lack of structure:

> *Your Lordship will, I hope, excuse the confused manner in which I have in this letter given an account of what has passed since I left the Cape of Good Hope. It has been written at different times, and my situation at present does not permit me to begin so long a letter again, the canvas house I am under being neither wind nor water proof.*

On 14 July, all was done, and the ships sailed out through the sandstone heads of Port Jackson and into the Pacific Ocean. Their departure left the settlement more isolated and alone than ever before.

London hears the news

On 22 March 1789, the *Prince of Wales* sailed into the deep-sea port of Falmouth in Cornwall, the first of the First Fleet ships to return after a very rough journey. The surviving crew were back on British soil after being absent for almost two years, but the presence of the ship went unremarked among the busy shipping port.

Over the next few days, letters and packages began to arrive in London. In Britain's capital, the nerve centre of the fledgling British Empire, news of the settlement was received, digested and then quickly circulated. Australian historian David Andrew Roberts describes Britain at this time as 'a society at the forefront of European enlightenment and modernity—the tangent of a nation rapidly reshaping itself through revolutions in science and industry, energised by innovation and inquiry'.[7]

London was also the seat of a growing empire, despite England's loss of the United States of America in 1776. Many newspaper and book publishers were located in London, and the city's status as the seat of government stimulated a thirst for information. The pace of life in the city in 1789 was probably similar to that of a twenty-first century capital. News may not have travelled as fast as it does today, but it came and went in large volume.

If Britain had forgotten about the First Fleet up to now, the arrival of the transport ships with their news sparked a new wave of interest and commentary. Newspapers were full of news summaries.

One of the first people who received news from the *Prince of Wales* was Sir Joseph Banks. Banks had inherited a significant fortune and estates when still a young man, which had allowed him to accompany Captain Cook on his journey to observe the transit of Venus in Tahiti, and to conduct surveys and discoveries in the Southern Hemisphere. He advocated to the British Government for the settlement at Botany Bay, and would continue to be actively engaged in the colony's affairs up to the time of his death in 1820.

Among Banks' papers in the State Library of New South Wales are two pages of notes in Banks' hand about the new settlement. It is not known for sure where Banks got the information from, but it is possible that Samuel Moore, who had taken over command of the *Prince of Wales* following the death of its captain from scurvy en route, travelled to London and had an interview with the man who was so influential in the establishment of the colony.

The notes provide a fascinating insight into some of the key events of the colony's founding. 'Prince of Wales: Captain Samuel Moore' is the heading on the first page. Under it:

> *John White, surgeon, complains of the lack of* [supplies?] *to aid the operation of the hospices such as blankets for the hospital, sugar, soap, barley, rice, oatmeal, currents, spices, vinegar, portable soup.*

Following this are short notes on different aspects of the new colony:

> *This Colony must for some years depend on supplies from England ... The Sirius will be sent to the northward for livestock ... A convict who fled to the woods returned in 10 days ... he said the natives were dying of famine ... 3 convicts executed for theft ... Port Jackson is a very fine harbour three leagues north of Botany Bay.*[8]

With the arrival of the *Prince of Wales* and the *Borrowdale*, book publishers swung into action. On 28 March 1789 (days after the ships' arrival), an advertisement appeared in *The World* newspaper: 'In a few days will be published: A Narrative of the Expedition to Botany Bay. By Captain Tench of the Marines. Printed by Debrett'. Tench's manuscript, of which he had presumably had at least one copy made, had been rushed to Debrett's offices in Piccadilly. When published, it became an instant success, with editions also released in French, German, Dutch and Swedish.

Later accounts of the colony from Governor Phillip, surgeon John White and judge-advocate Lieutenant David Collins would all prove enormously popular. Tench's follow-up, *A Complete Account of the Settlement at Port Jackson*, would also become a bestseller and be translated into many languages.

Opposite page: Sir Joseph Banks was eager for information about the establishment of the penal colony at Sydney Cove and wrote these notes after information arrived on the *Prince of Wales*.

Prince of Wales
Captn John Mason

Sidney Cove Port Jackson July 4 1788. 11

John White Surgeon complains of the want of necessaries to aid the operation of medicines as Blankets for the hospital, Sugar Sago Barley Rice Oatmeal Currants spices vinegar Portable Soup Tamarinds

Governor Phillip July 5.

~~Botany Bay~~ Rio de Janeiro
. a stock in spirits at ~~Botany Bay~~ Rio de Janeiro & serves to soldiers wives as well as soldiers the Flax plant is found & cost nothing Sheep do not thrive

July 10
on the 9th 20 natives came down to the boat & took by force the Fish that had been taken in the Sein orders had been given that a share should always be delivered to them on their asking for it a box of letters from Perouse

Acc^t of live stock May 1st

1 Stallion 3 mares 3 Colts 2 Bulls 5 Cows 29 sheep 19 Goats 49 hogs 25 pigs 5 Rabbits 18 Turkeys 29 geese 35 Ducks 122 fowls 87 chickens

3 Sheep dead & the Cows & Bulls lost Sheep thrive ill here

July 9
This Colony must for some years depend on supplies from England, the Sirius will be sent to the northward for live stock & an Isle called by Perouse des navigateurs, the Lieut Govr has about 4 acres in Cultivation I have 8 or 10 in Wheat & Barley the officers will raise enough to maintain their live stock all the corn we shall raise this & the next year must be saved for seed if necessity should oblige us to use it it will give but a few days support to the Colony there are many Shots the Crops are uncertain they have had much thunder & lightning some trees have been riven ~~[illegible]~~ & sheep
& hogs killed in the Camp most of the stock brought from the Cape is dead & all the governors sheep the cows have been missing 3 weeks supposed to be killed by the natives the horses do well

The officers decline ~~all~~ government of the Convicts & think it a hardship to sit in the Criminal Court as they are not paid for it & have been told, if 50 farmers & their Families were sent it would do more to render the Colony independent than 1000 Convicts 3 Convicts have been killed by the natives probably there are 1500 in Bot. Bay port Jackson & Broken bay. Cloths bad, axes & Tools as bad as possible, part of the Corn from England has been destroyed by the weevil, the rest is in good Condition

a shock of an Earthquake on June 22 afternoon slight lasted a few seconds attended with noise like a loud Cannon shot

the Climate is Fine night Cold 38 degrees variation between 8 in

Disturbing reports about the penal colony were common in private letters. Some of these reports reached the newspapers.[9] A few months after the arrival of the first ships, a female convict's letter was published in a regional newspaper. The letter may have been sent with the *Fishburn* and the *Golden Grove*—the last two transports to depart Sydney Cove—both of which left on 19 November 1788. The unknown writer had, perhaps, a predisposition to pessimism, but her words reflect the feeling of being disenfranchised, exiled and left with little hope:

> *I take the first opportunity that has been given us to acquaint you with our disconsolate situation in this solitary waste of creation ... we have now two streets ... if four rows of the most miserable huts you can possibly conceive deserve that name.*[10]

The writer goes on to say:

> *As for the distresses of the women, they are past description, as they are deprived of tea and other things they were indulged in in the voyage, by the seamen; and as they are totally unprovided with clothes, those who have young children are quite wretched. Besides this, though a number of marriages have taken place, several women, who became pregnant on the voyage, and are since left by their partners, who have returned to England, are not likely even here to form any fresh connections. We are comforted with the hopes of a supply of tea from China. The separation of us to an uninhabited island* [Norfolk Island?] *was like a second transportation. In short, every one is so taken up with their own misfortunes that they have no pity to bestow on others. All our letters are examined by an officer, but a friend takes this for me privately. The ships sail tomorrow.*

Despite such negative views, Phillip's dispatches sufficiently encouraged the Admiralty to send a Second Fleet to Port Jackson with more convicts and supplies. The first ship, the *Lady Juliana*, sailed in July 1789.

The journey of the Second Fleet was far more traumatic for the convicts than that of the First Fleet, with almost one in four dying as a result of the poor arrangements made for their health on the trip to Sydney Cove. But the ships also carried crucial stores and news for Phillip. That very human commodity, information, had completed its journey around the globe and back.

Meanwhile, in Sydney

By June 1790, Phillip was struggling to keep the settlement from starving. No news had been received from Britain. Clothes were rotting, and despair had taken hold of many of the convicts and their guards. There was almost nothing to link them to their homeland. In a kind of reverse form of communication, they clung to the artefacts brought with them from their birthplace: books and newspapers and other reminders of their home and culture.

In their 1988 article, 'Bound for Botany Bay', librarians Colin Steele and Michael Richards sought to identify the surviving books brought to Australia with the First Fleet.[11] They found at least one Bible, held at St Philip's Church in Sydney, although it is known there were a good many

A western view of Sydney Cove in 1979, painted in England by Edward Dayes likely after a drawing by Scottish artist and convict Thomas Watling, who arrived in the colony in 1792.

The English press was fascinated by the penal colony but often played on satirical notions involving convicts, a long way from the reality of their harsh circumstances.

other Bibles, New Testaments and tracts brought by the humane and conscientious Reverend Richard Johnson, the chaplain of the First Fleet. Lieutenant George Johnston brought *The Annals of Agriculture* and volume one and volumes three to eight of the 1753 Edinburgh reprint of *The Spectator* (which no doubt helped with educational and recreational reading). Another item he brought was the *Discourse of Epic Poetry of the Excellence of the Poem of Telemachus*, which was inscribed by Johnston 'Norfolk Island 1790'.

While many of the marines and convicts could not read or write, a significant number could. The late eighteenth century was a boom period for publishing, and a growing reading public would have been reflected in the members of the First Fleet. Drama was particularly popular, alongside fiction and travel collections. Author Thomas Keneally novelised the convict performance of George Farquhar's popular drama *The Recruiting Officer*—held in honour of the King's birthday at Sydney Cove on 4 June 1789—in his 1987 book *The Playmaker*.

It is difficult to ascertain what other literature the First Fleet brought. Captain Watkin Tench, for example, could quote Milton's *Paradise Lost* from memory, and therefore it is unclear if he had a copy with him for reference. Tench also quoted often from Shakespeare and Latin and Greek classics. And he had a good grounding in contemporary English and French literature, some editions of which he must have brought out with him. Oliver Goldsmith's *Deserted Village*, for example, was a favourite.

In the end, though, these small items were of only temporary comfort and were meaningless to most convicts. By the start of June, the colony was in despair. But things were about to change. Watkin Tench recorded the arrival of the *Lady Juliana*, on 3 June:

I was sitting in my hut, musing on our fate, when a confused clamour in the street drew my attention. I opened my door, and saw several women with children in their arms running to and fro with distracted looks, congratulating each other, and kissing their infants with the most passionate and extravagant marks of fondness ...

A few minutes completed our wishes, and we found ourselves on board the Lady Juliana transport, with two hundred and twenty-five of our country women whom crime or misfortune had condemned to exile ... We continued to ask a thousand questions on a breath ... 'Letters, letters!' was the cry. They were produced, and torn open in trembling agitation. News burst on us like meridian splendour on a blind man. We were overwhelmed with it: public, private, general and particular ... We now heard for the first time of our sovereign's illness, and his happy restoration to health. The French revolution of 1789, with all the attendant circumstances of that wonderful and unexpected event, succeeded to amaze us.[12]

The ship's arrival revived the colony. Historian Geoffrey Blainey writes:

News of her arrival was signalled from the long-idle flagstaff [at South Head]*, and passed from mouth to mouth until it reached the hungry men hoeing hungry ground at the most distant clearing. Within a few days her letters and newspapers from England and, above all, a little of her flour were ashore. The famine was over.*[13]

In the coming days, other ships of the Second Fleet arrived. First communications with Britain had been established. Sydney Cove was on the map. On 20 June, there was more rejoicing when the store ship the *Justinian* arrived at Sydney Cove. Mr Benjamin Maitland, its master, had managed the trip efficiently, with a fast passage of only five months.[14] The arrival of the Second Fleet, however, would bring an unexpected focus on the conditions for convicts.

We can only imagine where the young female convict was when she wrote the letter that would later be published throughout England. Perhaps she sat on a log by her tent in the late afternoon sun to write it. She had stepped off the *Lady Juliana* only three weeks earlier. Here is an extract from the letter she penned to an unknown recipient:[15]

> *We arrived here safe after a long voyage, in very good health, thanks to our good agent on board ... as we had every thing that we could expect from them, and all our provisions were good. We landed here 223 women and 12 children; only three women died, and one child; five or six were born on board the ship; they had great care taken of them ...*
>
> *This place was in a very starving condition before we arrived, and on allowance of only 2lb of flour, and 2lb of pork for each man for a week, and these were almost starved ... and the ground won't grow any thing, only in spots here and there; there is a place called Rose Hill, about twenty miles from this, where they say there are four corn fields ... we have hardly any cloaths; but since the Scarborough, Neptune and Surprize arrived, we have had a blanket and a rug given us.*[16]

She then wrote the lines that would cause a sensation:

> *Oh! if you had but seen the shocking sight of the poor creatures that came out in the three ships, it would make your heart bleed; they were almost dead; very few could stand, and they were obliged to sling them as you would goods; and hoist them out of* [the] *ship, they were so feeble; and they died ten or twelve of a day when they first landed; but some of them are getting better; there died in their way here on board the Neptune, 183 men and 12 women, and in the Scarborough 67 men, and in the Surprize 85; they were not so long as we were in coming here, but they were confined and had bad victuals and drinking water; the Governor was very angry, and scolded the Captains a great deal, and I heard intended to write to London about it; for I heard him say it was murdering them—it to be sure was a melancholy sight.*

A *trompe l'oeil* letter rack showing newspapers, notes, a quill pen, a penknife, a stick of red sealing wax and a tortoiseshell comb.

The letter written, she addressed it and sought out the sailor who had promised to take it back to England on her behalf. Then she likely returned to her duties.

It was a very long way from Sydney Cove to the newspaper offices in London, but the letter eventually got there. It appeared in the British press in a number of newspapers as an 'extract of a letter from one of the women convicts that sailed from England in the *Lady Juliana*'.[17] Dated Sydney Cove, Port Jackson, 24 July 1790, it first appeared in *The Diary, or, Woodfall's Register* on 3 August 1791.[18]

But who had the female convict addressed her letter to? To try to answer that, we need to look at the link between the publishers of the newspaper in which it first appeared and a colourful British aristocrat.

The Diary, or, Woodfall's Register was owned and edited by the brothers Henry and William Woodfall. The Woodfalls leaned politically towards the Whig party, which was in opposition at the time (the Tory Party under Pitt the Younger was in power and had made the decision to send the First Fleet to Botany Bay). The Woodfalls were also proprietors and editors of another newspaper, the London-based *Public Advertiser.* On 23 July 1791, two weeks before the appearance of the letter about the arrival of the Second Fleet, the following appeared in the *Public Advertiser*:

> *Yesterday Lord George Gordon received accounts from Botany Bay, containing very dismal intelligence. Many of the women convicts who went out in the Lady Juliana were drowned in their removal from Sidney Cove to Norfolk Island. The sickness that was reported to have carried off vast numbers of the men convicts, in other ships, is confirmed. The lists, containing the names of the women, and their different fates, would be too voluminous for a newspaper. Government, no doubt, are acquainted with the unhappy fate of the settlement, as the young man, who brought the news, went out in the Lady Juliana, and has been in town for some days.*[19]

Perhaps the 'accounts' received by Gordon included the convict's letter, which he gave to the Woodfalls for publication.

Another piece of evidence supports a relationship between Lord George Gordon and some of the female convicts aboard the *Lady Juliana*.

It is provided to us by the sailor John Nicol in his account of the voyage of the *Lady Juliana* to New South Wales:

> *We had one Mary Williams, transported for receiving stolen goods. She and other eight had been a long time in Newgate where Lord George Gordon had supported them. I went once a week to him and got their allowance from his own hand all the time we lay in the river.*[20]

Born in London in 1751 and educated at Eton, Lord George Gordon joined the navy where he rose to the rank of lieutenant. He fell out with his superiors in the navy when he argued for improvements to the conditions of the sailors. In 1774, he entered parliament and in 1779 organised the Protestant Association, formed to secure the repeal of the *Catholic Relief Act* of 1778. On 2 June 1780, he led a protest to the Houses of Parliament to present a petition against the Act. The protest turned into a very serious riot, with the mob getting out of control for several days, destroying several Catholic chapels, breaking open prisons and attacking the Bank of England. The military eventually quelled the riots, during which 450 people were killed or wounded. Tried for high treason, Gordon was acquitted, thanks to a skilful defence, on the grounds that he had no treasonable intentions.

Gordon's life 'was a succession of unlikely political and financial schemes'.[21] He was a political loose cannon, a champion of causes, and someone of whom the establishment must have been very wary after the events of 1780. Some, however, saw Lord Gordon as a revolutionary social activist: he opposed the death penalty and argued tirelessly for the rights of the poor and dislocated. He was a staunch opponent of transportation to New South Wales.

Despite his earlier acquittal, Lord Gordon did end up an inmate of Newgate gaol in London from 1788 up to his death from typhoid in that prison in 1793. He had been convicted in 1787 of libelling the Queen of France. His wealth allowed him to live in relative comfort in the gaol, and he was known to have a wide circle of friends and acquaintances within the prison walls.[22]

However it came to be published, the female convict's letter was neither the first nor the only news in Britain of the Second Fleet.

Paper and pen

When Governor Arthur Phillip wrote his first dispatch to the Admiralty in Britain from Sydney Cove in 1788, he would have likely laid his hands on paper and pen produced in England. Paper was manufactured across the country, although paper-hungry London was already becoming the focal point of production.

Paper was produced in workshop settings by mixing cotton or rags with water. The mix was pulped in a machine called a 'beating engine'. Once pulped, it was transferred to a large vat and a 'vatman' would place a mould in the mix and fill it with pulp. The vatman then passed the mould to a 'coucher', who would extract the paper, and press it between felts to remove water. The parchment was then 'sized', dipped in a gelatinous substance made from animal skins, to give it a sheen. Finally, the paper would be dried and cut, before being packaged and ready for the stationer.[23]

Governor Phillip would have written with a quill. Quill pens were the mainstay of writing in the eighteenth century and were only gradually replaced with pen nibs after Petrache Poenaru invented the fountain pen in 1827. Feather quills required hardening and sharpening (with the original 'pen knife') before they were able to be used to write with ink.

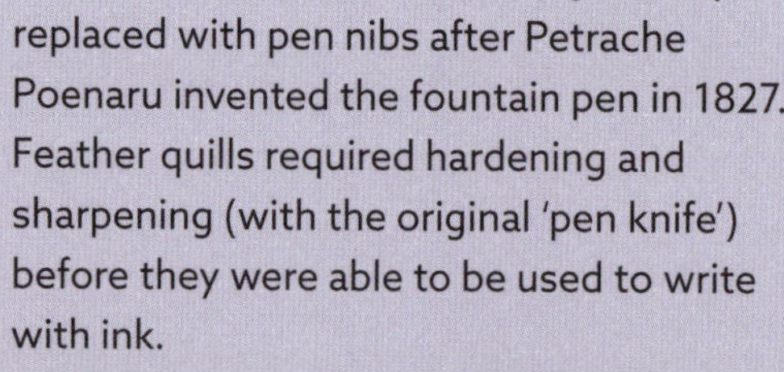

In eighteenth-century Europe, the most common ink was 'iron gall ink', which is a mixture of Oak Gall nuts (produced by oak trees as a reaction to wasps laying eggs under the bark of the tree), solvents, such as beer or wine, ferrous sulphate and gum or resin. The rusty brown colour of this ink is very recognisable from the eighteenth century.[24]

Jan Ekels' *A Writer Trimming His Pen* from 1784 shows the contemplative process of writing.

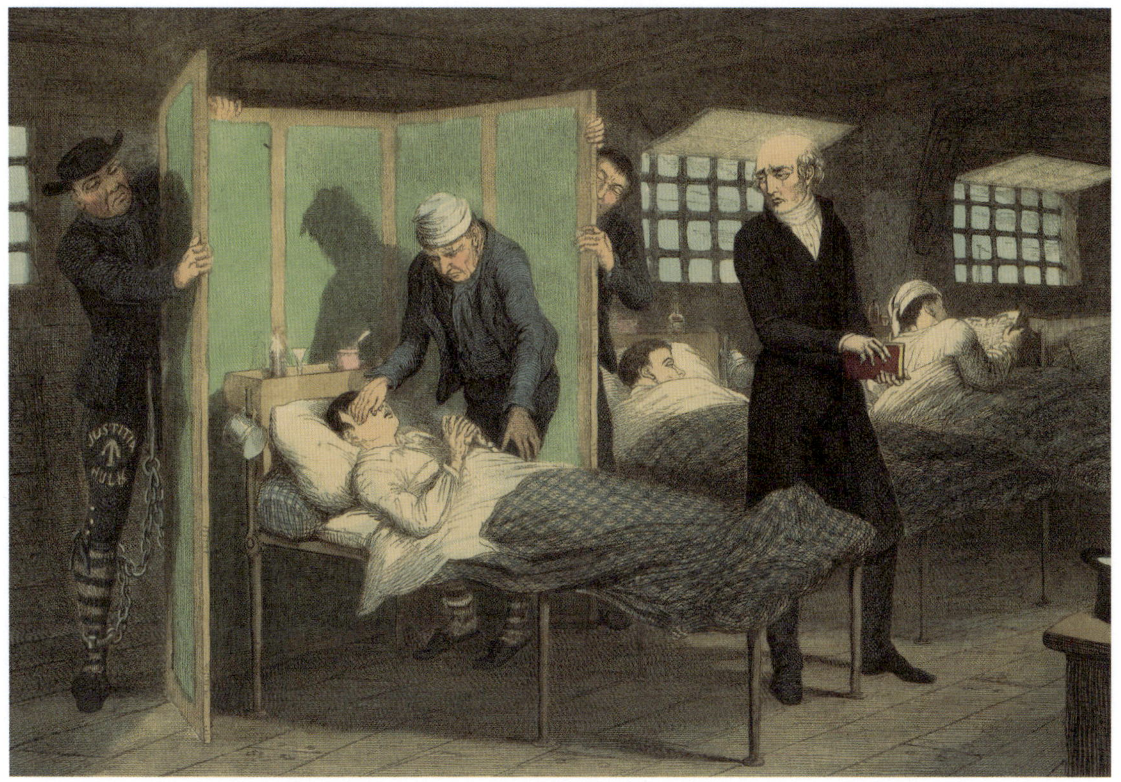

Hospital conditions for the sick and dying were often primitive by modern standards. With the arrival of the Second Fleet at Sydney Cove, Surgeon John White and his staff would be faced with a challenge that almost overwhelmed them.

The inhabitants of Sydney Cove were unprepared for the levels of illness and death among the new arrivals, a contrast to the relatively good standards of health of the First Fleet. The Reverend Richard Johnson, in a letter to a friend in Portsmouth, described going down into the *Surprize* where the convicts were held. He wrote: 'Beheld a sight truly shocking to the feelings of humanity, a great number of them laying ... unable to turn or help themselves'.[25]

The publication of the female convict's letter is recognised by historians as bringing to public prominence the neglect and mistreatment of convicts transported to New South Wales.[26] Eventually, the government was forced to act to improve conditions.[27]

A sackful of letters

By 1800, the penal colony of New South Wales had grown from a population of 850 to 5,217. Most lived in Sydney and Parramatta, but a number of new settlements had been established farther afield.[28] Britain was still sending convicts to Australia's faraway shores, and most convicts whose sentences had expired stayed because they had no other choice. An increasing number also found they had a better life in this strange new land than the one they would have had in England.[29]

Over the first two decades of the nineteenth century, New South Wales would grow further, not just in terms of population but also in potential. The issue of the colony's distance from England would, however, hamper decision-making and affect the colony's growth. It would also mean that exchanging information, personal and public, would be, for many years, worth a great deal to the often-lonely European settlers.

It took five to eight months for a letter to reach Britain by ship, and the same for it to return: a turnaround of at least 11 months (if a month was allowed for consideration and response). Then, in 1852, this period was cut drastically when an early steamship made the journey in 80 days. This was further surpassed during the golden age of the clipper sailing ships, with the clipper *Samuel Plimsoll* taking just 72 days from London to Sydney direct.[30]

There was no structured process for the encouragement of free settlers at the start of the nineteenth century, but they were beginning to arrive. There were about 160 free settlers in the colony in 1806.[31] They were looking for a new life, for room to move, and may have been encouraged by the more optimistic reports in the British newspapers and published accounts of the colony. With the growth in its population, the amount of mail and trade between New South Wales and the outside world also began to increase. Emancipated convicts and settlers still had connections with family and friends abroad. Post of a personal and business nature grew. As Sydney expanded, so did the demands on the port and its administration. The governor found himself dealing not only with the demands of a penal colony but also a growing centre of trade.

As New South Wales transformed from a penal settlement to a colony, the problems of distance and communication with the United Kingdom continued.

In 1803, the explorer Matthew Flinders returned to Sydney Cove after successfully circumnavigating New Holland, which he now proposed be called Terra Australis or Australia. Flinders was impressed by the improvements in the colony since his time there between 1796 and 1797, and even since he had touched base there the year before, in 1802. In *A Voyage to Terra Australis* he wrote about the advances he had seen, but also noted some of the issues holding back progress:

> *Amongst the obstacles which opposed themselves to the more rapid advancement of the colony, the principal were, the vicious propensities of a large portion of the convicts, a want of more frequent communication with England, and the prohibition to trading with India and the western coasts of South America, in consequence of the East-India-Company's charter.*[32]

Despite progress, the time and distance required to get advice from 'home' (Britain) was a major headache for successive governors. The situation was not helped by a degree of neglect from Britain as the

Napoleonic Wars raged. Historian David Mackay writes of the difficulties in finding policy direction in the records of the time:

> *This is not a period when the operations of the Government in general, or the Home Office in particular, are clearly discernible. Sydney, Grenville, Dundas and Portland, the relevant Secretaries of State, left little in their private papers on colonial affairs, probably an accurate reflection of their priorities in this period.*[33]

The lack of timely advice and support was a significant contributing factor to one of the most dramatic events in the fledgling colony's history, when Governor William Bligh was deposed by a military uprising.

Captain William Bligh, renowned for his epic open boat journey following the mutiny on the *Bounty*, arrived at Sydney Cove on 6 August 1806. He already had a reputation for being arrogant and blunt, and these character traits soon became evident in the colony.[34] These traits were, perhaps, the visible part of the 'iceberg', with a larger part being Bligh's over-reliance on formal authority and a lack of ability to read and potentially defuse differences of opinion. Bligh made efforts to remedy the many problems of the settlement: the monopoly on trading held by current and former officers of the New South Wales Corps ('the Rum Corps'), the run-down appearance of Sydney itself and the need for greater structure around a range of other activities.[35] He did not, however, have effective command of the military.

In January 1808, John Macarthur, formerly of the Rum Corps and the wealthiest man in the colony, clashed with the governor over an incident involving a ship owned by Macarthur, the *Parramatta*. Macarthur was probably arrested on Bligh's orders, but was released on bail by Rum Corps officers. Bligh was furious and ordered that Macarthur be arrested again the next day. Instead, ostensibly acting on a petition from the citizens of New South Wales requesting Bligh be removed as governor, Major George Johnston ordered several hundred of his troops to arms and went with four officers to arrest Bligh at Government House.

Opposite page: More free settlers arrived as the colonies grew, building rough bark huts for dwellings.

Bligh was placed under house arrest, and later allowed to board a ship for Britain, which he promptly directed to Hobart, Van Diemen's Land.

In exile on the Derwent River, Bligh wrote letters to a range of people in Britain, voicing doubts they would ever reach their intended audience. Writing to the secretary to the Admiralty, he argued:

> *In restoring this Colony to a state of great comfort and improvement, as well as happiness to all the good people in it, and supporting the civil government, I have been rebelliously deprived of my authority in a cowardly and dastardly manner.*[36]

As with the mutiny on the *Bounty*, time and distance had allowed Bligh to be overthrown; his reliance on the office of his authority was insufficient in a place where the power of an organised mutiny could be brought to bear.

The Rum Corps had exploited the vacuum created by the distance from London, where decisions took time to be made and communicated. The overthrow of Governor William Bligh showed how difficult it was to govern a colony thousands of miles away from the seat of power. It would take a long time for news of Bligh's removal to arrive in Britain, for the knots to be untied and action taken to restore order—the appointment of Lachlan Macquarie as governor and the replacement of the New South Wales Corps with the 73rd Regiment, which he was to lead. Macquarie entered Port Jackson on 28 December 1809, almost two years after Bligh was overthrown. In January 1810, he invited Bligh back to Sydney for a formal handover of responsibilities.[37]

Johnston faced a court martial in London in May 1811. The outcome of the case was of great interest to those associated with New South Wales but of little interest to anyone else. As part of his defence, Johnston made reference to the remoteness of New South Wales:

> *The distance of time and remoteness of the country at which the transaction in question took place; the death and absence of many persons whose evidence would have been of the highest importance to me; the seriousness of the charge, the extent to which it may affect my fortune, my liberty, and my life; all have their share in producing my uneasiness and embarrassment.*[38]

Left: The Rum Rebellion was made possible in part by the distance of New South Wales from the seat of government in the United Kingdom.

Below: After being deposed, William Bligh wrote a long and impassioned defence of his governorship to Sir Joseph Banks.

363

Copy

Government-House, Sydney,
New-South-Wales April 30th
1808

Sir

I have to acquaint you for the information of my Lords Commissioners of the Admiralty, that Since my last dispatch to their Lordships, by the Duke of Portland, on the 31st of October last, to the 26th Jan.y His Majestys Ship Porpoise has been employed in the evacuation of Norfolk Island.

Their Lordships will have been informed of my appointing Lieutenant John Putland to be acting commander of the Porpoise, who until extreme ill-health from a decline was a most valuable assistant to me. He died on Shore (while the Porpoise was at Sea under the charge of acting Lieutenant James Symons) on the 4th of January.

On

Johnston was found guilty, but he was only cashiered out of the army, rather than gaoled, returning to New South Wales to successfully continue developing his farming lands.[39] Britain did not have time to get too involved in the politics of this faraway colony. By sending Macquarie with his own regiment, the government addressed the issue pragmatically—and reasonably quickly, given the circumstances.

As New South Wales grew, so did the arrival of shipping, trade and the transport of mail.

Receiving a long-awaited letter

More than, perhaps, any other place in the world at that time, the penal colony of New South Wales needed mail from overseas for its social, personal and economic life. The exiles from England, Ireland, Scotland and Wales (and other countries also) longed to know what was happening in Europe and the rest of the world. They desperately wanted news from loved ones and relatives.

By 1809, ships were arriving more regularly, but the appearance of a sail in Port Jackson still prompted the same response. Kelly Burke writes in her history of Australia's postal service:

> *The commotion with which they were greeted remained the same. Crews were mobbed as eager settlers and freed convicts swooped on the ship's decks desperate to retrieve letters and news from home.*[40]

Many old letters held in museums across the world bear the telltale sign of an ocean voyage: seawater stains. When storms or heavy seas struck, ships were thrown around, cabins flooded, and furniture and people tossed from side to side. Almost everything got wet, including parcels and sacks of mail.

Disorganisation, and fraud, prompted the appointment of the settlement's first postmaster, in 1809.

A person sending a letter would need to wait for a departing ship and entrust the letter with the ship's captain. There were no guarantees that it would be delivered. And the five- to eight-month journey it travelled meant a long, long wait for a response. When mail arrived in 1804 for every officer but George Harris, the man who would later go on to co-found Hobart town sat down and penned a plaintive letter to his brother begging for a word from home.[41]

Once post arrived, it still had to be collected. By 1809, Sydney Cove had become the key settlement in the larger colony of New South Wales. There were settlements at Coal River (Newcastle) and Parramatta and at Hobart in Van Diemen's Land. Macquarie would soon introduce satellite towns near Sydney, including Windsor and Campbelltown. After the crossing of the Blue Mountains in 1815, the colony would expand rapidly. All this meant there needed to be a greater level of coordination. Like Britain at the time, there was no system of prepayment for mail. The recipient of the letter was obliged to pay for its delivery. It was a haphazard process.

Some system was needed, but was the colony ready for it? It was not like Britain, as Kelly Burke writes:

Such sophisticated a concept as a postal service, which Charles the First had instigated in England more than a century and a half earlier with the opening of the Royal Mail, had not been foreseen in a place that had started as an isolated dumping ground for incorrigible lawbreakers.[42]

On 25 April 1809, acting Governor Foveaux appointed Isaac Nichols to the position of postmaster at Sydney Cove. The rationale for this appointment was explained with a fairly direct reference in *The Sydney Gazette and New South Wales Advertiser*, on 30 April 1809, to the current state of disorder whenever a ship arrived:

Complaints having been made to the Lieutenant Governor, that numerous Frauds have been committed by Individuals repairing on board Ships, on their arrival at these Port, and personating others, by which they have obtained possession of Letters and Parcels to the great injury of those for whom they were intended.

Nichols was a former convict who had become a productive farmer and businessman in the colony. He took control of the receipt and distribution of mail arriving at Sydney Cove.[43] He was required to set up the first post office in his own home. Notices about the mail that had been received would appear regularly in *The Sydney Gazette and New South Wales Advertiser*.

It must have been a lively scene when post arrived by ship: Nichols boarding the ship on a dinghy from the shore and urgently seeking out the captain of the vessel, to advise him that he, Nichols, was now the official receiver of mail for the colony. The captain, tired after a long journey, relieved to be safely in port, gives orders to pass all mail to Nichols, who has brought attendants to help him transport it. Nichols fends off a number of settlers eager for long-awaited packages, citing his authority as the colony's newly appointed postmaster. Eventually, the mail is taken to his buildings at 8 George Street, just a few steps from the edge of Sydney Cove, and sorted. As agreed, a list goes up outside the building, and, after the majority of mail is collected and the fee paid, advertisements go in *The Sydney Gazette* for those who live further afield or are not expecting packages.[44]

News of the world!

An eighteenth-century newspaper can sometimes look haphazard, almost anarchic, by today's editorial standards. The pages are filled with short, often disjointed items of news, gossip and conjecture, piled on top of one another in columns of closely packed script. International news was not differentiated from domestic stories and news items were mingled without distinction.[45] Crimes, accidents and the details of everyday life were mixed in with court information and political reporting. One example is from the *Newcastle Courant* of 8 August 1724, which, in the space of half a page, reports on a plague in Constantinople, the movement of the King's baggage to Windsor, updates from the Dutch and Venetian ambassadors, and the trial of a man for seeking money under a counterfeit charity.

This desire for news was felt by all social classes at Sydney Cove. People would have sat and listened to the news as it was read aloud. St George's Coffee House operated in 1812 (although the advertisement listed nothing but alcohol for sale), where people most likely sat and read a newspaper while drinking coffee or liquor. By 1810, many inns had been established, and it is possible to imagine gatherings of patrons—if not too far under the influence of rum—gathering to listen to and discuss the news from far away. Similarly, at every farm or small settlement, newspapers would arrive, their contents to be absorbed and passed on among the populace. At times the news was momentous.

Napoleon defeated

The defeat of the forces of the French Emperor Napoleon at Waterloo in 1815 was one of the most significant events of the nineteenth century.

For many years, Napoleon, who had emerged from the chaos of the French Revolution as dictator, had seemed invincible, winning victory after victory in Europe as he created a French empire. Britain, ever mindful of maintaining a status quo of power in continental Europe, went to war with France. It was a long, hard and bitter struggle.

By 1803, Sydney Cove was a well-established colony with agriculture and livestock, a tempting target for capture by the French.[46] Following warnings from Britain of the dangers posed by French warships, the colonial government began to construct maritime defences around Sydney Harbour. The first battery was constructed at Obelisk Point, just south of Middle Head. A battery was also in place at Dawes Point.[47]

Napoleon's grip on Europe was only broken after his invasion of Russia in 1812, which resulted in disaster. After several subsequent defeats, Napoleon abdicated his throne and was sent into exile on the island of Elba.

In the extraordinary and unprecedented event known as 'The Hundred Days', in February 1815, Napoleon escaped with supporters from Elba. Landing at Cannes, France, he led 1,500 of his soldiers and supporters towards Paris. The recently crowned Louis XVIII fled, and Napoleon entered Paris one week later. Former supporters flocked to him and he formed a formidable army. England was once again under threat. On 25 March, Austria, Britain, Prussia and Russia agreed to an alliance against Napoleon. After a series of engagements, the two sides met on 18 June 1815, in what is now Belgium, for the Battle of Waterloo. Napoleon was defeated, and, after surrendering to the British, was exiled once again, this time to the more remote island of Saint Helena in the South Atlantic Ocean.

The existing gun emplacement at Dawes Point was expanded in 1819 by convict and architect Francis Greenway.

News of the battle did not reach New South Wales until seven months later. When it arrived, it caused a sensation, as this notice in *The Sydney Gazette and New South Wales Advertiser* of 20 January 1816 shows:

> *Government House Sydney,*
> *Friday 19 January, 1816*
>
> *By the ship Fanny, Captain Wallis, which arrived in this Port yesterday from England, His Excellency the Governor has received the gratifying Intelligence of some brilliant and most important victories obtained by our armies under the command of the illustrious Duke of Wellington, in Conjunction with those of our Ally, the King of Prussia, commanded by Prince Blucher, terminating in the total Defeat of Bonaparte, 'the Faithless Disturber of Europe and Destroyer of the human race', and finally in surrendering himself to the Commander of a British Man of War—His Excellency therefore orders and directs, that the following extracts from the London Gazettes shall be made public through this colony by the medium of a SYDNEY GAZETTE EXTRAORDINARY.*

The impact on the colony was huge. For most colonists, Britain was home. They were a small part of the empire, but they celebrated with functions and the naming of new suburbs and streets.[48] In June 1816, an *Ode for His Majesty's Birthday,* written by former convict Michael Robinson, appeared in *The Sydney Gazette.* Much of its rhetorical verse focused on the victory at Waterloo.[49]

By 1816, Governor Macquarie had already achieved much. Sydney was being developed—as a society, not a penal colony. He had pressed for the Blue Mountains to be crossed in June 1813, opening up more land for settlement. But his expenditure on public works led to raised eyebrows in Britain, and he would eventually be forced out of office as the government reasserted its efforts to maintain New South Wales and Van Diemen's Land as places of penal servitude.[50] This situation continued well into the 1860s, by which time booming wool exports and a gold rush had made the

Opposite page: The defeat of the French army under Napoleon on 18 June 1815 was understandably front-page news in *The Sydney Gazette and New South Wales Advertiser*.

Sydney Gazette Extraordinary.

PUBLISHED BY AUTHORITY.

SATURDAY, JANUARY 20, 1816.

GOVERNMENT AND GENERAL ORDERS.

Government House, Sydney, Friday, 19th January, 1816.

BY the Ship Fanny, Captain WALLIS, which arrived in this Port yesterday from England, HIS EXCELLENCY the GOVERNOR has received the gratifying Intelligence of some brilliant and most important VICTORIES obtained by our Armies under the Command of the illustrious DUKE OF WELLINGTON, in Conjunction with those of our Ally, the KING OF PRUSSIA, commanded by PRINCE BLUCHER, terminating in the total Defeat of *Bonaparte*, "the ruthless Disturber of Europe, and Destroyer of the human Race;" and finally in his surrendering himself to the Commander of a British Man of War:—His EXCELLENCY therefore orders and directs, that the following Extracts from the London Gazettes shall be made public through this Colony by the Medium of a SYDNEY GAZETTE EXTRAORDINARY.

By Command of His Excellency,

J. T. CAMPBELL, *Secretary.*

DOWNING STREET, *June* 22, 1815.—Major the Honorable H. Percy arrived late last night with a Dispatch from Field Marshal the Duke of Wellington, K. G. to Earl Bathurst, His Majesty's Principal Secretary of State for the War Department; of which the following is a copy:—

Waterloo, June 19, 1815.

MY LORD—Bonaparte having collected the 1st, 2d, 3d, 4th, and 6th corps of the French army and the Imperial Guards, and nearly all the cavalry on the Sambre, and between that river and the Meuse, between the 10th and 14th of the month, advanced on the 15th and attacked the Prussian posts at Thuin and Lobez, on the Sambre, at day light in the morning.

I did not hear these events till the evening of the 15th, and I immediately ordered the troops to prepare to march; and afterwards to march to their left, as soon as I had intelligence from other quarters to prove that the enemy's movements upon Charleroy was the real attack.

The enemy drove the Prussian posts from the Sambre on that day; and General Zieten, who commanded the corps which had been at Charleroi, retired upon Fleurus; and Marshal Prince Blucher concentrated the Prussian army upon Sombref, holding the villages in front of his position of St. Amand and Ligny.

The enemy continued his march along the road from Charleroy towards Bruxelles, and on the same evening, the 15th, attacked a brigade of the army of the Netherlands, under the Prince de Weimar, posted at Frasne, and forced it back to the farm house on the same road, called Les Quatre Bras.

The Prince of Orange immediately reinforced this brigade with another of the same division, under General Perponcher, and in the morning early regained part of the ground which had been lost, so as to have the command of the communication leading from Nivelles and Bruxelles, with Marshal Blucher's position.

In the mean time I had directed the whole army to march upon Les Quatre Bras, and the 5th division, under Lieut. General Sir Thomas Picton, arrived at about half past two in the day, followed by the corps of troops under the Duke of Brunswick, and afterwards by the contingent of Nassau.

At this time the enemy commenced an attack upon Prince Blucher with his whole force, excepting the 1st and 2d corps, and a corps of cavalry under General Kellerman, with which he attacked our post at Les Quatre Bras.

The Prussian army maintained their position with their usual gallantry and perseverance, against a great disparity of numbers, as the 4th corps of their army, under General Bulow, had not joined, and I was not able to assist them as I wished, as I was attacked myself, and the troops, the cavalry in particular, which had a long distance to march, had not arrived.

We maintained our position also, and completely defeated and repulsed all the enemy's attempts to get possession of it. The enemy repeatedly attacked us with a large body of infantry and cavalry, supported by a numerous and powerful artillery; he made several charges with the cavalry upon our infantry, but all were repulsed in the steadiest manner. In this affair His Royal Highness the Prince of Orange, the Duke of Brunswick, and Lieutenant General Sir Thomas Picton, and Major General Sir James Kempt, and Sir Denis Pack, who were engaged from the commencement of the enemy's attack, highly distinguished themselves, as well as Lieut. General Charles Baron Alten, Major General Sir C. Halket, Lieut. General Cooke, and Major Generals Maitland and Byng, as they successively arrived. The troops of the 5th division, and those of the Brunswick corps, were long and severely engaged, and conducted themselves with the utmost gallantry. I must particularly mention the 28th, 42d, 79th, and 92d regiments, and the battalion of Hanoverians.

Our loss was great, as your Lordship will perceive by the inclosed return; and I have particularly to regret His Serene Highness the Duke of Brunswick, who fell, fighting gallantly at the head of his troops.

Although Marshal Blucher had maintained his position at Sombrief, he still found himself much weakened by the severity of the contest in which he had been engaged, and as the fourth corps had not arrived; he determined to fall back, and concentrate his army upon Wavre; and he marched in the night after the battle was over.

This movement of the Marshal's rendered necessary a corresponding one on my part; and I retired from the farm of Quatre Bras upon Genappe, and thence upon the Waterloo the next morning, the 17th, at ten o'clock.

The enemy made no effort to pursue Marshal Blucher. On the contrary, a patrole which I sent to Sombrief in the morning, found all quiet, and the enemy's vedettes fell back as the patrole advanced.—Neither did he attempt to molest our march to the rear, although made in the middle of the day, excepting by following, with a large body of cavalry, brought from his right, the cavalry under the Earl of Uxbridge.

This gave Lord Uxbridge an opportunity of charging them with the 1st Life Guards, upon their debouche from the village of Genappe, upon which occasion His Lordship has declared himself to be well satisfied with that regiment.

The position which I took up in front of Waterloo crossed the high roads from Charleroy and Nivelle, and had its right thrown back to a ravine near Merke Braine, which was occupied, and its left extended to a height above the hamlet Ter la Haye, which was likewise occupied. In front of the right centre and near the Nivelle road, we occupied the house and garden of Hougoumont, which covered the return of that flank; and in front of the left centre, we occupied the farm of La Haye Sainte. By our left we communicated with Marshal Prince Blucher, at Wavre through Ohaim; and the Marshal had promised me, that in case we should be attacked, he would support me with one or more corps, as might be necessary.

The enemy collected his army, with the exception of the third corps, which had been sent to observe Marshal Blucher, on a range of heights in our front, in the course of the night of the 17th and yesterday morning; and at about ten o'clock he commenced a furious attack upon our post at Hougoumont. I had occupied that post with a detachment from General Byng's brigade of guards, which was in position in its rear; and it was for some time under the command of Lieut. Colonel Macdonel, and afterwards of Colonel Home; and I am happy to add, that it was maintained throughout the day with the utmost gallantry by these brave troops, notwithstanding the repeated efforts of large bodies of the enemy to obtain possession of it.

This attack upon the right of our centre was accompanied by a very heavy cannonade upon our whole line, which was destined to support the repeated attacks of cavalry and infantry occasionally mixed, but sometimes separate, which were made upon it. In one of these the enemy carried the farm house of La Haye Sainte, as the detachment of the light battalion of the Legion which occupied it had expended all its ammunition, and the enemy occupied the only communication there was with them.

The enemy repeatedly charged our infantry with his cavalry, but these attacks were uniformly unsuccessful, and they afforded opportunities to our cavalry to charge, in one of which Lord E. Somerset's brigade, consisting of the Life Guards, Royal Horse Guards, and 1st Dragoon Guards, highly distinguished themselves, as did that of Major General Sir W. Ponsonby, having taken many prisoners and an eagle.

These attacks were repeated till about seven in the evening, when the enemy made a desperate effort with the cavalry and infantry, supported by the fire of artillery, to force our left centre near the farm of La Haye Sainte, which, after a severe contest, was defeated; and having observed that the troops retired from the attack in great confusion, and that the march of General Bulow's corps by Enschermonte upon Planchenorte and La Belle Alliance, had began to take effect, and as I could perceive the fire of his cannon, and as Marshal Prince Blucher had joined in person, with a corps of his army to the left of our line by Ohaim, I determined to attack the enemy, and immediately advanced the whole line of infantry, supported by the cavalry and artillery. The attack succeeded in every point; the enemy was forced from his position on the heights and fled in the utmost confusion, leaving behind him, as far as I could judge, one hundred and fifty pieces of cannon, with their ammunition, which fell into our hands. I continued the pursuit till long after dark, and then discontinued it only on account of the fatigue of our troops, who had been engaged during twelve hours, and because I found myself on the same road with Marshal Blucher, who assured me of his intention to follow the enemy throughout the night; he has sent me word this morning that he had taken sixty pieces of cannon belonging to the Imperial Guard, and several carriages, baggage, &c. belonging to Bonaparte, in Gehappe.

I propose to move, this morning, upon Nevilles, and not to discontinue my operations.

Your Lordship will observe, that such a desperate action could not be fought, and such advantages could not be gained without great loss; and I am sorry to add, that ours has been immense. In Lieutenant Gen. Sir Thomas Picton, his Majesty has sustained the loss of an Officer who has frequently distinguished himself in his service, and he fell, gloriously leading his division to a charge with bayonets, by which one of the most serious attacks made by the enemy on our position was defeated. The Earl of Uxbridge, after having successfully got through this arduous day, received a wound, by almost the last shot fired, which will, I am afraid, deprive his Majesty for some time of his services.

His Royal Highness the Prince of Orange distinguished himself by his gallantry and conduct, till he received a wound from a musket ball through the shoulder, which obliged him to quit the field.

It gives me the greatest satisfaction to assure your Lordship, that the army never, upon any occasion, conducted itself better. The division of guards under Lieut. Gen. Cooke, who is severely wounded, Major General Maitland and Major General Byng, set an example which was followed by all; and there is no Officer, nor description of troops, that did not behave well.

I must, however, particularly mention, for His Royal Highness's approbation, Lieut. General Sir H. Clinton, Major General Adam, Lieutenant General Charles Baron Alten, severely wounded; Major Gen. Sir Colin Halket, severely wounded; Colonel Ompteda, Colonel Mitchell, commanding a brigade of the 4th division; Major Generals Sir James Kempt and Sir Dennis Pack, Major Gen Lambert, Major General Lord E. Somerset, Major General Sir W. Ponsonby, Major General Sir C. Grant, and Major General Sir H. Vivian; Major General Sir O. Vandeleur; Major General Count Dornberg. I am also particularly indebted to General Lord Hill, for his assistance upon this as upon all former occasions.

The Artillery and Engineer departments were conducted much to my satisfaction by Colonel Sir G. Wood and Colonel Smyth; and I had every reason to be satisfied with the conduct of the Adjutant General, Major General Barnes, who was wounded; & of the Quarter Master General, Colonel Delancy, who was killed by a cannon shot in the middle of the action. Lieutenant Colonel the Honorable Sir Alexander Gordon, who has died of his wounds, was a most promising officer, and is a serious loss to his Majesty's service.

General Kruse, of the Nassau service, likewise conducted himself much to my satisfaction, as did General Trip, commanding the heavy brigade of cavalry, and General Vanhope, commanding a brigade of infantry of the King of the Netherlands.

General Pozzo di Borgo, General Baron Vincent, General Muffling, and General Allava, were in the field during the action, and rendered me every assistance in their power. Baron Vincent is wounded, but I hope not severely; and General Pozzo di Borgo received a contusion.

I should not do justice to my feelings, or to Marshal Blucher and the Prussian army, if I did not attribute the successful result of this arduous day, to the cordial and timely assistance I received from them.

The operation of General Bulow, upon the enemy's flank, was a decisive one; and even if I had not found myself in a situation to make the attack, which produced the final result, it would have forced the enemy to retire, if his attacks should have failed, and would have prevented him from taking advantage of them, if they should unfortunately have succeeded.

I send, with this dispatch, two eagles, taken by the troops in this action, which Major Percy will have the honour of laying at the feet of his Royal Highness.

I beg leave to recommend him to your Lordship's protection. I have the honour, &c.

(Signed) WELLINGTON.

P.S. Since writing the above, I have received a report, that Major General Sir William Ponsonby is killed; and, in announcing this intelligence to your Lordship, I have to add the expression of my grief, for the fate of an Officer, who had already rendered very brilliant and important services, and was an ornament to his profession.

2d P.S. I have not yet got the returns of killed and wounded, but I inclose a list of Officers killed and wounded on the two days, as far as the same can be made out without the returns; & I am very happy to add, that Colonel De Lancey is not dead, and that strong hopes of his recovery are entertained.

KILLED AND WOUNDED.

KILLED.

Duke of Brunswick Oels.
Lieutenant General Sir Thomas Picton.
Major General Sir W. Ponsonby, K. C. B.
Colonel du Plat, K. G. L.
Colonel Ompteda, ditto.
Colonel Morris, 69th Regiment.
Colonel Sir W. Ellis, 23d.
Lieutenant Colonel Macara, 42d Regiment.
Lieutenant Colonel Cameron, 92d Regiment.
Lieutenant Colonel Sir Alex. Gordon, K. C. B. Aide de Camp to the Duke of Wellington.
Lieutenant Colonel Canning.
Lieutenant Colonel Currie, Lord Hill's Staff.
Major the Hon. Fred. Howard, 10th Hussars.
Major George Bain, Royal Artillery.
Major Norman Ramsay, ditto.
Major Cairnes, ditto.
Major Chambers, 30th Regiment.
Brevet Major Crofton, 5th Division.
Brevet Major Rosewiel, 2d Light Regiment.
Captain Bolton, Royal Artillery.
Captain Crawford, Guards.
Captain the Hon. — Curzon, A. D. C. to His Royal Highness the Prince of Orange.
Captain Chambers, A. D. C. to Lieut. General Picton.
Captain Charles Eles, 95th Regiment.
Captain Robinson, 73d Regiment.
Captain Kennedy, 73d Regt.
Captain Schauman, 2d Lt Bat. K. G. L.
Captain Holscowan, 1st ditto.
Captain Henry Marshal, 1st ditto.
Captain Cochen, ditto.
Captain Gunning, 10th Hussars.
Captain Grove, 1st Guards.
Lieutenant C. Manners, Royal Artillery.
Lieutenant Lster, 95th Regiment.
Ensign Lord Hay, A. D. C. to Gen. Maitland.
Ensign Brown, 1st Guards.

WOUNDED.

General His Royal Highness the Prince of Orange, G. C. B. severely.
Lieutenant General the Earl of Uxbridge, G. C. B. right leg amputated.
Lieutenant General Sir Charles Alten, K. C. B. severely.
Major General Cork, right arm amputated.
Major General Sir F. Barnes, K. C. B. Adj. General, severely.
Major General Sir J. Kempt, K. C. B. slightly.
Major General Sir Colin Halkett, K. C. B. severely.
Major General Adams, severely.
Major General Sir W. Dornberg, K. C. B. severely.
Colonel Sir J. Elley, K. C. B. slightly.
Colonel Harris, 73d Regt.
Colonel Quentin, 10th Hussars, slightly.
Colonel the Honorable Frederick Ponsonby, severely.
Colonel Sir William De Lancy, severely.
Lieutenant Colonel Lord Fitzroy Somerset, right arm amputated.
Lieutenant Colonel Hay, 16th Light Dragoons, severely.
Lieutenant Colonel Vigoureau, 30th.
Lieutenant Colonel Abercrombie, A. Q. M. G. slightly.
Lieutenant Colonel Hamilton, 30th Regt.
Lieutenant Colonel Cameron, 95th, severely.
Lieutenant Colonel Wyndham, 1st Foot Guards, severely.
Lieutenant Colonel Bowater, 3d Foot Guards, slightly.
Lieutenant Col. Macdonell, Coldstream, slightly.
Lieutenant Colonel Dashwood, 3d Guards, severely.
Lieutenant Colonel Sir R. Hill, Royal Horse Guards Blue, severely.
Lieutenant Colonel Norcott, 95th, severely.
Lieutenant Colonel Hill, severely.
Lieutenant Colonel Schreider, 8th Light Battalion.
Lieutenant Colonel Adair, 1st Guards, severely.
Lieutenant Colonel Miller, 1st Guards, dangerously.
Lieutenant Colonel Sir George Henry Berkeley, A. A. G.
Major Maclean, 73d Regt.
Major Beckwith, 95th, severely.
Major Jessop, Assistant Quarter Master General.
Major Buscae, 1st Light Bat. K. G. L. right arm amputated.
Major Parkinson, 73d, severely.
Major Parker, R. H. Artillery, leg amputated.
Major Robert Ball, Royal Artillery, severely.
Major Hamilton, Aide-de Camp to General Sir E. Barnes.
Major Lindsay, 69th regiment, dangerously.
Major Watson, 69th Foot, severely.
Brevet Major Eisem, dangerously.
Major Wilkins, 95th Foot, severely.
Major Miller, 95th Foot, severely.
Captain Smith, 95th Foot, severely.
Captain Tyler, A. D. C. to Sir Thomas Picton, slightly.
Captain Dance, 23d Light Dragoons.
Captain Johnston, 95th Foot.
Captain Chimers, 95th Foot.
Captain Darney, Royal Artillery, severely.
Captain Napier, Royal Artillery, severely.
Captain A. M'Donald, Royal Artillery, severely.
Captain Webber, Royal Artillery, severely.
Captain Dumaresques, Aide de Camp to General Sir J. Byng, severely.
Captain Whymates, Royal Artillery, severely.
Captain Barnes, Brevet Major Royal Artillery, severely.

Australian colonies important economic entities. In decades to come, the means to communicate across the vast continent and beyond would be an important part of Australia's colonial development.

Publishing letters home

British newspapers were exceptionally curious about the outside world, and news from abroad was a major part of their content. Since Britain was a maritime nation, journalists would wait at the ports and gather information from ships as they returned from around the globe.

During the second and third decades of the nineteenth century, letters from New South Wales continued to find their way into newspapers in Britain. Thanks to the efforts of libraries and research facilities across the world, newspapers are often now digitised, and there are rewards in trawling through these papers with the assistance of a search engine.[51]

One example of a personal letter that made its way into a regional newspaper from New South Wales was published in *Trewman's Exeter Flying Post* of 23 December 1819:

> *A letter of an unfortunate nature of a town in the neighbourhood of Bath to his wife, dated Sydney Cove (Botany Bay) February 14, 1819, contains the following interesting passages: 'I long to hear of you, my dearest wife, and of our dear children. I am with S.L. Esquire and work at cloth weaving. I could wish you to come to me, as it will be of great benefit to me and secure my freedom—may make us both comfortable and happy as I could gain a good livelihood. This country is the most beautiful and healthy in the world ... I can support you well, and therefore I propose this—the only means of our meeting again on Earth.'*

Regional newspapers seemed to take an interest in local people. This example is from the *Bury and Norwich Post* of 1817, about a woman transported for perjury:

> *By a letter just received from New South Wales, we hear that Miss Radford, who some time since was tried at the guildhall of Exeter, for perjury, and transported to Botany Bay, conducted herself so well on her*

Many families in the United Kingdom were interested in how their relatives or friends were faring in Australia.

> *passage hither, as to engage the most marked attention of all on board, and especially C.S****rs, Esq., a young officer, of good family and respectability, who was so enamoured with her amiable deportment, as to make honourable proposals of marriage, and a short time after their arrival they were united; the ceremony being performed at the church of Parramatta, by the Ref. Mr Marsden. The Governor afterwards granted permission for Mr S to become a resident of the colony.*[52]

Another item, headlined 'Rencounter between a Dog and a Shark' in the *Asiatic Journal* of 1821, is an early example of that perennial newspaper favourite—shark attacks in Australia:

Mr Cossar has a farm at the Long Reef, about ten miles north of the sea beach, as large as Sydney Cove, about a mile round it. The banks of the lagoon, though several feet above the highwaters' level, at spring tides, is forced into communication with the sea ... At a time within the present twelvemonth, when the sea and the lagoon had become become united ... a fine water dog was observed to dash into the water, at an erect moving spire, which had the appearance of a shark's back-fin, and was soon perceived to be engaged with this voracious fish[53]

It seems the dog had bitten off more than it could chew and was dragged into the water, from which it was rescued by two men; it survived, despite having been mauled by the shark. The shark got away.

Newspapers also carried many articles with updates about the colony and the relative speed with which some ships were now reaching New South Wales. The *Caledonian Mercury* reported in 1820:

The celerity with which communications to and from New South Wales have lately been accomplished, by vessels that have made the passage without loitering away time at intermediate ports, is cheering to those who purpose adventuring to this new world of enterprize. The Eliza, which sailed from the Thames in October, arrived within the Heads at Port Jackson in the short space of 96 days. The Prince Regent anchored in Sydney Cove in one hundred and three days from Spithead; and Admiral Cockburn brought home the intelligence of that vessel's arrival in three months and three days![54]

The same article comments on the growing prosperity of the colony and also remarks on the rapid emergence of wool as a major export:

it is gratifying to learn, the colonies were enabled to send off one season's growth, four hundred and fifteen bales of their wool. It has already been noticed how much the fine fleeces of New South Wales vie with the best qualities of Saxon and Spanish.

Post offices were prominent and stately buildings in colonial architecture.

The presence of a post office—a key point for the management of communications, and a link to the outside world—was a significant inclusion in many cities and towns in Australia. In her book *The Stamp of Australia*, Kelly Burke writes:

> *According to the Australian Heritage Council 'Government architects built enormous post offices in major provincial towns as statements of the authority and presence of the government'. 'These buildings were designed intentionally to make a statement that the Australian colonies were civilised British countries.' This ideological underpinning meant the great Australian post offices of the 19th century looked remarkably different from their equivalents in the frontier towns of the United States at that time. The post office was not as central to the identity of the American wild west, because there was not the same need to assert a sense of British civilisation. It was not unusual for town planners to incorporate the post office into a town's official precinct, which would typically include a police station, courthouse and sundry government administrative buildings.*[55]

Long live Queen Victoria!

The Australian colonial newspapers were avid reporters of the royal family. In the period 1830–1850, the colonies had not yet had the influx of population and ideas from the gold rushes that created a more complex political situation. The idea of empire reigned supreme, with a single focus on the colony's relationship with Britain. Ideas about nationhood beyond that were still nascent at best.

After the death of George III, who reigned for 60 years (1760–1820), two kings followed in quick succession: George IV (1820–1830) and William IV (1830–1837). William's successor, his niece Victoria, was much written about as a princess prior to her ascension to the throne. This item appeared in the *Sydney Herald* of 23 March 1837:

> *The Princess Victoria comes of age this year; Her Royal Highness is said to be accomplished in a high degree; she speaks with fluency and elegance nearly all the modern European languages, is a proficient in Latin, and has made great progress in the mathematics; she is also an excellent musician.*

Soon after this was written, Queen Victoria's life changed dramatically. William IV, who was 71 years old, died on 20 June 1837. As always, the news travelled by ship to Australia. Many Sydney-bound ships touched at Hobart first, and reports of William's death and Victoria's ascension to the throne were first read there, as recorded in *The Tasmanian* on Friday 20 October 1837:

> *On Thursday, at Twelve o'clock, according to usage, Her Majesty, Queen Victoria, was proclaimed in front of Government House, in presence of an immense assemblage of people, including the military and heads of departments. Before the hour appointed, great numbers had congregated, and an extreme interest was evinced in the business of the day: the military formed in line before the scaffolding, erected for the delivery of the proclamation.*

The reports, assembled from a range of British newspapers, included descriptions of William's illness and death and the text of Victoria's first speech, which focused on her determination to be a conscientious regent despite her youth:

> *The severe and afflicting loss which the nation has sustained by the death of His Majesty, my beloved uncle, has devolved upon me the duty of administering the Government of this Empire. This awful responsibility is imposed upon me so suddenly, and at so early a period of my life, that I should feel myself utterly oppressed by the burden were*

The interior of the settler's hut perhaps reflects the reality of conditions for many in Australia upon arrival from England.

> *I not sustained by the hope that Divine Providence, which has called me to this work, will give me strength for the performance of it, and that I shall find in the purity of my intentions, and in my zeal for the public welfare, that support and those resources which usually belong to a more mature age, and to longer experience.*

The news soon spread throughout the colonies. Victoria, whose reign was to last until 22 January 1901, became monarch of the British Empire. Australia grew out of all proportion during her reign, becoming a federated nation just weeks before she died. In that time, the Industrial Revolution expanded exponentially, bringing both progress and poverty. The British Empire reached its peak, with colonialism bringing a period of enormous growth and change.

News of gold

The discovery of gold in the colonies of Australia transformed society and supercharged colonial development. In the 1850s, the population of Australia tripled. Agriculture also expanded as more labourers became available. Indigenous communities were, on the other hand, decimated.

Traces of gold were found by European surveyors on the Fish River, near Bathurst, New South Wales, as early as 1823. In 1839, two geologists, P.E. Strzelecki and the Reverend W.B. Clarke, found gold specks in silicate near Hartley, New South Wales. Concerned at the possible disruption to society that a gold discovery could cause, Governor George Gipps asked for all mention of the Hartley find to be suppressed. 'Put it away, Mr Clarke,' Gipps is supposed to have said, 'or we will all have our throats cut!'[56]

Gipps was concerned by the large 'convict element' of the population; transportation to New South Wales only ceased in 1840. The appointment of a government geologist that same year showed that the colony was willing to look into mineral deposits more closely.

Many young workers from the Australian colonies travelled to California to try their hand at finding gold during the seismic rush of the 'forty-niners'. They brought back practical skills and an eye for finding gold. Two of these men were to lead the way in discovering gold in Australia.

On 12 February 1851, Edward Hargraves found a small amount of gold at a location near Bathurst he later named Ophir. Three colleagues, John Lister and the Tom brothers, later found payable gold there. Hargraves presented this gold to the colonial secretary, thus gaining primary recognition and a large reward.

These finds in New South Wales led to a huge rush across the Blue Mountains to Bathurst. In Victoria (which became a separate colony to New South Wales in July 1851), there was a serious decline in population due to the exodus to the New South Wales goldfields, and a Gold Discovery Committee was formed in 1851. A reward of £200 was offered to anyone who found a payable goldfield. Californian miner James Esmond won the reward by discovering gold near Clunes. Gold was then found near Ballarat.

Edward Hargraves was credited with the discovery of gold near Bathurst in February 1851.

The rush was on; the 'roaring days' had begun. People gave up their jobs to head for the goldfields, and news spread around the world.

The news must have travelled the same way it usually did at that time—by ship. There were no telegram links in place, no chance of the message leap-frogging ahead of ships and the mail they carried. In newspapers from the first half of 1851, there are references to New South Wales mentioning the discovery of new lands, the wool trade and other miscellany. Then there are the first references to gold, and soon a media rush.

This extract from the British *Worcestershire Chronicle*, of 3 September 1851, tells of the discovery of gold in New South Wales:

> *The Sydney Morning Herald of the 20 May* [1851], *contains an extraordinary statement relative to the discovery of a second California at Bathurst, in New South Wales, which professes to be taken from the Bathurst Free Press of the 17th. The substance of the statement made is, that a young gentleman named Neale found in the neighbourhood of Bathurst a piece of gold weighing eleven ounces—that a person named Austin bought it of him for 30/., and then started off for Sydney. The fact is subsequently stated, that an old man (whose name is not given) arrived in Bathurst with several pieces in mass, weighing in all from two to three pounds.*

In true Victorian style, the same *Worcestershire Chronicle* article conveyed the dramatic upheaval of the rush for gold:

> *We have then the natural supplemental account that the whole population of Bathurst became aroused, by the reports which reached them, into that state of half-frantic emotion which the passion for gold can equally stimulate in the north and the south. Magistrates deserted the seats of justice—merchants their counting houses—clerks their desks—domestic servants their ordinary engagements, to be converted by one felicitous adventure into so many Croesuses.*

The news spread around the world. There was much interest in California, the home of gold-rush fever, and some miners left the United States to try their luck in Australia. A letter home to California published in local newspapers commented about the lack of law and order:

> *A month's sojourn on Fryar's Creek has given me a deep insight into the morale of the diggings, and opened up scenes that I could not have anticipated during the rosy days when the wonders of Ballarat first flashed our imagination with the prospect of vast fields of illimitable wealth. At Ballarat, there was peace, unity, and security; but at Fryar's Creek these desirable qualities are reversed, and quarrels, dissensions, bloodshed, and danger of the direst description, reign supreme. The*

The gold rushes in Australia made news around the world. This dramatic picture shows the 'rush' aspect of getting to the goldfields.

"OFF FOR THE DIGGINGS," AT BATHURST.

tea. They call Penrith a town. I should call it a village; it stands on the river Nepean, which stream we crossed the next morning on a floating bridge or punt worked by men. On reaching the opposite side we crossed the Emu Plains, which are the grazing ground or "lays" for graziers. They leave their

WASHING CRADLE.

cattle on the Emu plains after they have brought them up from the interior, whilst they go on to Sydney to fetch up butchers to buy them.

The Nepean, which bounds the plains, is one of the finest rivers in this part of the colony; it is about the size of the Birmingham Canal, and always flowing. Soon after crossing the plains we had to cross a bridge, thrown over a fearful abyss, and began to ascend the celebrated Blue Mountains, which formed an impenetrable barrier to the first colony, until after many attempts a pass was discovered across them in 1813. Since that period a capital road has been constructed, planned, and executed by Sir Thomas Mitchell, over a country which in physical difficulties may be compared to the route executed by order of Napoleon over the Alps. As we ascended Lapstone Crag the road wound along the sides of the mountains; crag towering over crag, and rocks overhanging, seemed every moment about to fall and crush us. For miles the road zigzags to find a gradient over which drays can travel—in some places cut through solid rock. We did not halt until we reached the Weatherboard Inn, so called from the materials of which it was first built, distant twenty-two miles from Penrith. Travelling in these regions is dear, but good—no less than £2 a day for myself and horse. We had roast fowl, ham, beefsteak, and potatoes served as well up as at any roadside inn in England.

After dinner we rode over a very fair macadamised road, up and down like the dales and hills of Derbyshire, occasionally passing over a wooden bridge uniting two mountains meeting on the skew. At the next inn, Pulpit Hollow, we only took a glass of brandy and water, without dismounting, and went on to Blackheath, which is 70 miles from Sydney, where we slept.

The inn at Blackheath is on the top of a high mountain, one of the coldest dwellings in the colony, exposed to continual rain, with snow and rain for a change. Potatoes grow here, which they won't do to perfection on the Sydney side. Here we had a capital dinner and supper combined—good vegetables, with roast fowls, a bottle of colonial wine, and pancakes. I mention these things to show how comfortably we got along, so different to the accounts from California. For the horses there was a good warm stable well bedded down, and plenty of corn. The next day we arose at daylight and rode to the foot of Mount Victoria, so named in 1832, after our Queen, then Princess, by the Governor, Sir Richard Bourke, when Sir Thomas Mitchell, the Surveyor-General, by means *of convict labour*, cut a road through the mountain, which any dray can now descend locked, and can ascend with a full load and ten bullocks; thus superseding a dangerous pass by Mount York. Our railway cuttings have nothing more formidable than this Victoria Pass.

We were now within fifty miles of Bathurst, but instead of keeping the mail road we turned off over one of the old tracks used before the road was cut, to visit a friend of my companions.

ASCENDING A PASS IN THE BLUE MOUNTAINS.

Government is palsied, whilst the ill-doer runs on a career of unchecked crime and rapine, or at the most is checked by an occasional pistol shot, or similar act of summary justice, responded to by a groan; and the effect manifested next morning by blood stains; when a few observations are bandied about from tent to tent that a man was shot, and no more is heard of the matter.[57]

Another Californian newspaper compared the Australian goldfields with those of California:

notwithstanding the immense 'nuggets' that are found in those gold fields, they are not to be compared to our diggings, and that men do not average anything like the wages they do in this country. As proof of this he says, that ten shillings per day is the highest wages paid mechanics in Sydney. Many of his companions returned with him, all perfectly satisfied that California, in every respect, is superior to Australia for the working man.[58]

The description of lawlessness was certainly justified in many cases. Riots and the massacre of Chinese were by far the most serious events, occurring in Buckland Valley and Lambing Flat. The canvas towns that were set up, sometimes within the space of a week, had populations of up to 40,000, predominantly men. If the field was more permanent in nature—such as at Bendigo, Ballarat or Mount Alexander—houses, dance halls and hotels would soon appear.

Coach services became the main method of communication. Cobb & Co. is the most famous. The sight of its coaches was familiar on the goldfields, and poet Henry Lawson immortalised the scene in 'The Roaring Days':

Oft when the camps were dreaming,
And fires began to pale,
Through rugged ranges gleaming
Would come the Royal Mail.
Behind six foaming horses,
And lit by flashing lamps,
Old Cobb and Co.', in royal state,
Went dashing past the camps.[59]

The 'Cobb' of Cobb & Co. was Freeman Cobb, a young American from Brewster, Massachusetts. In 1853, aged 23, he established Cobb & Co. with three associates in Victoria to convey mail and passengers between the port of Melbourne and the Victorian goldfields. The first journey of a Cobb & Co. coach was from Collins Street, Melbourne, to the Forest Creek diggings (now Castlemaine) on 30 January 1854. The coach completed the voyage in half the time of its competitors.

The company became very popular because of its reputation for speed and efficiency. Two reasons explain why Cobb & Co. coaches were so fast. The first was the way the coaches were designed. Most coach companies in Victoria used English-built vehicles, which had very heavy bodies and

A race between Cobb & Co. and rival company the Bendigo to Castlemaine Coaches.

stiff steel springs. These were not well suited to Australia's often very rough bush roads. Cobb, on the other hand, used American-built coaches. As Kathy Riley wrote in *Australian Geographic*:

> *Freeman instead imported Concord coaches, which had been designed for travel in the American West. They had rounded, lightweight and supple bodies resting on leather straps called thorough braces. The result was a much smoother, faster ride—although the back and forth rocking motion of the carriage prompted one passenger to liken the experience to riding 'a baby camel in a hell of a hurry'.*[60]

In addition to these carriages, Cobb & Co. had changing stations only 10 to 20 miles (16 to 32 kilometres) apart. This meant their horses were much fresher than those of the competition and were able to keep up a better pace for the journey.

As money flowed from the goldfields, the population of Australia grew significantly. Before 1851, Australia's total European population was about 77,000. Most of those had been convicts sent by ship over the previous 70 years, although free settlement had been steadily increasing.

The gold rush completely changed that. In the two years that followed Edward Hargraves' discovery at Bathurst, Australia's population increased rapidly. In the decade from 1850 to 1860, there was an increase in population of approximately 740,000.[61] Melbourne and Sydney grew from large towns into cities. Further immigration followed. The impact of the gold rushes was to drive Australia towards becoming a nation, although it would be another 40 to 50 years before the colonies could agree on a single constitution and take the proposal to a successful referendum.

The individual stories of people arriving in Australia survive through letters and diaries. Rachel Henning was not happy when she first arrived in Australia in 1854, a year after her brother and sister had come out to make a new life. Her brother had suffered from scarlet fever and it was thought the climate would do him good. On the trip out, she exercised her powers of observation. The *Australian Dictionary of Biography* records:

> *Her 'slightly mordant sense of humour' first showed in her shrewd comments on her fellow passengers: 'Mr and Mrs Donaldson are in their*

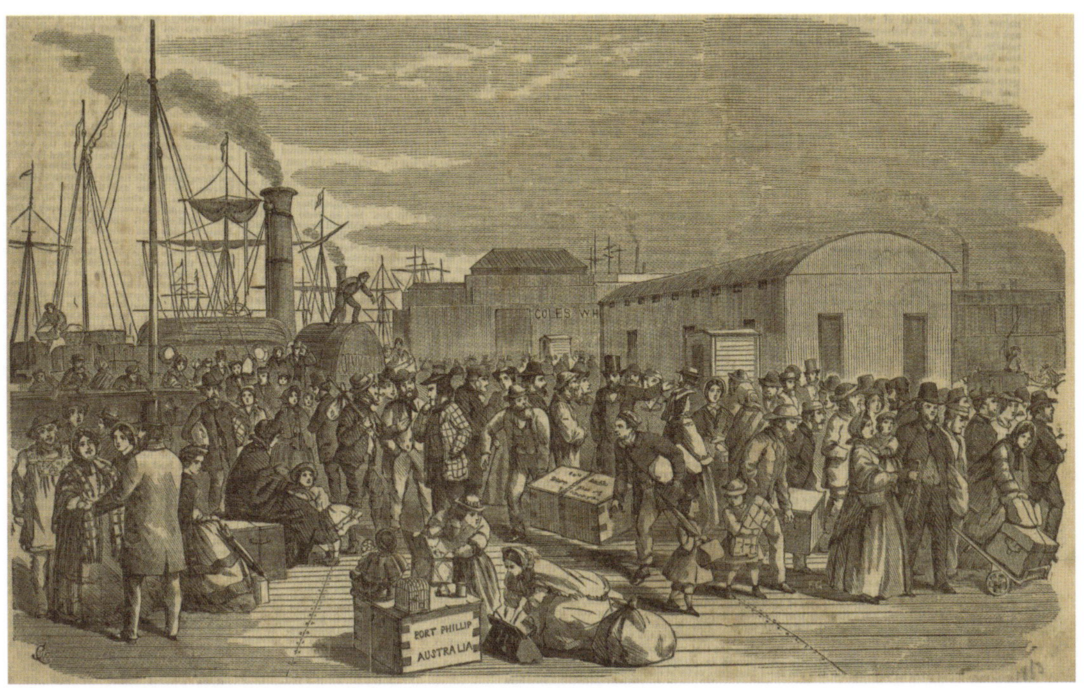

The gold rush transformed the fledgling Australian colonies, causing huge new waves of arrivals from overseas.

own eyes the great people on board, he being actually a member of the Australian Parliament (I did not know they had one)'.[62]

Henning found little appeal in her new surroundings:

After a placid existence in English country houses, Rachel disliked the heat and the bush life 'extremely' and 'did not care enough about Australian flowers' to make a botanical collection or to use two letters of introduction from Sir William Hooker of Kew. Miserably homesick she went to England in the Star of Peace ... In 1861 she returned to Australia in the [SS] *Great Britain.*

She started to discover the beauty of Australia and became a keen gardener. She continued to be a productive letter writer, corresponding with her sister Etta, who remained in England, and also with her sister Amy, who had married and now lived in Bathurst. She died in 1914.

Handwritten letters in the digital age

Letters and the mail were a key part of Australia's communications with the world until the late 1990s, when letters began to be replaced by emails. Personal letters have now largely disappeared from postal communications, although they remain popular for special occasions, such as when a child wants to send a letter to Santa Claus.

Although email is an incredibly useful tool, something was lost in this change to digital communication; emails and texts still include news, but they do not have the tactile, three-dimensional quality of a letter, and they lack key personal elements. So much of a person goes into a letter: the choice of paper and envelope, the handwriting, drawings or objects, small keepsakes, news and expressions of love and desire. Receiving a reply becomes an event, heavy with anticipation, as evidenced in this anonymous poem from a soldier in World War II, waiting for mail:

No mail.
The answer comes each day
and you, quiet, turn away,
knowing that that is that
and nothing can be done.

You write.
Letters into limbo,
composing thoughts, feeling,
black words on white paper,
a man's life in his own mind
committed to actuality
on foolscap and envelope,
postage threepence.

You write.
Letters posted into blackness
south through the sky,
taking you,
man living, man thinking, man feeling,
in an air-mail envelope
south to a silence
that gives no response,
just accepting, not commenting,
void as the sky it cleaves.[63]

A number of books mourn the decline of handwritten letters, including Philip Hensher's *The Missing Ink*, Ian Sansom's *Paper* and John O'Connell's *For the Love of Letters*.[64] Part of the essence of what is missing is the style of handwriting, the receipt of a physical, tactile object in the post, and the time taken to consider and write down passages, rather than typing rapidly, as

Above: Settlers eagerly awaited letters from their families back in the United Kingdom and other countries.

Right: The mail was an important link for the gold miners, a chance to rest from their harsh life and think of others far away.

we often do with an email. But despite modern developments in electronic communication, mail remains a critical part of life, especially for packages and business. And in some locations it provides a vital personal link.

Close to Sydney, on the Hawkesbury River, you can join the mailboat that delivers mail and supplies up and down the river:

> *As mail runs go, it's an absolute beauty of a gig. There are only seven stops to deliver to, and they're spaced along a flooded river valley surrounded by thick green bushland, mangroves and handsome sandstone cliffs.*
>
> *The catamaran putters along for about three hours, doubling up as a pleasure cruise for most of those on board. But despite having passengers to feed and entertain, the crew members know that their first priority is to get letters and parcels to tiny communities that are otherwise cut off.*
>
> *The cruise—and mail run—starts from Brooklyn, where trains from Sydney and Newcastle pull in. The neighbouring rail bridge crosses the river, and gives those living on the settlements on either bank a connection to normality. But many smaller settlements—generally just a handful of houses, many of which are waterside holiday homes that have been passed down through generations—can be accessed only by boat. Aside from the houses that have been grandfathered in, there is a smattering of artists and writers who love the isolation and have set up home on the wild banks of the Hawkesbury.*[65]

Two women collect their supplies on the upper reaches of the Hawkesbury River in about 1952.

2

Connecting to the world

1850–1876: The arrival of the telegraph and telephone in the Australian colonies

By the 1850s, the Australian colonies were booming, their populations and economies driven by the discovery of gold and the strength of the emerging wool and agricultural industries.[1] The country's days as a penal colony were fading: all transportation to New South Wales ceased by 1840, and the last convicts were sent to Perth, Western Australia, in 1868. By 1835, about 300 ships reached Sydney Cove in one year, 60 of them from Britain.[2] Sydney and Melbourne—particularly Melbourne—were jumping ahead in leaps and bounds.

The Australian colonies struggled with their communications with Britain, the centre of the empire. Many political and commercial decisions were made in the 'home country'. A monthly mail service was provided by the Peninsular and Oriental Steam Navigation Company, but this still involved a considerable turnaround time.[3]

The desire for news from Britain and continental Europe continued unabated. A painting by renowned twentieth-century Australian maritime artist John Allcot, titled *The Race for the News in the 'Fifties'*, depicts a dinghy racing out to Sydney Heads to meet a ship arriving from Britain in the 1850s, in order to get the 'scoop' of the latest news from the other side of the world, likely to be about three months old.

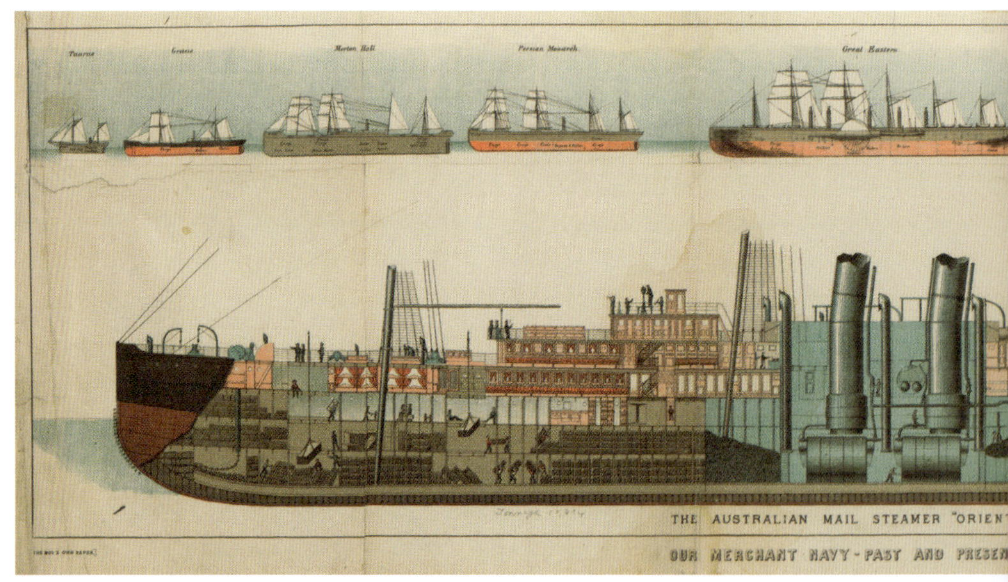

In Sydney, newspapers raced to meet new shipping arrivals, eager to be first to get news from abroad.

New technology would soon arrive to solve the communications dilemma for Australia. The age of invention was in full swing around the globe. Key discoveries in science, transport and health had already transformed everyday life, and communications were soon to be revolutionised with the invention of the telegraph system.

Mail steamers provided a regular service, carrying substantial amounts of post to and from the Australian colonies.

The telegraph

The idea of sending communication signals from fixed points had long existed. Methods of communication included smoke signals, beacons and the introduction of the semaphore or flag system.

Some historians argue that the first step in a long line of cumulative experiments that led to the invention of telegraphy came in 1746, when Jean-Antoine Nollet conducted his experiment with 700 monks connected to a Leyden jar, each receiving an electric shock at virtually the same time. He had demonstrated that electricity moved instantaneously over a distance.

Nollet's experiment inspired the theory that messages could be sent using electrical currents over copper wire. In the early nineteenth century, two key developments paved the way for this concept to move towards becoming a reality. In 1800, the Italian physicist Alessandro Volta invented a battery that could store an electric current, which could later be discharged. Then in 1820, the Danish physicist Hans Christian Oersted showed that a magnetic needle could be deflected with an electric current. This principle was later applied to the telegraph: as a telegraph key is alternated up and down, it connects—or disconnects—an electric circuit, controlling the electric pulse and sounds that are transmitted.

Inventors developed a number of early workable electric communication systems, including those in Britain by Sir William Cooke and Sir Charles Wheatstone. The breakthrough, though, occurred in the United States, when the artist-turned-inventor Samuel Morse, working with his colleagues Leonard Gale and Alfred Vail, produced a single-circuit telegraph. An operator pushed down a key to complete the electrical circuit of the battery. This action sent the electrical signal across a wire to a receiver at the other end. The system only required a key, a battery, wire and a line of poles to carry the wire between stations. Messages were known as 'telegrams'. The system was successfully trialled between Washington, DC, and Baltimore, Maryland, on 24 May 1844.

The simplicity of the process, when combined with the code developed by Morse (Morse code), meant a telegram could now be sent to multiple destinations. Morse patented his invention and the telegraph system was born. The telegraph immediately began to revolutionise communications

A telegraph set comprising a telegraph key, a relay and a register.

around the world. Australia's first telegraph line began operation between Melbourne and Williamstown in 1854. The 17-kilometre line was overseen by a Canadian, Samuel McGowan. By the end of the same year, the line was extended further to Geelong and Ballarat.[4] Within four years, Sydney, Melbourne and Adelaide were connected.[5]

McGowan was a scientist and administrator. Born in Londonderry, Ireland, in 1829, he emigrated to Canada with his family. At age 18, McGowan began to take a great interest in telegraphy, and after learning directly from Samuel Morse, gained experience with several telegraph companies in North America.[6]

Hearing of gold discoveries in Australia, McGowan travelled to Victoria in 1853. He was interested in forming a company to provide telegraphic linkage between the larger urban centres of Melbourne, Sydney and Adelaide as well as the goldfields. The government, however, decided to make all telegraph lines a public monopoly. In September 1853, tenders were called for the construction of an experimental line between Melbourne and Williamstown, and McGowan's was successful. On 1 March 1854, he was appointed general superintendent of the Electric Telegraph Department of Victoria. Just two days later, the first telegraph service south of the equator was opened. By December, under McGowan's guidance, the experimental line had been extended to Geelong. In 1857, all main centres in Victoria were connected, with lines running from Melbourne westwards to Portland and northwards to the Murray River. By the end of 1858, telegraph communication between Melbourne and Sydney, and Melbourne to Adelaide, had been established. It was a remarkable achievement.[7]

Two key problems had still to be overcome before Australia could be linked by telegraph to the world. The first was how telegraph wires could be laid over or under the seas, so that continents could be linked. The second, for the colonies of Australia, was to work out if the great heart of the continent could be crossed. Could a line be run from the south-east, where the main population centres were, to the north, where the undersea cable would come ashore?

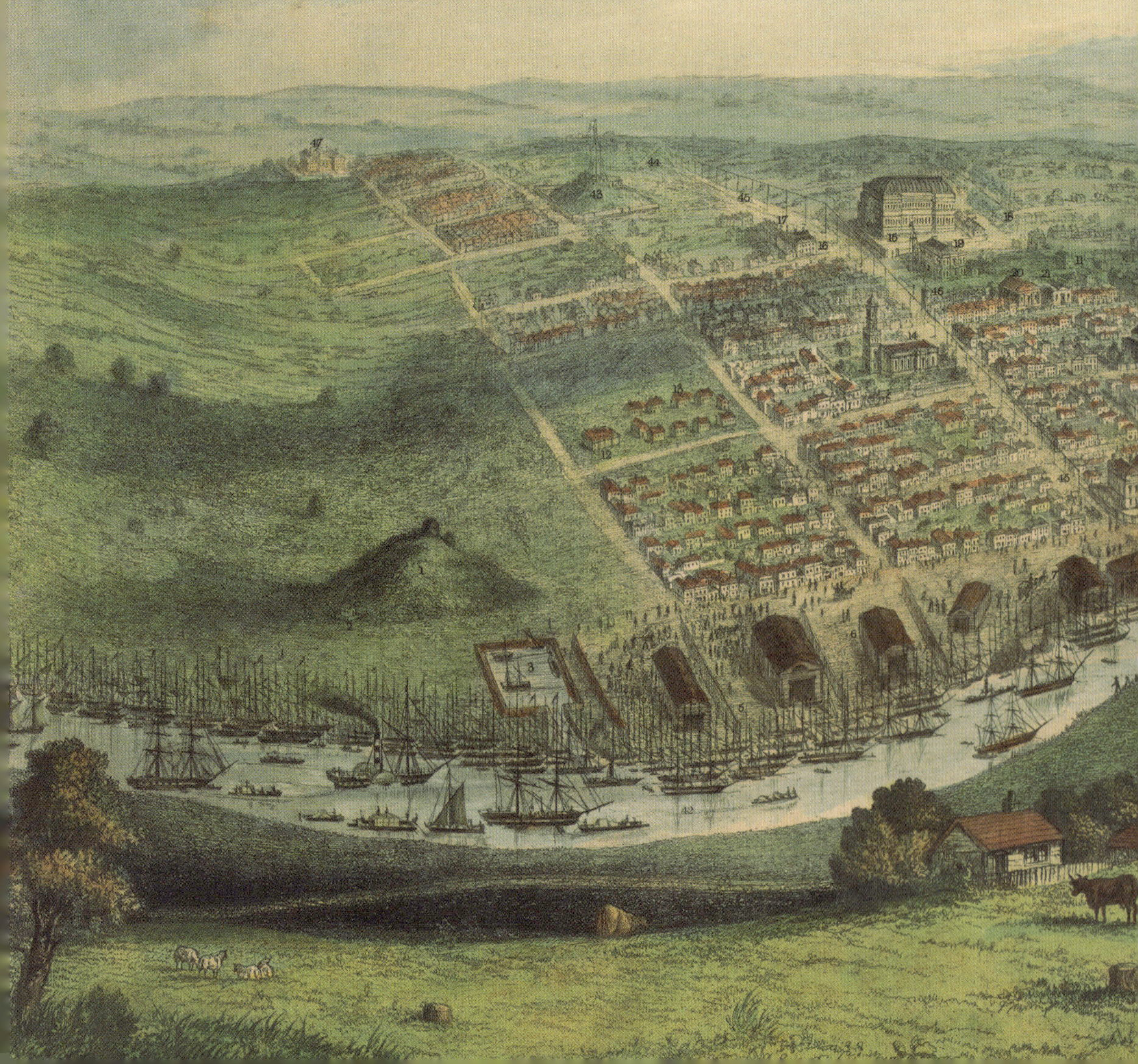

Melbourne grew rapidly, with wealth and numerous new arrivals due to the gold rushes.

Laying cables along the seabed to create an intercontinental telegraph system was a major challenge. Researchers, inventors and telegraph companies experimented with different types of copper-core wires and waterproof coverings. As early as 1850, a successful cable covered in gutta-percha (a form of latex rubber) was laid across the relatively short distance of the English Channel from England to France. As with many innovations, problems had to be identified and the technology improved before the invention could be rolled out more broadly. There were many issues to be considered, including sharks and worms, as described by historian Mary Godwin:

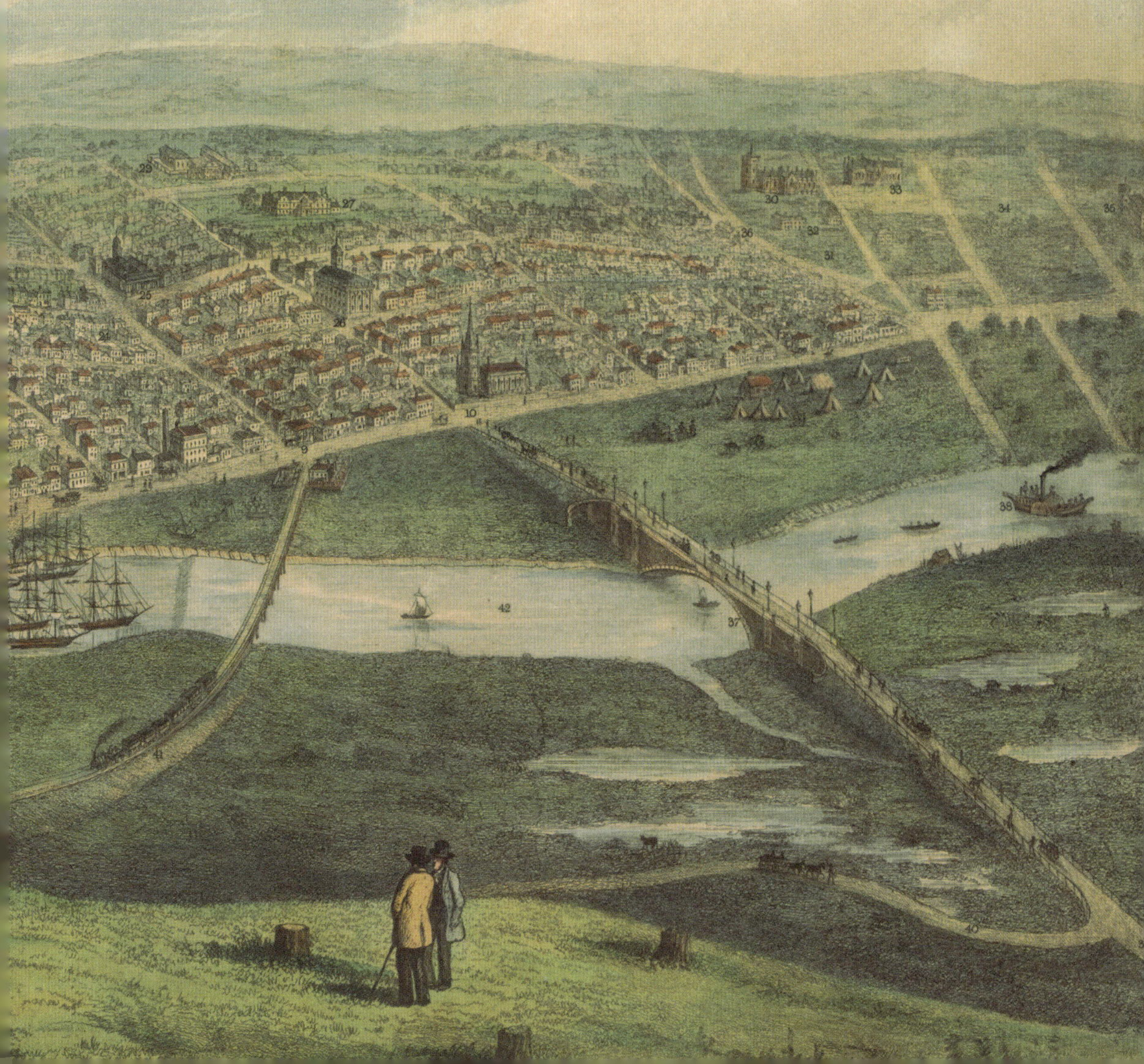

Probably one of the major problems was the nature of the bottom of the ocean. Really, you had to know the profile of the bottom of the ocean because you had to lay a cable that fitted snugly along the ocean bed and there are things like undersea volcanoes and also things living in the sea. Sharks have been known to decide to bite them, there were worms called Teredo worms, which used to like to eat the gutta percha, which was used to insulate the copper wire at the core of the cable. It was the Victorian equivalent of going to the moon 100 or so years later and it attracted the great minds and great amounts of money and the challenges in the same way.[8]

In 1865, the first successful transatlantic cable was put in place between Ireland and Newfoundland, on the north-eastern coast of North America. For the first time, news could travel almost instantaneously across a distance that would take five to six weeks to travel by sailing ship.

By 1870, there were telegraph cables linking Britain with places as far away as Japan and Java.[9] The possibility of radically improving Australia's connection with the rest of the world was now within reach. But first a route for the line had to be identified.

During the 1850s and 1860s, settlers had been pushing further into the interior of Australia. One question had to be answered: what lay in the centre of the continent? Little was known of central Australia. Many thought it was uncrossable, with speculation that there was a great inland sea that would prevent a land crossing from south to north.

In 1839, John McDouall Stuart arrived in South Australia from Scotland. He worked as a surveyor before joining Charles Sturt's expedition into the desert in 1844. Between 1859 and 1862, Stuart led a number of expeditions to try and find a way northwards, through central Australia, to the northern coast of the continent.

The first five expeditions failed due to the terrain, lack of water and illness.

Samples of the submarine telegraph cables that would soon begin to connect countries through undersea lines.

Stuart's sixth expedition found a way to the northern coast of Australia, opening the route that the Overland Telegraph Line would later follow.

Stuart was an alcoholic, and his health was poor, but he persevered. He mounted a sixth expedition with some support from the South Australian Government. Departing from Adelaide, after a difficult and exhausting expedition they reached their goal. The following is the entry from Stuart's diary of 24 July 1862:

> *Thursday, 24th July, Thring Creek, Entering the Marsh. Started at 7.40, course north. I have taken this course in order to make the sea-coast, which I suppose to be distant about eight miles and a half, as soon as possible; by this I hope to avoid the marsh. I shall travel along the beach to the north of the Adelaide* [Adelaide River, in what is now the Northern Territory]. *I did not inform any of the party, except Thring and Auld, that I was so near to the sea, as I wished to give them a surprise on reaching it ... Crossed the valley, and entered the scrub, which was a complete network of vines. Stopped the horses to clear a way, whilst I advanced a few yards on to the beach, and was gratified and delighted to behold the water of the Indian Ocean in Van Diemen*

Gulf, before the party with the horses knew anything of its proximity. Thring, who rode in advance of me, called out 'The Sea!' which so took them all by surprise, and they were so astonished, that he had to repeat the call before they fully understood what was meant. Then they immediately gave three long and hearty cheers.[10]

Stuart had found the pathway for the colony of South Australia to progress into the north. South Australia became responsible for the Northern Territory in 1863 and established two settlements at the mouth of the Adelaide River: Adam Bay (later abandoned as a European settlement) and Palmerston (modern-day Darwin).

Now that new technologies were available to allow cables to run along the seabed, the colonies competed to be the one to have the final link running from Java to Australia. Queensland almost secured the deal, until South Australia won by offering to pay for laying the cable across the desert, from Port Augusta to Darwin. On 18 June 1870, the South Australian Government entered into a contract with the British Australian Telegraph Company, which was laying the undersea cable to Darwin, to build the line 'by 1 January 1872 with a budget of £128,000. South Australia hoped that being the first point of contact between Australia and the rest of the world would stimulate the colony's business environment'.[11]

The work was supervised by the postmaster-general of South Australia, Charles Todd. Born and educated in London, Todd was appointed as an 'astronomical calculator' at Greenwich Observatory in 1841. He went on to work at Greenwich as the supervisor of a galvanic system for the transmission of time signals. This involved regular cooperation with the Electric Telegraph Company and C.V. Walker, an electrical engineer who was an early proponent of submarine telegram cables.

Todd became intensely interested in telecommunications, and when South Australia requested Sir George Airy, the Astronomer Royal, to recommend an observer and superintendent of electric telegraph, he nominated Charles Todd.

Members of the Overland Telegraph Line team: the Port Darwin postmaster John Archibald Graham Little, leader of the northern section, Robert Charles Patterson, Charles Todd and surveyor Alexander James Mitchell.

Todd was appointed to the position and reached Adelaide in November 1855. He worked with his Victorian counterpart, Samuel McGowan, to recommend a set-up using the Morse system for links between Adelaide, Melbourne and Sydney.[12] These projects were implemented during the 1860s. In 1866, British companies put forward a number of new proposals to complete the international telegraph link. When South Australia negotiated the rights to lay the Australian line from Adelaide to Darwin—via the route pioneered in 1862 by John McDouall Stuart—Todd was appointed head of the project. His enthusiastic leadership proved crucial to overcoming the range of challenges that arose. Trusted by his employers and employees, he also had a quirky sense of humour, delighting in puns such as 'I would be odd without my T'.[13]

Todd split the route into three main sections—southern, central and northern—with work occurring simultaneously on each. The central section of 1,000 kilometres, from Macumba River to Tennant Creek, was the least known territory to the planners, with only Stuart's journals providing them with a map and understanding of the terrain. Before a new line could be laid, however, they needed a helper to get them out into the desert.

There is a scene in the opening of the 1981 film *Gallipoli* when Archie Hamilton and Frank Dunne decide to head to Perth across the desert to enlist in the army. They are lost—badly lost—and are starting to lose concentration and energy. Then they spot the silhouette of an animal in the desert—a camel. 'It would have to be your lucky day,' says the laconic camel driver in the film. To remind us just how big the world was before the advent of modern travel, he says, 'I almost went to Perth once'. His trusty camel provided everything for him. It carried his water and supplies and was a stoic and resilient companion in the desert. These 'ships of the desert' would, equally, provide a great support to the Overland Telegraph Line.

The first camel arrived in Australia in 1840, imported from the Canary Islands. A larger shipment of 24 camels from India and Palestine arrived soon after. The camels were brought out specifically for the Burke and Wills expedition of 1860–1861. They were renowned for their ability to retain water and travel long distances in arid or desert landscapes.

The track record of explorers' use of camels was not strong. In 1846, John Horrocks led an expedition towards Port Augusta that included Aboriginal goatherd Jimmy Moorhouse and artist S.T. Gill. They left Penwortham in the Clare Valley north of Adelaide on 29 July 1846 for a planned four-month journey. In mid-August, the expedition crossed the Flinders Ranges via what is now known as Horrocks Pass. Horrocks found that the camel was temperamental but could carry heavy loads, which meant they could transport more water. On 1 September, Horrocks was preparing to shoot a bird on the shores of Lake Dutton. When he was reloading his gun, the camel moved and the rifle was discharged, causing injuries that resulted in Horrocks' death on 23 September.

The expedition led by Robert O'Hara Burke and William Wills left Melbourne in August 1860 for the northern coast of Australia with 26 camels, as well as horses and wagons. From their advance depot on Cooper Creek, Burke and Wills set out with six camels, one horse and two other men. They eventually reached the coast at the Gulf of Carpentaria.

On the disastrous return journey, three of the men died (including Burke and Wills), two camels and the horse were eaten, another two camels were abandoned and two became bogged and were shot.

Although the expedition ended in tragedy, the camel had proved itself as a useful form of transport in the outback. Australian breeding programs were soon underway, and by 1866 Australia was exporting camels to the world. At the same time, camels were continuing to be

Camels were ideally suited to supporting travellers in the outback and deserts of central Australia, as seen in this S.T. Gill watercolour of the Horrocks expedition.

brought into Australia, this time accompanied by Afghan cameleers, known as 'Ghans'. A camel party could travel up to 40 kilometres per day, and each camel could carry up to 600 kilograms. They soon became a reliable and essential form of transportation:

> *The camels and their cameleers helped carry supplies inland for the mining and sheep industries, aided the building of the Overland Telegraph Line, the Canning Stock Route, major fence lines and the Trans-Australia and Central Australian railways. They carried pipe sections for the Goldfields Water Supply, supplied goods to inland towns, mining camps, sheep and cattle stations and also Aboriginal communities. Wagons hauled by Camels moved wool from sheep stations to railheads, pulled scoops in the construction of dams, and helped with ploughing and other farm work.*[14]

It was the northern section that proved the most difficult for Todd. The wet season severely affected the work, and managing the supply chain from the coast proved onerous. Work came to a standstill at King River, about 3,500 kilometres from Palmerston. The government overseer dismissed the contractors, and the government railway engineer R.C. Patterson was put in charge. He arrived at Port Darwin in August 1871.[15]

The work was hard. The historian Ann Moyal describes it, at its most regular, like this:

> *So just to give you an idea of how the men worked: the overseers were responsible for maintaining discipline and the health of their men and they had to report every day on how many poles each labourer had put in and how much wire had been constructed across. And they got their men up at 5.30, had breakfast and worked of course till about 11, and then across the heat of the day they had a rest till 2, then they worked till nightfall. They had to put in 20 poles to every mile and in an area like the centre of Australia, which is the highest lightning area in Australia, every second pole was fitted with a lightning rod.*[16]

The work was also dangerous. Two entries from a sample of the journal of engineer Walter Rutt, an overseer on the northern section, held at the State Library of South Australia, show that the dangerous conditions of the crossing led to tragedy and also conflict with the Indigenous owners of the land:

> *5 November 1871: Late at night Sub-Inspector* [Leas...?] *rode into camp with news that Bowman, one of Mr Hack's bullock drivers, had died suddenly with symptoms of apoplexy hastened by sun-stroke ...*
>
> *6 November 1871: Mr Patterson had the men called together and his* [Mr Bowman's] *effects sold by auction for the benefit of the relatives. Nothing known of him except that he was a Sydney man, believed to be from Leicestershire, and had been a gold digger. He complained on Saturday morning of pain in the back of his head but it did not appear to be dangerous until an hour before his death, when he was taken with a fit while driving his team and never regained consciousness.*[17]

The construction of the Overland Telegraph Line was a laborious undertaking. As well as laying poles, the workers were also clearing vegetation.

In his detailed technical report, Charles Todd describes just how difficult the vegetation was to clear:

> *From Daly Waters to Frew's Iron-stone Pond the poles are very sound, being mostly of blood-wood, and of the full size. The clearing over this length was exceedingly heavy; I believe by far the heaviest on the continent—the line being carried for the greater part of its length through a dense mulga scrub, which here attains a height of over 40 feet, and hedge tree, through which it was impossible to lead a horse.*[18]

Workers had to cope with extreme heat. They were up from 5:30am, had a break in the middle of the day, and would then work until nightfall.

The two ends of the overland cable were finally joined at Frew Ponds at 3pm on 22 August 1872. R.C. Patterson recorded the event in his diary. Judging by the entry, excitement clearly got in the way of risk management:

Half the party seized hold of me and the wire, and the other half of the other end, and stretched with all might and main to bring the two ends together. All our force could not do this. I then attached some binding wire to one end. The moment I brought it to the other end a current passed through my body from all the batteries on the line. I had to yell and let go. Next time I proceeded more cautiously and used my handkerchief to seize the wire. In about five minutes I had the joint made complete and Adelaide was connected with Port Darwin. It would have been with England had not the [overseas] *cable broken down.*[19]

It had been a massive undertaking. The line was made up of 36,000 telegraph poles and 11 repeater stations 200 kilometres apart (one of which was Alice Springs Telegraph Station, the beginnings of what would become this major township) needed to boost the electrical signal.[20]

Unfortunately, in June 1872, a fault had developed in the submarine cable between Port Darwin and Java, and there was dead silence on the line.[21] The newspapers voiced disappointment, proving that modern-day complaints about infrastructure have many precedents:

> *The repeated delays and disappointments in the opening of through communication with the Australian colonies have had the effect of deadening public interest in the subject. According to present appearances, it will probably be several months before messages can be sent through direct. For although, as the last mail informs us, the continental line was expected to be completed in all its sections by the close of August, the submarine line is still unrepaired. I learn from the officials of the company that the injury in the cable is somewhere near the Port Darwin end, and is supposed to have been occasioned by abrasion on the coral formation in that region of the sea.*[22]

The undersea cable from Java to Darwin was back in action by 21 October, a stream of messages was sent and received, and celebrations commenced. Now the newspapers were jubilant:

> *English news Twenty-Four Hours Old! If any doubt has up to this time lingered in the minds of the public as to the actual establishment of a wire connection between Australia and Great Britain, it must be effectually dispelled by the overwhelming evidence to be found in subsequent columns. We have been so long accustomed to look upon telegraphic communication with the old country through the qualifying medium of gaps in the land line and breakages in the cable, of estafettes and steam express services, that it is difficult to realize the fact of our having finally dispensed with all these adventitious aids, and become dependent upon the electric current alone. Never until now have we been able finally to appreciate the importance of the new era that has dawned upon these Southern colonies ... A comparison of dates will show that*

not much more than twenty-four hours elapsed between the dispatch from the London Office of a message which will be found elsewhere and its publication here. This is by far the most memorable event that has yet occurred in the history of news-catering in the colony.[23]

The colonies of Australia were now linked to the world. Modernisation was coming to Australia. The infrastructure put in place by the Overland Telegraph Line opened up the land to pastoralists. The devastating impact on the culture, land and livelihoods of Indigenous people continued.

From telegraph to telephone

The telegraph was a great marvel, but to use it, you had to go to a central point, such as a telegram or post office. From there, messages were received at the 'cable head', the terminal receiving point, and would be translated from Morse code and collected by, or distributed to, the recipient. However, success soon bred success when it came to the telegraph line; technologies continued to improve.

Research focused on how to send several messages over a single wire. In 1868, American farmer-turned-telegraphist Joseph Stearns invented the duplex, a system that transmitted two messages simultaneously over a single wire. The Western Union Telegraph Company bought the rights to Stearns' duplex system.

Teacher of the deaf and inventor Alexander Graham Bell was interested in this research and worked on developing designs able to subdivide a telegraph line into ten or more 'channels'. The next step was 'harmonic telegraphs' (which used tuning forks that responded to specific acoustic frequencies), and after that, the voice.

On 10 March 1876, Bell made the first telephone call. Having achieved success in transmitting the human voice, Bell and his assistant, Thomas Watson, took the invention to the Western Union Telegraph Company. The verdict: 'After careful consideration of your invention, while it is a very interesting novelty, we have come to the conclusion that is has no commercial possibilities'.[24]

Fortunately, others saw differently, and Bell became very wealthy from his invention. Another inventor, Elisha Gray, had worked on a very similar invention, but lodged his patent after Bell.

Telephones had the potential to bring communications into the workplace and the home, and by the 1880s phones were commonplace in the United States and spreading internationally.

Like many inventions during the late nineteenth and early twentieth centuries, telephones—along with electric light, running water and sewerage systems, radio, television and the refrigerator—brought

Left: The post and telegraph office became the mainstay of communications across Australia.

Below: Bell's experimental telephone receiver that presaged a new transformation in communications: a device that carried the human voice over distance.

increased livability into the home. In his book *Made in America*, Bill Bryson writes of the scale of inventions in the 'frantic last quarter of the nineteenth century'[25]. America had a tradition of productive 'tinkering', which was reflected in the domestic nature of many of the inventions—that is, inventions to make life easier for the average person in their home.

In Australia, news of the invention of the telephone was greeted with amazement and amusement. In Victoria, the *Mount Alexander Mail* published an article on 5 December 1876, stating:

> [The new invention could transmit] *the sound of the human voice through a thousand miles of telegraph line so distinctly that the words uttered by the operator at one end of the line can be distinctly made out at a thousand miles distance by the receiver at the other end. It would seem as if this was the highest possible triumph of telegraphy.*

On 18 November 1876, a writer for the *South Australian Register* saw the humorous side of the invention:

> *Who then can foretell the future of the telephone? Doubtless before you and I, my incredulous public, are many years older, Edwin in Adelaide will be able to have a whole Saturday afternoon's talk with his Angelina in London, at which time he may appropriately exclaim in the language of the song: 'Although I listen to your voice Your face I never see'.*

Australians were soon adopting the telephone with gusto. The first phone was used by the Robinson brothers in Melbourne and South Melbourne in 1879.[26] As in England, it was colloquially called 'the blower', after an earlier version of a telephone-like system. Melbourne's first telephone directory from 1880, published by the Melbourne Telephone Exchange Company, lists 44 services.[27] An Australian racehorse was soon given the name Telephone.[28] Journalists seemed to enjoy reporting on the use of the telephone, with, for example, a regular 'Our telephone' section in the Melbourne *Herald* appearing in the 1890s. In an article in the Sydney *Evening News*, from 31 December 1910, the retiring postmaster of the suburb of Balmain reflected on the progress he had seen: 'the telephone was started with 10 subscribers; today there are 400'.

Early telephones were powered by a battery in the home where the telephone was located. As systems grew, a larger, common battery was installed at local exchange centres, and the government introduced regulations to control the networks.

Access to the telephone was more complex for rural Australians, given the vast distances involved. But it did happen, although often after some time. For example, in Queensland, the Brisbane Central Exchange started a service in April 1883, by which time 175 subscribers were already connected. The demand was growing in the city, especially for businesses, but the charges were high. Operations in Queensland were more expensive than for those further south due to both the long distances and the smaller number of subscribers.[29]

By the beginning of the twentieth century, telephone lines had extended into rural areas. The first country exchange in Australia opened at Maryborough, Queensland, in 1882. The technology quickly spread.

From small beginnings (and three-digit telephone numbers), evident in this telephone directory from around 1882, the technology would soon become a mainstay of our work and personal lives.

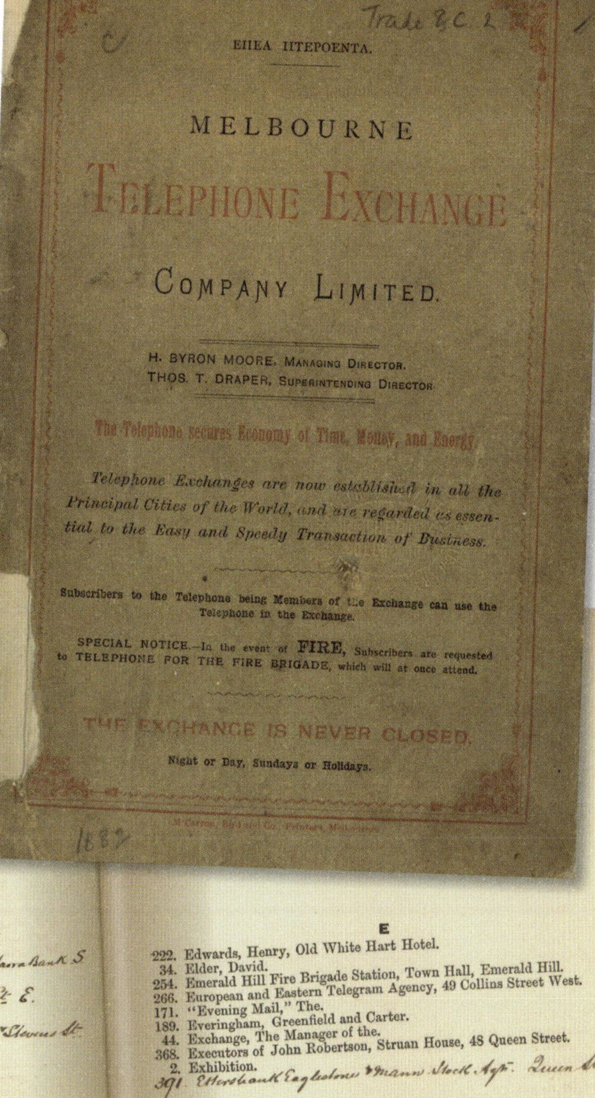

A. Currie

ΕΠΕΑ ΠΤΕΡΟΕΝΤΑ.

MELBOURNE

TELEPHONE EXCHANGE

COMPANY LIMITED.

H. BYRON MOORE, MANAGING DIRECTOR.
THOS. T. DRAPER, SUPERINTENDING DIRECTOR.

The Telephone secures Economy of Time, Money, and Energy.

Telephone Exchanges are now established in all the Principal Cities of the World, and are regarded as essential to the Easy and Speedy Transaction of Business.

Subscribers to the Telephone being Members of the Exchange can use the Telephone in the Exchange.

SPECIAL NOTICE.—In the event of FIRE, Subscribers are requested to TELEPHONE FOR THE FIRE BRIGADE, which will at once attend.

THE EXCHANGE IS NEVER CLOSED.

Night or Day, Sundays or Holidays.

M'Carron, Bird and Co., Printers, Melbourne.

1882

4 *Melbourne Telephone Exchange Company.*

338. Corbett and Son, A. G., Machinery and Iron Merchant[s] Street.
354. Couche, Calder and Co., William Street.
54. Cowan and Co., Wholesale and Manufacturing Stationers.
111. Crisp, Lewis and Hedderwick, Solicitors.
319. Croker, William H., Solicitor, &c., 8 Market Buildings, W[...]
48. Crosby, W., and Co., Merchants and Shipping Agents.
369. Crouch, T. J., Architect, 46 Elizabeth Street.
336. { Cuming, Smith and Co., Chemical Works, Yarraville. / Campbell, Charles, and Co., William Street.
92. Cuningham, Hastings, and Co.
61. Curcier and Adet, Wine and Spirit Merchants, Importers.
70. Custom House.
386 Cameron Laing & Coy 112 Flinders Lane E.
381 Caughey A. R. Wine merch[an]t 4 Collins St W. & Yarra Bank S
394 Coffee Tavern Coy Ltd 89 Bourke St E.
393 Do Do Registered office 82 Collins St E.
385 Cook J. McG Mutual Provident Buildings
404 Cohen Bros & Coy Furniture warehouse. Lonsdale & Stevens St.

D

113. "Daily Telegraph" Newspaper.
62. Dalgety, Blackwood and Co., Merchants, &c.
55. Danby & Gilmour, Accountants, Trade Assignees, &c.
124. Danks, John, Brassfounder.
50. Davey, Cole and Flack, Trade Assignees, &c.
215. Davies, M. H., Solicitor, 6 Collins Street West, and Mathoura Road, Toorak.
203. Davies and Campbell, Solicitors, 22 Collins Street East.
203. Davies, J. M., Boundary Road, Toorak.
234. Dean, William, and Co., 91 Flinders Lane East.
80. De Castella and Rowan, St. Hubert's Wine Cellars.
252. Denis Brothers, Bourke Street East.
291. De Paula, Mackley and Co., 24 Market Buildings, Collins Street West.
21. Derham and Co., Grain Merchants.
3. Derwent and Tamar Fire and Marine Assurance Company.
72. Detmold, William, Wholesale Stationer, Bookbinder and Manufacturer.
223. Dillon and Burrows, Latrobe Street and A'Beckett Street.
238. Dodgshun, James, and Co., 23 Flinders Lane East.
209. Donaldson, H. B., and Co., Beach St., Sandridge.
210. Douglas and Sons, 100 Collins Street East.
326. Dresden Marine Insurance Company, Queen Street.
284. Duckett, Edward, Lonsdale Street East.
226. Dudgeon and Arnell, 125 Lonsdale Street West.
392. Dickins R & Coy 25 Market St

5

E

222. Edwards, Henry, Old White Hart Hotel.
34. Elder, David.
254. Emerald Hill Fire Brigade Station, Town Hall, Emerald Hill.
266. European and Eastern Telegram Agency, 49 Collins Street West.
171. "Evening Mail," The.
189. Everingham, Greenfield and Carter.
44. Exchange, The Manager of the.
368. Executors of John Robertson, Struan House, 48 Queen Street.
2. Exhibition.
391 Ettershank Eaglestone & Mann Stock Agts. Queen St.

F

176. Falk, P., and Co., Wholesale Jewellers, Importers, and Merchants, 30 Little Collins Street West.
5. Fanning, Nankivell and Co., Merchants.
257. Federal Bank of Australia, corner of Collins and Elizabeth Streets.
230. Felix, John } Spencer Street.
230. Finlay's Hotel }
213. Feldheim, Jacobs and Co., Queen Street.
235. Felton, Grimwade and Co., Flinders Lane West.
182. Fergusson and Mitchell, 27 Collins Street West, Engravers, Lithographers, Printers, and Account Book Manufacturers.
98. Fergusson and Moore, Printers.
55. Fire Insurance Association, Limited (The).
106. Fire Insurance Companies' Brigade Association.
317. Fitzgerald Bros., Errol Street, Hotham.
93. Fitzgerald, T. N., Surgeon.
147. Ford, Wm., and Co. (Geo. Swift), Pharmaceutical Chemists and Medical Agents.
452 Forbes & Rowden Burwood Rd Hawthorn
453 Forbes & Rowden High Street St Kilda

A country exchange was opened at Townsville in 1883, Rockhampton followed in 1884, Bundaberg in 1886 and Charters Towers in 1891.[30]

Eucla: A vital link in the telegraph network

The town of Eucla was established in 1877 as the site of a manual repeater station for the telegraph line between Albany, Western Australia, and Adelaide. The town is located within Western Australia, just 11 kilometres from the South Australian border. It sits within sight of the sea, on the edge of the Great Australian Bight. To support the town, a jetty was built with a one-kilometre tramline to haul supplies and equipment. During the late nineteenth century, the town acted as the centre for both South Australia and Western Australia in receiving and forwarding messages.[31]

Public servants from both colonies operated out of Eucla's telegraph station. Before Morse code was adopted, Eucla acted as a translation station between two different telegraph codes; South Australian staff employed what was known as the 'Victorian Alphabet', and Western Australian telegraphers used the 'Universal Code'.

Eucla itself is a town of about 50 to 60 people today, a stop-off on the Eyre Highway. The remains of the telegraph station are a local tourist attraction, but in its heyday, the station was buzzing with constant activity. Photos show lines of workers busily processing and passing on messages, maintaining the link between South Australia (and therefore the world, via the Overland Telegraph Line) and Western Australia.

The last days of Morse code

With Federation in 1901, the Commonwealth of Australia took over responsibility for communications from the colonies (now states), including telecommunications. This made sense, as one of the key goals of Federation was to improve connections across the entire continent. The first Commonwealth postmaster-general was responsible for the management of telephones and systems across Australia.

Inside the Eucla Telegraph Station in 1914.

The telephone arrived soon after the telegraph, but did not entirely replace it for many years; the telegraph was a simpler system. Morse code was still used extensively in World War II. On 13 December 1962, the last Morse code telegram sent in New South Wales was transmitted from the Sydney General Post Office to the Bombala Post Office.[32] In the same year, the TRESS system (Teleprinter Re-perforator Exchange Switching System) replaced telegraphy. In 1987, the teleprinter was replaced by a facsimile system that produced 'Lettergrams'. The last Australia Post Lettergram was sent from the Tamworth Post Office to the Tamworth Powerstation Museum on 30 September 1993.[33]

In 1997, when stopping their use of Morse code for maritime distress calls, French authorities sent a final message: 'Calling all. This is our last cry before our eternal silence'.[34]

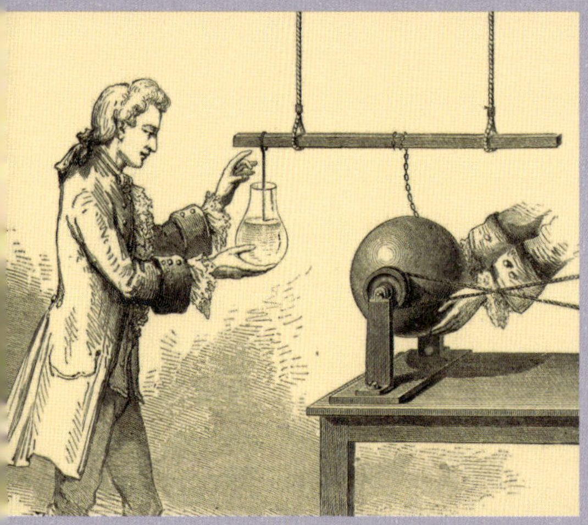

The Leyden jar was an early electric battery which was used in electrical experiments.

Jump-starting the telegraph

Like many innovations, the invention of the telegraph came about at the end of a chain of other discoveries. Before the telegraph was invented, the potential of electrical energy was discovered, a method of storing that energy was conceived and the ability to conduct electricity along metallic wires was fine-tuned.

Electrical energy was first described by William Gilbert (1544–1603) in his work *De magnete ...* (*On the Magnet ...*). A physician to Queen Elizabeth I, Gilbert was a rigorous scholar. He conducted many experiments, testing myths, and was one of the first people to use an objective form of experimental methodology. Gilbert also conducted experiments on the way objects like amber, when rubbed, can attract light objects, which he termed 'electrics', from the Greek word for amber. Gilbert used a needle turning on a vertical point to measure the strength of charges.[35]

Then came the first capacitator, or battery, capable of storing electricity. The early battery was a Leyden jar, invented by physicist Pieter van Musschenbroek in the town of Leiden, in the Netherlands. The Leyden jar was a glass flask, part-filled with water, with a wire wound around the inside, able to hold a large electrical charge. The end of the wire stuck through the cork lid. The jar was charged by attaching the end of the wire to a device that generated static electricity.[36]

Jean-Antoine Nollet was one of the first to experiment with conducting a charge along wire. In England, Henry Cavendish (1731–1810) was also researching conductivity—the ability to carry an electrical current—in the second half of the eighteenth century.

With these three crucial elements, the path was open for the invention of the telegraph. The development of a transmitter key and a receiver would change the world.

3

'Seeking Awarua Station'

1911–1916: Wireless radio and the heroic age of Antarctic exploration

On 1 January 1901, the colonies of Australia were federated by an Act of the British Parliament, becoming a single nation. After many years of bickering and negotiating, the colonies had finally reached agreement on a way forward.

By 1901, the country had a population of 3,773,801, not including Indigenous Australians.[1] The young nation was eager to prove itself in the international arena and, in 1912, the Commonwealth Government supported scientist Douglas Mawson's proposal for an Australian expedition to Antarctica.

Mawson was born in Yorkshire, England, but emigrated to Australia as a young boy with his family. He studied geology at the University of Sydney and was working as an academic when he joined Ernest Shackleton's Antarctic *Nimrod* expedition of 1907–1909. In 1911, he secured private and government backing for the Australasian Antarctic Expedition, with a strong focus on scientific research.[2]

Mawson decided to make use of a relatively new invention, wireless radio, to establish direct communication from his base in Antarctica back to the world, via remote Macquarie Island and Hobart, Tasmania.

His decision to try and establish wireless communication was a bold one. There were four expeditions heading to the Antarctic during the period 1911–1912. They represented four countries. Two parties—those of Captain Robert Falcon Scott (Britain) and Roald Amundsen (Norway)—would be in a race to reach the South Pole. The Japanese Antarctic Expedition headed south for scientific purposes, as did the Australians.

The role of wireless technology

Wireless technology, which had been invented in the late 1890s, allowed messages to be communicated by electromagnetic waves to (potentially, mobile) points, at first by Morse code, but then, as radio evolved, by voice. It works through the use of an electrically charged transmitter, which sends a signal through the airwaves. The signal is picked up and interpreted by a receiver.

Douglas Mawson's decision to link his expedition back to Australia by wireless was a bold experiment which eventually proved its worth.

The theory of electromagnetic radiation was first proposed by James Clerk Maxwell in 1864. But two key men—Nikola Tesla and Guglielmo Marconi—have been identified as responsible for applying that theory to invent the first wireless radio. In 1893 in St Louis, Missouri, Tesla demonstrated the first wireless radio. However, Marconi filed the first patent for wireless telegraphy in Britain (in 1896) and was the first person to transmit radio signals across the Atlantic Ocean (in 1901). In 1899, when he equipped two ships with wireless radio to report on the America's Cup yacht race, the take-up of this invention grew exponentially.[3]

Wireless radio was critical to shipping, allowing a moving craft to communicate to a fixed station (ship to shore) or to another ship. When the *Titanic* struck an iceberg on 14 April 1912, it sent out Morse code emergency distress (SOS) signals that summoned ships to pick up survivors.

For the Australasian Antarctic Expedition, Mawson purchased a German-made Telefunken 1.5-kilowatt 'spark' transmitter, which used long-wave and Morse code telegraphy.[4] The expedition would land a party at Macquarie Island to maintain the radio station to be constructed there. There were to be two radios used in Antarctica, the first at Mawson's main base at Commonwealth Bay, and the second at Western Base, which was led by veteran Antarctic explorer Frank Wild.

What advantages would the wireless bring? It would allow Mawson's party to communicate key findings or issues with Australia, encouraging interest in the expedition. It was also an important tool in the case of an emergency. Unfortunately, things did not start smoothly with the wireless.

Mawson's journey into the unknown, 1911–1914

Macquarie Island is a subantarctic island, lying about 1,500 kilometres south-east of Tasmania. It is 34 kilometres long and 5 kilometres wide at its greatest breadth. The island teems with penguins, seals and birds, most seeking a nest in the earth to have their offspring.

Mawson's expedition left Hobart on 2 December 1911, steaming south through heavy seas. Part of the bridge of their ship *Aurora* was destroyed on 5 December, when a huge wave struck the vessel. Mawson wrote:

> *The wind increased from bad to worse, and great seas continued to rise until the culmination about 4 a.m. on the morning of December 5, when one struck the bridge, carrying the starboard side clean away. Toucher, the officer on watch, had a narrow escape; fortunately, he happened to be on the other side of the bridge at the time.*[5]

They reached Macquarie Island on 11 December. The island already had inhabitants: shipwrecked sailors from the *Clyde* and half a dozen sealers who lived on the island for the summer months.

Walter Hannam, a radio officer on the Australasian Antarctic Expedition, spent many hours at his station, listening for signals.

The men unloaded the equipment for the station, including a hut and supplies, and selected a site for the wireless masts:

> *It was decided that the best site for the wireless station was the summit of* [an] *isolated precipitous hill—Wireless Hill. We had then to face the serious difficulty of transportation of the heavy masts and engine parts from the beach to the summit—a vertical height of over three hundred and fifty feet.*[6]

Five men formed the Macquarie Island party, charged with managing the wireless station and undertaking scientific observations. Among them was telegraphist Arthur Sawyer, who was to be chief wireless operator.

Mawson and the rest of the expedition continued south, and set up their main base at Commonwealth Bay, Adélie Land. Here they hurried to erect a purpose-built hut and prepared to see out the winter, before launching their key journeys of discovery in the spring and summer.

With the help of others, radio officer Walter Henry Hannam, a wireless operator and mechanic, laid the strong foundations necessary for the petrol motor and the generator of the wireless installation. The floor of the workroom was then built around these, and the walls and roof added. Hannam continued to unpack and mount the wireless equipment.[7] He sent a number of messages, some of which were heard by Sawyer at Macquarie Island. But on 13 October a hurricane struck, destroying one of the masts. Mawson wrote of the event:

The Australasian Antarctic Expedition made significant discoveries, but tragedy was about to strike.

October 13 was known as Black Sunday. We were all seated at dinner and the Hut was quivering in the tornado-like gusts which followed a heavy 'blow' reaching a maximum hourly average of 91 miles. One mighty blast was followed by a crack and the sound of a heavy falling body. For a moment it was thought that something had happened to the Hut. Then the messman ran out to the trap-door and saw that the northern wireless mast had disappeared.[8]

For the next few months, Hannam constantly struggled to bring the radio back to life.[9] The wireless was still not operating when, on 10 November 1912, Mawson set out with his colleagues Xavier Mertz and Belgrave Ninnis to explore the unknown section of the Antarctic continent known as King George Land.

It was a journey into the unknown. Mawson titled this group the 'far-eastern party', which was to 'push out rapidly overland ... mapping more distant sections of the coast-line'.

In a tragic set of circumstances, on 14 December, Ninnis, with his team of dogs and sledge, fell into a seemingly bottomless crevasse, and all were lost. Mawson and Mertz called for three hours, but there was no answer.[10]

Mertz and Mawson had to immediately turn for home, as most of their supplies had gone with the sledge. Mertz became ill with poisoning from the dogs' livers they had eaten. He died during the night of 7–8 January.[11] In a feat of endurance, Mawson returned alone to Commonwealth Bay.

As he stumbled towards the hut, on 8 February 1913 the *Aurora*, which had returned to Commonwealth Bay, departed, intent on leaving before the ice pack closed in again with the end of summer. With no sign of Mawson or his party, a group of volunteers was left behind for a second winter in the Antarctic. Later that day, they witnessed Mawson's return, a ghostly figure emerging out of the ice.

While Mawson recovered, the new radio operator, Sidney Jeffryes, got the radio working. On 15 February, they picked up signals from Macquarie Island. The signals became more distinct until, on 20 February, a message from Commonwealth Bay reached Sawyer at Macquarie Island, who immediately responded by saying 'good evening'.[12]

With no daylight for several months, party members had to focus on keeping busy, planning their expeditions and undertaking daily tasks.

On 21 February, they were able to exchange information. They spoke about the fate of their own party, and learned that Captain Scott and his party had perished returning from the South Pole. The signals went from Macquarie Island to Hobart, and then were shared with the world at large. Mawson sent the news of the tragic deaths of his two companions, with special messages to their relatives.

Mawson wrote: 'The first news from the outside world was the bare statement that Captain Scott and four of his companions had perished on their journey to the South Pole'. Mawson had already heard from the returning *Aurora* that Amundsen and his party had reached and returned from the pole.[13]

The joy of communication was clear:

> *It was now a common thing for those of us who had gone to bed before midnight to wake up in the morning and find that quite a budget of wireless messages had been received. It took the place of a morning paper and we made the most of the intelligence, discussing it from every possible point of view.*[14]

It was difficult work, though, with Jeffryes often spending a whole night on one message. The noise at their hut on Cape Denison, at the head of Commonwealth Bay, was constant, with the wind very strong and the dogs barking nearby. And the signal itself was sometimes faint or crackly due to St Elmo's fire, the discharge of static electricity in the atmosphere which sometimes appears as a faint light, but which can also affect radio signals.[15] The Australian Antarctic Division notes how difficult it was for these pioneers:

> *Due to atmospheric static and auroral activity, the quality of signals at Commonwealth Bay varied greatly. Battling these conditions, along with the constant howling of the wind and sledge dogs outside, radio operator S.H. Jeffryes could spend entire evenings trying to transmit or receive a single message. After the main radio mast was damaged by winds, expeditioners experimented unsuccessfully with kite aerials ... Contact was re-established with Wireless Hill* [on Macquarie Island] *by rebuilding the masts in a new configuration.*[16]

Tragically, the radio operator, Jeffryes, was affected by the long hours and the isolation of their situation. His behaviour became erratic, and he was heard transmitting messages in Morse code to the expedition's base

Previous pages: Members of the Australasian Antarctic Expedition back on board on their way back to Australia.

on Macquarie Island, saying that the other members of the party were trying to kill him. He was relieved of his duties on the radio.[17] When they returned to Australia, Jeffryes had to be committed to a mental asylum, where he remained for the rest of his life.[18] Today it would have most likely been possible to manage his condition and return him to his much-loved radio work.

The *Aurora*, under Captain Davis, returned to Commonwealth Bay on 12 December 1913, a welcome sight to the party. The expedition prepared to depart for home on 23 December. Mawson wrote:

> *An hour later the motor-launch, with Madigan and Bickerton, sped away for the last load through falling snow and a rising sea. Hodgeman had battened down the windows of the hut, the chimney was stuffed with bagging, the veranda entrance closed with boards, and, inside, an invitation left for future visitors to occupy or make themselves at home.*[19]

The *Aurora* and the party reached Adelaide on 26 February 1914, to a tumultuous reception. The expedition was over. Much had been achieved, but the loss of two of the expedition members meant that it was marked by tragedy.

The radio was brought back from Commonwealth Bay. It was not, however, the last time that it would be used in Antarctic waters.

Shackleton's Imperial Trans-Antarctic Expedition, 1914–1916

Alongside Captain Robert Falcon Scott and Roald Amundsen, Sir Ernest Shackleton stands as one of the key leaders of the heroic age of Antarctic exploration. His proposed crossing of Antarctica, known as the Imperial Trans-Antarctic Expedition, has become famous for the expeditioners' feats of survival when the expedition ship *Endurance* was crushed by ice in the Weddell Sea. It is tantalising to think what events may have been avoided if it had been possible to have radio contact with the outside world, as Mawson had done. Radio communications—its strengths and its weaknesses—played a key role in determining the outcome of Shackleton's attempt to cross the Antarctic continent.

21st-century Antarctica: Getting your news fix in 24-hour darkness

Antarctica is 14.2 million square kilometres in size, and although there are now 70 stations on the continent, with a population of about 5,000 people, those stations are minute specks in a truly vast land. During winter, the sun does not appear for four months. Entertainment must be especially important at this time. What happens when the staff want to stream entertainment online in their downtime?

Internet services are received via satellite, but are prioritised for essential communications and the purposes of research, including communicating scientific data and conducting medical consultations. The introduction of satellites has revolutionised communications between Australia and the Antarctic bases, and equipment and bandwidth are updated as technology changes. A separate satellite system provides in-field communications, such as radio, for staff using handheld sets and on vehicles.[20] In addition, today's Antarctic expeditioner is normally able to access news and social media online, and to receive regular mobile phone calls.

Inspecting the VHF repeater, a combination receiver/transmitter, near Davis Research Station, 2019.

Shackleton's 1907–1909 expedition, when he and his companions reached a point within 100 miles (160 kilometres) of the South Pole, was widely recognised as being a critical turning point in southern polar exploration. He showed the way to the pole, ascending a massive glacier and struggling on, at altitude, until he had to make the decision to turn back with his companions, or be lost.

Shackleton was a restless soul, and kept returning to the Antarctic. He rightly had a reputation for looking after his men when hardship struck. His methods of raising money were less admirable; he often overcommitted and left debts that could affect others, such as leaving expedition members unpaid on their return to civilisation. His proposal to cross the Antarctic continent from the Weddell Sea side (below South America) to the Ross Sea side (below New Zealand and Australia) was highly ambitious. He secured funding for the venture—including promissory notes, a contract with a media organisation and loans—after a long and arduous process.

The Imperial Trans-Antarctic Expedition would comprise two parties—the Ross Sea party, with Douglas Mawson's old ship *Aurora* and the radio equipment used on the Mawson expedition—and the Weddell Sea party—with the ship *Endurance,* also equipped with a radio receiver, but no transmsitter.[21] Shackleton's plan was to use sled dogs to carry him and other members of the Weddell Sea party to the South Pole and down the Beardmore Glacier, where stores laid by the Ross Sea party along the mighty Antarctic Barrier would support their journey back to the Ross Sea. This lifeline of supply depots would be 360 miles (580 kilometres) long. Shackleton would lead the Weddell Sea party. For the Ross Sea party, he appointed Aeneas Mackintosh as the leader, with Chief Officer Joseph Stenhouse in charge of the *Aurora.*[22] The expedition prepared to leave England as World War I began, receiving dispensation from Winston Churchill, First Lord of the Admiralty, to proceed.[23]

Sailing into the pack ice of the Weddell Sea on 11 December 1914, the *Endurance* was caught fast in the ice before the expedition could make landfall. The ship was crushed on 27 October 1915, and Shackleton and his party made camp on the pack, which drifted northwards until the ice began to break up. Without a transmitter, which were quite common on board ships at this time, *Endurance* was unable to send a distress signal. This would have serious consequences for both the men on the *Endurance* and those members of the expedition on the Ross Sea side of the Antarctic continent.

The men took to the ship's small boats on 9 April 1916 and reached Elephant Island, a feat of enormous endurance in itself. Shackleton and a selected crew then departed Elephant Island on 24 April 1916 and sailed the open boat, *James Caird*, across more than 800 miles (1,300 kilometres) of the worst seas in the world to reach South Georgia Island, where there was a whaling station. They landed on 10 May 1916.

The Ross Sea party knew nothing of this, because it was not possible due to technical limitations at that time for the Ross Sea and Weddell Sea land parties to communicate directly by wireless transmitters.[24]

The *Aurora* did have a receiver and transmitter on board, the same one used at Commonwealth Bay by Mawson. It was operated by Lionel Hooke, who was a great radio enthusiast. He had been so anxious to join the expedition, he had claimed to be 20 when he was in fact 18 years of age.[25] He was fascinated by electricity. At 17, he had joined Melbourne Tramways, the department responsible for the electrification of the city, as an apprentice. He then trained as a marine wireless operator, on behalf of Amalgamated Wireless (Australasia) Ltd.[26]

As far as the Ross Sea party was aware, Shackleton and his group were on their way, and it was imperative that supply bases be laid up to the foot of Beardmore Glacier. The *Aurora* had successfully reached Cape Evans in the Ross Sea, and a party had gone ashore with the first of many stores. The plan was for *Aurora* to find a safe anchorage and stay in Antarctica for the winter. The radio transmitter would stay on board *Aurora* at her winter quarters. The party would attempt to establish communications with Macquarie Island once a tower was erected on the ship.

Disaster struck. A tempest burst on Cape Evans in the early hours of 6 May 1915, and *Aurora,* with 18 men aboard, broke free of her moorings. Chief Officer Stenhouse and the crew were awakened by 'the hysterical fury of the storm'.[27] In her book *The Lost Men: The Harrowing Saga of Shackleton's Ross Sea Party*, Kelly Tyler-Lewis writes:

Shackleton's epic journey by open boat from Elephant Island to South Georgia Island to seek help for his party has become the stuff of legend.

> *Before they reached the companionway, two explosive reports boomed like artillery blasts. On deck, broken wires whipsailed shrilly through the air as* [James Paton] *raced towards the bulkhead, hurricane lamp in hand, shouting, 'She's away wi' it!'*[28]

The *Aurora* was adrift, and the ten other members of the Ross Sea party were stranded on land without most of its supplies. Fortunately, Cape Evans had been the headquarters of Captain Scott's expedition just

S.Y. AURORA.
A.A.E.

two years before, and there were still many supplies left behind, just enough to lay the depots they believed had to be put in place in order for Shackleton's team to survive.

The *Aurora* was caught in the pack ice. As autumn arrived, the ship drifted with the ice slowly northwards. Over the next 11 months, *Aurora* and her crew drifted 700 miles (1,130 kilometres) in the pack ice. As the southern summer of 1915–1916 approached, the crew hoped that the ice would open up and the ship could break free. It was not to be, and the ship was in danger of being crushed. Finally, in March 1916, *Aurora* broke free of the pack ice. The ship was leaking and could only use a 'jury rudder' (a temporary rudder) to cover the 2,000 miles (3,220 kilometres) to New Zealand.[29]

During this time, Hooke tried hard to get the radio working. As Tyler-Lewis writes:

> *Hooke persisted with the wireless set, modifying the generator and the transmitter to try to increase the range. In late August* [1915], *he caught occasional snatches of messages from Macquarie Island and Awarua* [Bluff Point, New Zealand]. *Then, on September 5, the mizzenmast was torn off in hurricane-force winds, carrying the attached wireless mast and aerial with it. Hooke's experiments came to an abrupt end. 'Hooke dismantled wireless,' wrote Stenhouse. 'Heartsick'.*[30]

With Stenhouse's encouragement, Hooke nonetheless continued to experiment with the repair of the wireless. On 14 March, they cleared the pack, but they were in a sorry state, with little ballast and a makeshift rudder—two things that would sorely test their ship in the Southern Ocean's ominous storms.[31]

The *Aurora*, photographed here by Frank Hurley during the Australasian Antarctic Expedition, also supported the Ross Sea party of Shackleton's Imperial Trans-Antarctic Expedition. *Aurora* was swept away from Cape Evans by a storm on 6 May 1915, and become trapped in pack ice until March 1916.

Hooke persisted and rebuilt the transmitter tower. After more than a year, it seemed hopeless, but either because of the changes made by Hooke or the closer range, on 24 March it burst into life with a string of messages coming through.[32] Hooke then started to transmit messages.

So it was that on a quiet evening at Bluff Station on the tip of the South Island of New Zealand, the radio operator at the Awarua receiving station was startled when a crackling message was received. It began with snatches of Morse code, CT VLB VLB, 'Seeking Awarua Station'.[33] It was from *Aurora*, a distress signal and details about their situation. In freak atmospheric conditions, the message had got through. The world now knew of their plight, and help arrived.

Back in Antarctica, the rest of the Ross Sea party were marooned at the world's end. After the *Aurora* left, the ten men were to undertake a journey across the ice to establish a critical line of supplies for Shackleton's Weddell Sea party, which they were expecting to come from the other side of the continent.

The men set out to lay the depots in May 1916. With the *Aurora* gone, taking most of the supplies with it, they reorganised the supplies left behind by Scott from his expedition of 1912 and set out on the trip across the Great Ice Barrier. In the face of the most difficult and challenging circumstances, they laid the depots for a party that would never come. One of them, the Reverend Arnold Spencer-Smith, died of scurvy on March 1916 on the return journey, only days away from the relative safety of Hut Point, on the shores of the Ross Sea. Two others—Aeneas Mackintosh and Victor Hayward—disappeared when they tried to cross from Hut Point to Cape Evans on the springtime ice.

The remaining men were alone. They had no communication with the outside world, and the strain of their isolation began to have an impact on their mental state.

After returning to civilisation, Shackleton was determined to reach this party he had sent southwards. But he was no longer in control. The Australian Government funded the relief of the men, using the *Aurora* again. Shackleton travelled with the ship, which reached the party on 10 January 1917. They had been in complete isolation for two years and, like Shackleton, they were shocked by news of World War I.

With the *Endurance* sunk, crushed in the pack ice, Shackleton and his Waddell Sea party of the transantarctic expedition spent months drifting slowly north on the ice.

If communication had been available, would the tragedy have been averted? Douglas Mawson—and his radio operators Hannam and Jeffryes—and Hooke on the *Aurora*, had pushed the boundaries using new technology and had been successful in overcoming the odds to send some vital messages: Mawson, to let the world know the fate of the expedition; and Hooke to alert the world to the plight of the *Aurora* and the men of the Ross Sea party.

Antarctic radio heroes

There are many attractions in Hobart, but for an Antarctic enthusiast, a trip to Mawson's Huts Replica Museum gives a great insight into the living conditions of this pioneering party. A replica of the radio, the

German-made Telefunken 1.5-kilowatt 'spark' transmitter, has pride of place. In 2017, the museum also secured remains from radio masts used at Macquarie Island. As the museum spokesperson, Warwick Arnold, said, 'It was "cutting-edge technology" when it was erected on Macquarie Island in January 1912, by the Australasian Antarctic Expedition'.

The three radio men involved were all Australians. Walter Hannam was a strong believer in radio communications, particularly for Australia's security following World War I. He served in the army during the remainder of the war and was a founding member of the Wireless Institute of Australia. He was awarded the Polar Medal in 1914 for his services in Antarctica. He died in 1965 at the age of 80.

Sidney Jeffryes showed great dedication and significant ability in managing the radio in the second winter at Commonwealth Bay. It is a tragedy that he developed a debilitating illness. He was awarded the Polar Medal, but spent the remainder of his life in mental hospitals. When he died, aged 58, he was buried in an unmarked grave. In October 2018, the Mawson's Huts Foundation organised a plinth and memorial plaque for his grave.[34]

Lionel Hooke served in the military during the remainder of World War I then rejoined Amalgamated Wireless (Australasia) Ltd (AWA). He played a key role in encouraging radio broadcasting in Australia (see Chapter 5). He became managing director of AWA in 1944.

A Telefunken Morse key used with radio spark transmitter, from around 1910–1920.

Amundsen's success, Scott's tragedy

Roald Amundsen's return to Hobart, on 7 March 1912, was unheralded by wireless. Wireless existed, but in order for it to have any range it needed to have staging posts. Mawson had pioneered a connection in January that year, when he established a mid-point at Macquarie Island. But wireless was not practicable for Scott or Amundsen on their expeditions.

Amundsen anchored his ship, the *Fram*, in the Derwent River and ordered his crew to remain aboard while he went ashore, proceeding directly to the General Post Office to send a telegram to the young King Haakon VII of Norway.

He and his party had reached the South Pole through a combination of risk, expertise and meticulous planning. Whereas Scott chose a well-established area on terra firma at Cape Evans, Amundsen built his headquarters on the ice shelf in the Bay of Whales. Amundsen also chose to use dogs, rather than the ponies Shackleton had used in 1907–09 when he got within 160 kilometres of the South Pole, and he risked making a new route for himself, rather than following the road up the Beardmore Glacier pioneered by Shackleton and his party.

After one false start, Amundsen left his base, Franheim, on 19 October 1911 with four other men, 52 dogs pulling four sledges and enough supplies for 60 days.[35] Experts on skis since childhood, and brought up to master dog teams, the members of party made strong progress, never having to subject themselves to the terrible hardships of man-hauling of sledges, which Scott and his party endured on their tragic return from the South Pole.

The party reached the South Pole on 14 December. They spent three days surveying and marking the area and then set off on their return journey. Scott's party arrived on 17 January 1912.

The *Fram* sailed in, unannounced, to Hobart. Word spread that Amundsen—who a number thought was a tramp when he arrived at a hotel to check in—had returned to civilisation. Once identified, he was surrounded by journalists desperate to find out what his party had achieved.[36] He had an exclusive deal, however, with the *Daily Chronicle* in Britain, and Frank Bowden, manager of telegrams at the

When he returned to Hobart, Roald Amundsen kept his successful expedition to reach the South Pole a secret until he had fulfilled his contractual obligations to inform the *Daily Chronicle*.

post office, transmitted Amundsen's dispatches to the King of Norway and the *Daily Chronicle* in strict confidence.[37] Other papers could only speculate:

> *Captain Amundsen, when seen yesterday afternoon by a 'Mercury' reporter, gave an outline of the movements of the Fram, but declined to enter into any details regarding his movements in the Antarctic, stating that he was bound at present not to give this information. He added that he was very sorry that this was so, in view of the fact that this was his first port of call after his return from the Antarctic regions, and that he had already received much kindness since his arrival here. As soon as he could do so he would be very glad to take the inquirer on board the Fram, show him the charts and everything of interest, and give the fullest possible information, but for the time being he had regretfully to keep silent on the very points which people seemed most anxious to know about.*[38]

A rumour spread that Amundsen had said Captain Scott had also reached the pole. Amundsen was quick to deny this rumour. Twenty-four hours later, on 7 March 1912 (British time), the *Daily Chronicle* declared the news of Roald Amundsen's success. Suddenly the Hobart postal exchange was extremely busy, as letters and telegrams of congratulations arrived from around the world.[39] Such was the sophisticated and weblike network of the telegraph by this point, that within 24 hours the news had burst onto the world.

Amundsen was feted in Hobart. He then undertook a two-week lecture tour of Australia entitled 'How I reached the Pole', beginning in Adelaide. His many well-wishers included the chief justice and the masters of the Norwegian sailing barques in Port Adelaide, Melbourne and Sydney, where he ended his tour on 6 April 1912.[40]

A memorial plaque in Hobart at the place where Amundsen sent his message carries this inscription:

> *Roald Amundsen and Race to the South Pole*
>
> *Roald Amundsen reached the South Geographic Pole on 14 December 1911, the first human to do so. His first stop on the way home was in Hobart where he arrived on 7 March 1912 in his ship, the Fram. He sent a coded message to King Haakon VII of Norway from the Hobart General Post Office. The telegram was sent by the Manager for Telegraphs, Hobart, Frank Bowden, who was sworn to secrecy until the official announcement was made in London.*

As Amundsen arrived in Hobart, Scott's expedition was still out on the snow, struggling to return from the South Pole as extreme storms and cold closed in. Scott's last diary entry was on 29 March 1912. He and the other five members of his party all perished, with the last three, Scott, Bowers and Wilson, found in a tent by the search party the next spring.

Roald Amundsen was one of the great explorers of the 'heroic' age of Antarctic exploration. News of his successful expedition to reach the South Pole was sent from the GPO in Hobart.

4

Running the line

1914–1918: Getting the message through on the deadly battlefields of World War I

Messages often have to travel vast distances. Humans have used a range of communication methods throughout history to achieve this, including mounted riders, who were a key form of messenger in many cultures for many centuries—riding alone, in groups or by carriage. Getting news to London of the victory at the Battle of Trafalgar in 1805, for example, was an incredible feat of endurance that required a mounted messenger to travel at phenomenal pace. The smallest but fastest British warship in the battle fleet, the schooner HMS *Pickle*, was selected by Vice Admiral Collingwood to convey his dispatches to London. The ship's commanding officer, Lieutenant John Richards Lapenotière, was left in no doubt about the urgency of his task. Collingwood, who had overseen the victory of the British fleet over a superior combined French and Spanish force after the death of his friend, Vice Admiral Lord Nelson, implored Lapenotière to use 'every exertion, that a moment's time may not be lost in their delivery'.

It took Lapenotière 11 days, from 26 October to 6 November 1805, to deliver the news from the fleet, positioned in the Atlantic Ocean off Spain, to the Admiralty in Whitehall. The final stage of his journey, nonstop by post-chaise from Falmouth to London, took only 37 hours to cover the 271 miles (436 kilometres).[1]

Communications are, of course, often critical in military campaigns. The development of the telegram and Morse code in the mid-nineteenth century started to complement the use of semaphore or visual signalling and was adapted by the British Navy in 1867 to use for signalling from ship to ship with lights. The British first made use of a telegraph line during the Crimean War of 1853–1856, and it was a decisive form of communication during the Indian Mutiny of 1857.[2] It was then used extensively during the American Civil War.

The use of the telegraph was important at a strategic level. It has been argued that, in 1914, the German Army, in spite of extensive planning of their invasion of Belgium and France through the Schlieffen Plan, did not provide for the necessary level of communication between strategic headquarters and the rapidly advancing armies that were driving into Belgium. This enabled the French and British to stabilise their line, leading to the stalemate of trench warfare for the next four years.[3]

When World War I began, on 28 July 1914, Australia, as a young nation of the British Empire, was almost tripping over itself to join the empire's cause against Germany. It is perhaps difficult, with our twenty-first-century understanding of the terrible consequences of both World War I and World War II, to relate to this powerful social phenomenon. An army of volunteers for the Australian Imperial Force (AIF) expeditionary force was assembled and on its way to the Middle East by 1 November 1914, when the troopships left Albany, Western Australia, their final Australian port of call.

One of the first tasks the British requested the Australian forces to undertake was to attack German wireless installations in the Dutch East Indies. Germany had invested significant resources in these installations. They allowed Germany to communicate with its colonies without using Britain's 'Red Line' of telegraph cables around the world. Before 1914, Germany had built wireless stations in Africa, East Asia and the Pacific. At the request of the British, Australian forces attacked and took over a German wireless station on the island of New Britain on 11 September 1914. Campaigns were also mounted against other German wireless stations in these first stages of the war.

Capturing or destroying German wireless stations in German colonies close to Australia was an early focus of Australian military action following the outbreak of World War I, such as here in Bitapaka, New Britain.

The expeditionary force that Australia sent overseas needed to be properly equipped for modern warfare, and communications were a critical part of this preparedness. The AIF, like the British Army, was equipped mainly with telegraph cables and telephones for communications between the front line and commanders. However, wireless technology progressed as the war went on.

Training for signallers lasted about ten weeks. It included drills that could be considered 'basic training'—armed and unarmed combat, bayonet fighting and marching. Signallers were also trained in semaphore and the use of Morse code.[4]

What was life like for these signallers on the front line? What risks did they take? How did they get their equipment to work?

Signallers soon learned when they got to the front line that there was a large gap between establishing effective communications as set out in a textbook—an ordered and orderly network of wired communications from headquarters to the front line—and the experience of the battlefield itself.

The famous English author J.R.R. Tolkien was a signaller in the British Army at the Battle of the Somme in 1916. His biographer, Humphrey Carpenter, described the chaotic and makeshift conditions Tolkien was operating in—a mass of tangled wires, faulty equipment and ad hoc alternatives to wires—which were a far cry from what he had been exposed to during his training.[5]

Despite the challenges, these men knew that often the lives of others depended on signals getting through and undertook extraordinary acts of bravery to get their work done. In his book about the AIF's Signal Service in the war, Desmond Lambley writes of the unique role of the signaller:

> *Sometimes he was called 'The Spook' because he could mysteriously tap or buzz on his machine and call up all sorts of unknown sprits from afar off. Communications were the mainspring of the modern battle and enabled the higher commander to control men and supplies operating on a wide front, and they enabled him to fling in his reserves at the critical moment ... And 'The Sig' with his little buzzer, sitting in a corner of a dugout, or under a thin piece of tarpaulin, sent on this information, which meant so much to the man waiting in the rear. In*

the open warfare stunts, he sent back the information with his flag or flapper or his wonderful O.L. Lamp—that little winking eye of white in the daylight and red at night, which saved the weary feet of tired runners and leapt over space in a few seconds.[6]

When telegraph lines were cut by shellfire, it was the signallers' job to get out of the trench and fix them. The signallers had to go out at any time of the day or night, under fire, in order to repair the damage. They went into action with their companies, and when they reached an objective, they had to take up the task of establishing communications in a shell hole, with a lamp and little or no cover.[7]

Signallers were part of a Divisional Signal Service Company for each division, under the Australian Engineers. In practice, signallers operated in small groups, attached to fighting units and headquarters. On their shirts, signallers in the Australian Army wore, along with their battalion colour patch, a patch with blue and white flags, crossed diagonally.

A very high percentage of signallers received decorations for bravery—almost 13 per cent of Australian signallers enlisted—reflecting their constant exposure to risk, and being required to exercise their initiative to get critical messages to and from the front line.[8]

For signallers, much of war was routine work, sometimes mundane in nature, followed by periods of great danger and stress. When time and space allowed, signallers and engineers would often lay out key communications structures, which were highly organised. In battle, it was at the ends that they became frayed, which was unfortunately where they mattered the most.

Australian ground forces fought in three key campaigns during World War I: Gallipoli, the Middle East and the Western Front. Each campaign posed its own challenges.

Above: Signallers had a dangerous role in running telegraph lines across open ground.

Evading enemy ears

Despite the need for a range of communications in the trenches of the Western Front, cable communication by telegraph or telephone was the most important, at least until the arrival of wireless in the closing year of the war.

Cable allowed direct communication between a commander and his units. A major cause for concern was that the wire could easily be tapped by enemy forces, who would listen in.

A British officer, Major A.C. Fuller, was quick to come up with an adaptation to try and address this problem. Realising it was the alternating current that could be detected, Fuller devised a means of using a weak direct current instead. The resulting equipment was called the Fullerphone, which included both Morse code and speech facilities. Although it was very effective, there were manufacture and supply issues throughout the rest of the war.[9]

The Fullerphone was invented in an attempt to circumvent messages being intercepted by German forces.

Gallipoli: April to December 1915

The Australian and New Zealand Army Corps (ANZAC) landed on the Gallipoli Peninsula on 25 April 2015 as part of Britain's campaign to take the Dardanelles, march on Constantinople and push for Turkey to exit the war. Their main landing was at Gaba Tepe, soon to be known also as Anzac Cove. The Turkish forces were waiting for them, and used the steep ridged land to their advantage.

After the first day of bloody fighting, the Australians had gained just a toehold at Anzac Cove, but they had consolidated their position at a series of key points and had established a divisional office. Signallers, working out in the open, had laid wires between that office and the advanced brigades, and by midnight the headquarters' signallers were in contact with the men in the forward trenches. It was the era of modern communications in warfare.

The experiences of signallers, however, showed how deadly the job was. Ellis Silas was born in London in 1885 and migrated to Australia in 1907. He was living in Perth when, in 1914, at the outbreak of war, he joined the 16th Battalion. Silas was an artist and kept a diary. He was not a natural fit for the army, hating the crowded and boisterous nature of life in camp. But he was determined to 'do his duty'. He landed at Anzac Cove on 25 April 1915 and was immediately in the thick of the action, often running messages between key locations.[10] His diary entry from 26 April gives a graphic account of the chaotic and fatal scenes on the second day at Anzac Cove:

> *Pope's Hill—daybreak—down in the Valley, in the midst of this frightful hell of screaming shrapnel and heavy ordinance, the birds are chirping in the clear morning air and buzzing about from leaf to leaf, placidly going about its work, is a large bee—to think of what might be makes me weep, for fighting is continuing in all its fury.*
>
> *Our signallers have been nearly all wiped out—I suppose I'll get my lead pill next. It has been now a ceaseless cry of 'Stretcher bearers on the left'—they seem to be having an awful time up there—one poor fellow has just jumped out of his dug-out, frightfully wounded in the arm; I bound it up as best I could, then had to dash off with another message.*

Signallers were active in Gallipoli, laying vital communications between the trenches. Once in place, signal lines provided vital networks for the ANZAC Headquarters to the front lines.

All along the route, scrambling along the side of the exposed incline, my comrades offered me a dug-out for me to take cover as the snipers are getting our chaps every minute, but as the messages are important, I must take my chance. All along the route I keep coming across bodies of the poor chaps who have been less fortunate than I.[11]

Silas was recommended for a decoration, but it was never progressed. After several more days of managing non-stop dispatches and messages, Silas fell into a delirium with shell shock. On 17 May, he wrote in his diary:

> *17 May 1915: was much worse last night—am told that I was quite off my head. Am told to go down immediately to the M.O.* [Medical Officer] *but I will not do so until our Battalion is relieved which will be in a few hours. See the M.O. who tells me that I had better go away for a week or two. I say good-bye to Colonel Pope, who says 'I'm sorry you are going, Silas, you have done some valuable work for us.' When I tell Margolin I am going he exclaims 'Yes, Silas old chap, it's about time too, you're not cut out for this kind of thing; I hope you will get into the A.M.C.* [Army Medical Corps] *as you always wanted to do.'*[12]

Silas was evacuated from Anzac Cove, sent back to Egypt and was discharged the following year, 1916, as medically unfit. That same year he published his book describing his experiences.

The battle at Gallipoli continued. In August, Lance Corporal Cyril Bassett won the only Victoria Cross awarded to a New Zealander at Gallipoli. He was engaged in laying and repeatedly repairing telephone wire from the headquarters of the New Zealand Infantry Brigade on Walker's Ridge across to Pope's Hill on 7 August.[13] Pope's Hill was a key point during the August 1915 offensive, in which the beleaguered ANZAC forces launched one more attack aimed at breaking the Turkish hold on the high ground of Gallipoli. A new position required new communications. Basset received his Victoria Cross when:

> *under a continuous and heavy fire,* [he] *succeeded in laying a telephone line from the old position to the new on Chunuk Bair. He has subsequently been brought to notice for further excellent and most gallant work connected with the repair of telephone lines by day and night under heavy fire.*[14]

Finally, the British commanders realised the Turkish resistance was too strong and the casualties too high. By 20 December 1915, the Anzacs had evacuated, with the British departing in early January 1916. The AIF had suffered a terrible toll at Gallipoli; there were 26,111 Australian casualties, including 8,141 deaths. They had fought valiantly, and the signallers had conveyed hundreds of messages in the heat of battle to support the overall coordination of movement and tactical response.

The Western Front, 1916–1918

After Gallipoli, the ANZAC forces were reorganised. The AIF in Egypt was expanded: I ANZAC Corps was made up of two Australian divisions and one New Zealand division, and II ANZAC Corps comprised two Australian divisions. They were transferred to the Western Front. The AIF's 3rd Division arrived in France in November and became part of II ANZAC Corps in Flanders. Created in Australia in February 1916, the division had been training at Salisbury Plain in England.[15]

By 1916, when the Australians arrived at the Western Front, trench warfare had already claimed many thousands of lives. It was a deadly place where the weapons of modern war could kill men in their hundreds and thousands in a day, and where two forces (the French and British on the one hand, the Germans on the other) fought over trenches for months and years, with no end in sight.

The Australians were to confront trench war at its worst. In a poorly considered attack at Fromelles, over the night of 19 to 20 July 1916, the 5th Division suffered more than 5,500 casualties. Days later, the 1st, 2nd and 4th Divisions joined the battle at Pozières, part of the Battle of the Somme. They launched many attacks and gained ground, but some 23,000 AIF men were killed or wounded.[16] If Gallipoli hadn't already shown the Australian public the true cost of the war, the Western Front would drive the lesson home.

The Somme was a terrible battle. It was intended to turn the course of the war, but it failed. On 1 July 1916, the first day of the battle, British forces suffered close to 60,000 casualties—including about 20,000 soldiers killed. The battle has become infamous for being the most futile operation in history.[17] By the time the campaign ended, five months later, more than three million soldiers had been engaged in fighting, and more than one million had been killed or wounded.

J.R.R. Tolkien's experiences as a signals officer at the Battle of the Somme, trying to support communications, are vividly described by John Garth in his book *Tolkien and the Great War*:

> *A vast buried cable system had been installed prior to the Battle of the Somme, but of course it extended no further than the frontline. Beyond its reach soldiers worked in a zone of mystery, in which thousands of them simply disappeared. The job of the signaller was to shed some light on the mystery by helping to set up a battlefield communication system and using it.*[18]

In practice, this was a terribly difficult and often futile task. Tolkien soon discovered how hard it was:

The entrance to a signaller's dugout in Laviéville, France, in 1918. The photographer, Guy Herwald Parker, had inscribed the image 'Spooks dugout'.

The battalion's signallers carried coils of wire ready to set up new phone stations in captured territory. The surface lines, however, were easily tapped and Morse buzzers could be heard within three hundred yards as the signal leaked into the chalky ground ... Flags, lamps and flares simply drew fire from the enemy ramparts. Most messages were sent by runner ... Orders from the generals at corps HQ took at least eight hours to reach the attacking troops.[19]

Tolkien led a number of missions to set up advanced communications, including a battalion headquarters further north, under shellfire. Four of his companions were killed that day. In late October, Tolkien fell ill from trench fever, and was eventually sent back to England. Two of his best friends were killed at the Somme. His experiences made a strong impression on him in terms of the importance of fellowship and friendship in the face of danger and death.

As at Gallipoli, telegraph lines were the most commonly used tools for signallers on the Western Front. During 1917, the Australian forces were involved in a number of campaigns to try and break the German lines.

During World War I, runners were used over short distances, usually on the front line. These runners were subject to great danger from shelling and snipers. One such was Private Stephen Clucas, from Bendigo in Victoria. He was 18 years old when he enlisted. At Gallipoli, he was wounded and evacuated to Malta. After he recovered, he returned to his unit, now on the Western Front in France. In August 1917, he was detached for duty with the Signal Office at the 2nd Infantry Brigade headquarters. The citation for his Military Medal showed the bravery of his actions:

In the operations East of Hooge on the evening of 21 September 1917, when telephone communications between Cable Head and Brigade had been cut by shellfire, Private Clucas volunteered to take an important message through. He successfully carried out this task and returned with the reply under very heavy shellfire.[20]

To get wires through, signallers had to get out of their defensive zone of the trenches and into the open—an action that risked death. Although cables were laid underground where possible, shellfire might break or disable them. Surface lines would instead have to be run out, a dangerous enterprise.

Technological change

In the first years of World War I, the telegraph was the mainstay of communications, operated by a signaller, one way at a time, using Morse code. However, the wired phone became increasingly popular, allowing a direct, two-way exchange of information. The key risk was that these messages could be, and often were, intercepted by German forces, by attaching a line to the existing one.

Engineers leave a signal office on Westhoek Ridge, laying a surface telephone line to a forward unit.

Division and battalion headquarters were a key point along the Western Front. As one observer wrote:

This spot constitutes the nerve-centre of the army in the field, the central point of the spider's web. The tracery of the web is formed by the threads of messages ceaselessly passing to and fro, not only from every part of the sphere of action, but also from the bases of supplies in England. All methods of transmission are employed and the total number of messages of all natures, and from all quarters, averages no fewer than 3,000 the majority of which run to a far greater length than the average telegrams of peace time ... radiotelegraph bears its full share of the burden.[21]

Amid the chaos of the Western Front, armies were constantly sorting out and innovating to create a network of communications, a 'Tele-net' as science writer Paul Gannon calls it:

The 'Tele-net' describes the co-existent networks that, although not directly interoperative, did provide the 'coverage' needed for the new warfare. As the 1914–1918 conflict unfolded the Tele-net was loaded with an ever-extending array of connected technologies and applications such as direction-finding, artillery aiming and ranging, and air defence.[22]

The use of wires, and telegraph and telephones, continued to be the mainstay of battle until 1916. But despite, or because of, the challenges faced on the front line, communications evolved over the course of the war, and the communications available in 1918 were significantly different to those available in 1914. Wireless sets began to be used, but they had drawbacks at first:

[Wireless] *sets were bulky and unwieldy, requiring wagons and horses to transport them from location to location. An added complication was that they did not have battle-zone robustness built into their design: this made them impractical for use by the infantry on the move, so they were given to those troops with horses and thus, the logic ran, the means to transport them.*[23]

Communications on the Western Front were both sophisticated and—near the front line—often compromised or destroyed, requiring replacement.

One of the developments was a new multi-wired system that stopped messages being tapped just by putting receivers in nearby ground. And towards the end of the war, wireless communications became more frequently used:

> *Wireless sets became small enough for troops to carry, or even to install in attack vehicles—as was the case at the Battle of Cambrai (November–December 1917), where some tanks had wireless sets on board in an effort to overcome the ever-present communications relay problem; there was also a tank in the field tasked with communications cable laying.*[24]

As trenches became static along large parts of the Western Front, almost like a semi-permanent fixture, signallers worked to improve the resilience of their communications networks. Lines running above or along the ground were subject to destruction from shelling. Experiments and experience showed that communications lines buried six feet (1.8 metres) below the surface were reasonably safe from being damaged.

The Battle of Hamel and the AIF campaigns of 1918

Radio came to be the solution to a number of communications problems. Anywhere bare metal wires touched the earth, messages being sent on them could be intercepted—and they often were. The soldiers who operated the transmitters also found themselves marked out as targets.[25] The use of aircraft and tanks also posed problems. At first, hand signals or squares of white cloth laid out in different patterns over the ground were used to communicate messages, but it was difficult to change them quickly with emerging circumstances.

The use of wireless by the British Royal Flying Corps was a key factor in its effectiveness, as pilots were able to communicate directly with artillery units and headquarters.[26]

At the Battle of Hamel, which was launched in July 1918 as a counter-attack following German advances, the coordination of artillery, aircraft, tanks and foot soldiers, often using wireless equipment, was carried out in a highly successful manner. The campaign was planned by ANZAC General Sir John Monash. It was described as a great success. In two hours, all objectives were gained, and 1,400 German prisoners were captured.[27]

General Monash's use of good communications helped him to win both the Battle of Hamel and the offensive that would be the first to break the Germans' Hindenburg Line, precipitating the defeat of Germany and the signing of the Armistice in November 1918. Monash, an engineer by profession, carefully planned and coordinated all arms of his forces—infantry, artillery, tanks and even the air force—to strike with maximum effectiveness against the German line. In the final 'hundred days', communications had to be changed to suit a more open style of warfare as the Germans retreated, and wireless (which had become more portable) was increasingly used.

A short wave mark 3 radio tuner, a radio receiver designed in 1917–1918, used for receiving wireless messages, including from aircraft.

In Palestine, heliographs were used to communicate between military units.

Campaigns in the Middle East, 1916–1918

At the same time that fighting was taking place on the Western Front, Australian forces—part of the British Desert Mounted Corps—were facing Turkish forces in Palestine. Following some early battles around Gaza, ANZAC mounted troops were involved in the capture of the strategic town of Beersheba on 31 October 1917.

The Australians also played an important role in the capture of Jerusalem in December 1917. Despite the loss of the many experienced British troops sent to the Western Front in 1917–1918, the Corps defeated an attack by the German Asia Corps at Abu Tellul in April 1918. In September, the Corps played a significant role in the advance to Heifa and Semakh, entering Damascus on 1 October 1918. Turkey signed an armistice at the end of that month, by which time Corps units had reached Aleppo.

While telegraph and wireless were used in the Middle East, one item used more than on the Western Front was the heliograph. A heliograph is effectively a solar telegraph, which transmits signals by flashes of sunlight reflected through a mirror.[28]

The heliograph was well suited to the conditions of Palestine and Syria. To telegraph messages over the great distances of the deserts of Sinai and

Palestine in support of their division's efforts in the field, ANZAC signallers would set up their long-range communications equipment, including heliographs, atop hills, in order to give themselves clear lines of sight over which to transmit and receive intelligence. This same high ground also gave them a vantage from which to survey their surrounds.[29]

Signallers played an important part in this campaign, working to get messages through where they were needed. Corporal Francis Burrell received a Military Medal for conspicuous gallantry in action while laying a four-kilometre cable to the 8th and 3rd Light Horse regiments operating on the left flank of the brigade during the operations at Tel Khueilfeh:

> *This NCO* [non-commissioned officer] *displayed great courage in crossing the open under very heavy fire. Three places had to be crossed which were covered by enemy machine guns from commanding hills. As the fire was too heavy to cross with the pack set, he laid the last mile of line by hand.*[30]

On 1 January 1925, the Australian Corps of Signals was formed. Its motto is 'Certa Cito', which means 'swift and sure'.

The Royal Australian Navy: Learning with wireless

The Royal Australian Navy (RAN) was formed in July 1911, ten years after Federation. The first British-built ships for the RAN, the destroyers *Parramatta* and *Yarra*, arrived in Australia in October 1913. They were equipped with standard Marconi radio sets, not the more specialised British Admiralty models.[31]

A training base was established at Williamstown, Victoria, along with a wireless station. Signals and radio training began as more ships arrived, with signallers also learning their skills on board the training ship HMAS *Tingira*.[32] To communicate, ships and shore stations used wireless telegraphic communication, with Morse code.

In the years leading up to the outbreak of World War I, the Commonwealth Postmaster General's Department (PMG) built two wireless stations, one at Sydney, the other at Fremantle. The RAN would have preferred British imperial-standard stations, but the PMG engaged the German company Telefunken. These two stations were taken over by the RAN at the beginning of the war.

The RAN was active in the Pacific region during the first months of the war. Navy ships and personnel were involved in the capture of German colonial bases in present-day Papua New Guinea and Samoa. A radio signal from a British colonial outpost led to the RAN's first major action of the war.

In September 1914, the German cruiser *Emden* began to sink British shipping in the Bay of Bengal. German cruisers were spotted off the coast of Samoa. In November 1914, the RAN cruisers *Melbourne* and *Sydney* were protecting a convoy of troopships when they received a radio signal from the wireless station at Direction Island, in the Cocos Islands, reporting that an unrecognisable warship was approaching. It was the *Emden*, which was about to land a raiding party to take over the outpost.[33]

HMAS *Sydney* was sent to intercept the ship. In a major naval engagement, the *Sydney* crippled the *Emden*, which then surrendered.

After the German presence in the Pacific was no longer a threat, the British Royal Navy requested that the ships of the RAN be sent to other theatres of war. The RAN subsequently served in a range of locations, including on the Royal Navy's China Station, based out of Singapore, and in the Mediterranean.

The use of wireless radio at sea became increasingly sophisticated as the war progressed. The German Imperial Navy, like the Royal Navy, used coded telegraph signals, and efforts were made by the Allies to break these codes. Powerful shore stations enabled ships to communicate from 'ship to shore', and vice versa, effectively sending, receiving and relaying messages across vast distances.

By the end of World War I, the RAN was highly experienced in the management of communications at sea. Visual signalling continued to be an important part of the make-up of a signaller's role on navy ships.[34] Signallers formed the nucleus of skilled operators who would support the growing maturity of the RAN.

5

Fireside comfort

1925–1939: The wireless radio in Australian homes, and the coming of airmail

Fifty mighty Argonauts, bending to the oars
Today will go adventuring to yet uncharted shores
Fifty young adventurers today set forth
And so we cry with Jason 'Man the boats, and Row! Row! Row!'

(Theme song of the ABC *Argonauts Club* radio program)[1]

Broadcast radio in Australia was introduced in the early 1920s, survived and even grew during the Depression years (1929–1939) and blossomed in the 1940s. In many ways, radio was more transformative than television and the internet because of the magnitude of the change. It meant those who could afford a radio in their home could be informed, could relax listening to music or drama and could feel connected to the world.

In Australia, the first experiments in wireless transmission, as distinct from Morse transmissions, began towards the end of World War I. With broadcast radio, a strong signal is broadcast from a sending station to a very large set of receivers—radios.

On 13 August 1919, wireless promoter and businessman Ernest Fisk gave a demonstration transmission in Sydney. It was followed by others in Melbourne. Shortly after, a successful transmission of tests took place between Tasmania and the mainland.

Fisk was a key figure in promoting the progress of broadcast radio in Australia. He was the general manager of Amalgamated Wireless (Australasia) Ltd—better known as AWA—and had worked with the prime minister at the time, Billy Hughes, on promoting wireless technology at the 1922 Imperial Conference in London.[2]

Fisk's lobbying for broadcast radio reflected a worldwide growth at that time. The technology was based on that of wireless radio, but was focused on transmission from a studio. Through the use of broadcast technology and infrastructure, radio receivers could then pick up the programs.

In 1920, the experimental Detroit station in the United States, 8MK, announced the results of the 1920 Harding–Cox presidential election to the approximately 500 locals with receivers.[3]

The FIRST DIRECT WIRELESS MESSAGES from ENGLAND to AUSTRALIA.

The Right Hon W.M. Hughes P.C. K.C. LL.D.

The Right Hon. Sir Joseph Cook G.C.M.G., P.C.

AMALGAMATED WIRELESS (Australasia) LIMITED
WIRELESS HOUSE, 97 CLARENCE STREET, SYDNEY, N.S.W.

No. 1. Wahroonga OFFICE Sept 22nd 1918
Handed in at London — Carnarvon (direct) 1.15 pm E. T. Fisk
CHARGES TO PAY

To Sydney for Publication.

I have just returned from a visit to the battlefields where the glorious valour and dash of the Australian troops saved Amiens and forced back the legions of the enemy, filled with greater admiration than ever for these glorious men and more convinced than ever that it is the duty of their fellow-citizens to keep these magnificent battalions up to their full strength.
W. M. Hughes. Prime Minister

AMALGAMATED WIRELESS (Australasia) LIMITED
WIRELESS HOUSE, 97 CLARENCE STREET, SYDNEY, N.S.W.

No. 2. Wahroonga OFFICE Sept 22nd 1918
Handed in at London — Carnarvon (direct) 1.25 pm E. T. Fisk
CHARGES TO PAY

To Sydney for Publication.

Royal Australian Navy is magnificently bearing its part in the great struggle. Spirit of sailors and soldiers alike is beyond praise. Recent hard fighting brilliantly successful but makes reinforcements imperative. Australia hardly realises the wonderful reputation which our men have won. Every effort being constantly made here to dispose of Australia's surplus products
Joseph Cook. Minister for Navy.

These messages were transmitted by arrangement with Senatore G. Marconi, G.C.V.O., D.Sc. & Godfrey C. Isaacs Esq. Managing Director, Marconi's Wireless Telegraph Company, Limited, from the Marconi Transatlantic Station at Carnarvon, Wales, at 3.15 a.m. & 3.25 a.m. (Greenwich mean time), September 22nd, 1918.

Received instantaneously at 1.15 p.m & 1.25 p.m (Sydney time) by Mr E.T. Fisk, Member Institute of Radio Engineers & Managing Director, Amalgamated Wireless (Australasia) Limited, — at his Experimental Wireless Station, Wahroonga, New South Wales, with apparatus designed and manufactured in Sydney by Mr Fisk and the Staff of Amalgamated Wireless (Australasia) Limited.

Wireless messages across the globe were another game changer in communications.

The *Smithsonian* magazine's summary of expansion of the radio in the United States shows the exponential nature of growth:

> *As more events were captured on the radio, more fans built and bought sets. From 1922 to 1923, the number of radio sets in America increased from 60,000 to 1.5 million. In 1922, there were 28 stations in operation;*

by 1924, there were 1,400. Among the biggest commercial broadcasters were the National Broadcasting Company and the Columbia Broadcasting System, formed in 1926 and 1927, respectively, and still familiar as television networks NBC and CBS.[4]

Back in Australia, a number of government inquiries were held in the early 1920s to determine the future of radio. To supplement commercial broadcasters, the Scullin Labor government established the public broadcaster, the Australian Broadcasting Commission (ABC), in 1932. Radios were only available to listeners who paid a subscription to a particular broadcaster, and a licence fee to the government, but these costs did not stop the popularity of the new service.

2KY Radio Station in Kings Cross, Sydney, aroun 1920–1945. Australians took to radio with increasing enthusiasm.

Growth in Australia kept pace with the United States in proportionate terms (given Australia's much smaller population). Mike Osborne, writing for Museums Victoria, has traced radio's coming of age in Australia:

> *Growth in the first years of radio was very rapid, tapering off at the end of the 1920s with the advent of the Great Depression. Between 1924 and 1929 the number of licensed listeners grew from over 1,200 licences (0.2 % of population) to over 300,000 (approx. 4.7% of a population of 6,400,000). With an average household size in metropolitan areas of about 4.2 people (based on 1921 and 1933 censuses), this meant that 20% of households in Australia had radio by 1929. These figures conceal the city focus of radio use: by the end of 1929 there were 19 licensed stations but only three were in regional cities: Newcastle, Toowoomba and Bathurst.*[5]

A huge range of information and entertainment was available: classical music, religious services, crooning singers, jazz, drama, sport (such as cricket), children's shows, and news and current affairs. Radio continued to grow despite the Depression. By the end of 1938, there were more than one million radio licences (approximately 16 per cent of a population of 7 million or 66 per cent of households).[6] Radios improved in quality and became cheaper: they changed from being complex battery-powered devices with confusing controls, to mains-powered devices with easy controls suitable for the domestic environment, mounted in attractive pinewood and elegantly shaped furniture.

Black Tuesday, 29 October 1929

During the late 1920s, economies were struggling with sluggish growth. The Wall Street Stock Crash of 29 October 1929, sometimes called Black Tuesday, precipitated a terrible economic depression around the world. Black Tuesday hit Wall Street as investors traded some 16 million shares on the New York Stock Exchange in a single day. Billions of dollars were lost, wiping out thousands of investors. Subsequent panic rushes on bank accounts, and a drastic decrease in demand, led to very high unemployment and swept away the optimism of the 1920s.

Right: An advertisement for the Healingram 'Vaucluse', produced by the A.G. Healing manufacturing firm.

Below: An AWA Radiola Broadcast Receiver from 1927. Radios (or radiograms) were quite large, looking like a part of the furniture when they arrived in the home.

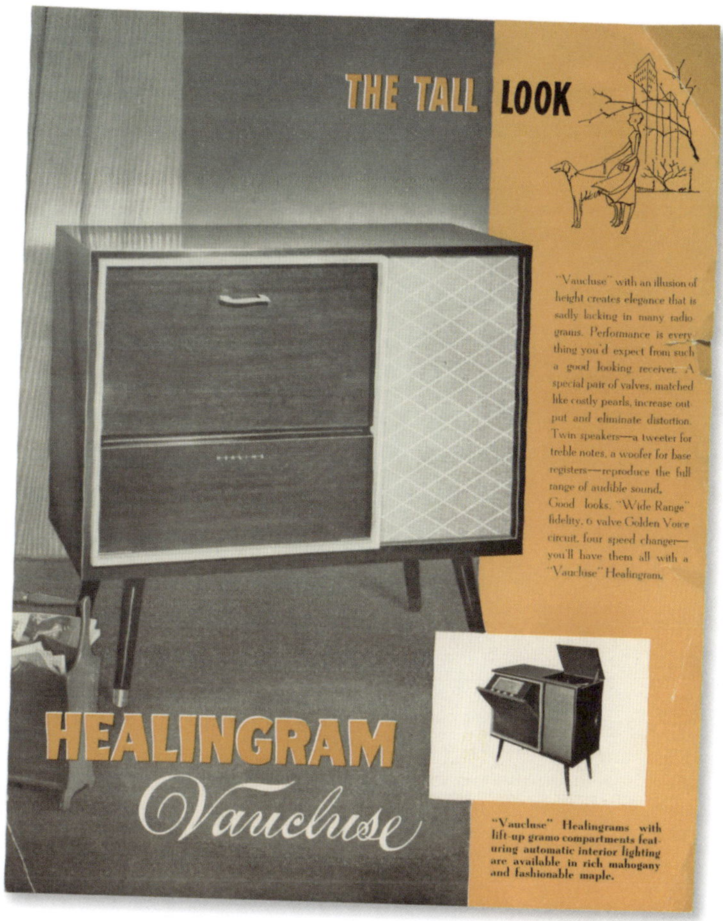

In Australia, the Depression hit hard. Worldwide demand for wheat and wool—Australia's two economic mainstays—plummeted. Unemployment rose sharply, throwing households into distress. Politicians made use of the radio to communicate more directly with a panicking public. The most famous of these broadcasts was Franklin D. Roosevelt's fireside chats. In 1933, the newly elected president quickly grasped the opportunity of using this mass medium to explain some of his more dramatic changes. With the country in the grip of the Great Depression, Roosevelt believed he should explain the problem and the need for the public to trust the banking system and not withdraw money.

On the evening of 12 March 1933, Roosevelt outlined his program for reforming the banking industry and asked for the public's cooperation. The broadcast was successful, having an automatic impact by stabilising the banks. Roosevelt used the broadcasts to explain a range of policy issues. He was also inspirational, with famous quotes such as 'The only thing we have to fear is fear itself'.[7] His voice became familiar to the public. Here is part of his second fireside chat, delivered on 7 May 1933:

> *Today we have reason to believe that things are a little better than they were two months ago. Industry has picked up, railroads are carrying more freight, farm prices are better, but I am not going to indulge in issuing proclamations of over-enthusiastic assurance. We cannot ballyhoo ourselves back to prosperity. I am going to be honest at all times with the people of the country. I do not want the people of this country to take the foolish course of letting this improvement come back on another speculative wave. I do not want the people to believe that because of unjustified optimism we can resume the ruinous practice of increasing our crop output and our factory output in the hope that a kind Providence will find buyers at high prices. Such a course may bring us immediate and false prosperity but it will be the kind of prosperity that will lead us into another tailspin.*[8]

Roosevelt felt confident in talking in detail to all Americans. By using the radio, his calm explanation of the way forward during the Depression was carried into people's homes.

Radio gave politicians access to a new form of mass communication, as in American President Frederick D. Roosevelt's 'fireside chats'.

Joseph Lyons, then prime minister of Australia, used a very similar format to great effect, providing the essential stability needed at that time. This radio broadcast from New Year's Eve 1934 shows the tone was friendly, stoic and optimistic:

> *Good evening, listeners. The wheel of time has turned another cycle. We turn our backs on a year that has passed and we face the year that is to come ...*
>
> *For many, I know only too well, 1934 has been a year of trial. To many it has brought suffering; to these, words can be of small comfort, but*

I cannot refrain from expressing my unbounded admiration for the manner in which thousands of our people have borne their sufferings with fortitude, have faced life and its problems so courageously. The world these days seems to be out of joint in many respects and the economic crisis through which we have been passing has left its mark ...

To them, to you who are listening tonight, we owe our thanks. The road to economic recovery is painful but I have not a doubt that the road the Australian people have taken is the correct one and that its goal will be worth the effort of attaining it.

For those who have known sorrow in the past year I pray that there will be better times ahead. For those who have been more fortunate I pray that there will be a continuance of good fortune. And I would conclude with the words of Robert Louis Stevenson 'To travel hopefully is a better thing than to arrive and the true success is to labour'.

Good night and a happy new year to you all.[9]

The Australian economy did improve, but it took time. Lyons served three terms and died suddenly when still in office, on 7 April 1939.

Radio was also one of the necessary means of communicating the beginning of World War II to Australians. On 3 September 1939, the prime minister, Robert Menzies, used a radio broadcast to make the fateful declaration of war against Nazi Germany to the Australian people:

Fellow Australians, it is my melancholy duty to inform you officially that in consequence of a persistence by Germany in her invasion of Poland, Great Britain has declared war upon her and that, as a result, Australia is also at war. No harder task can fall to the lot of a democratic leader than to make such an announcement. Great Britain and France, with the cooperation of the British Dominions, have struggled to avoid this tragedy. They have, as I firmly believe, been patient. They have kept the door of negotiation open. They have given no cause for aggression. But in the result, their efforts have failed and we are therefore, as a great family of nations, involved in a struggle which we must at all costs win and which we believe in our hearts we will win.[10]

Above: Australian Prime Minister Joseph Lyons used radio to address the public about the Great Depression in 1934.

Right: Menzies also used it in 1939 to tell Australians when the nation entered the war against Germany.

Music to the home

The radio provided a sense of home and comfort. Many American songs of the 1930s and 1940s, always popular in Australia, connected back to 'home', at a time when service men and women were away at war.

Radio stations would play popular songs such as *My Home in Tennessee, Happy Days are Here Again, Ol' Man River, We'll Sing in the Sunshine* and *Home on the Range.*

Music broadcasts became a part of the ABC's program in the 1930s. But the radio schedule included a range of content, such as the children's session with *Bobby Bluegum* and the first pilot for *The Argonauts Club,* race calls from Sydney's Royal Randwick Racecourse on *Racing Notes,* cable news from London including stock exchange reports and shipping news, ABC Women's Association broadcasts of housekeeping advice, and a schedule of assorted dramas, plays, sketches and lectures. From 1934, music broadcasts became a mainstay following the appointment of Sir Bernard Heinze as conductor and musical adviser to the ABC.[11]

The ABC also established an orchestra and choral group in every major Australian capital.

Radio drama

Radio drama took time to grow in Australia. Writers and producers needed to adapt their style from the theatre, where they had learned their craft. In the early days of drama on radio, everything was done live. In the 1920s, plays were often only five- or six-minute 'mini' plays, and actors would need to perform live, sometimes quite late at night. In the 1930s, His Master's Voice began to produce very large 16-inch (41-centimetre) records that could hold longer recordings. This helped to record plays that could be broadcast later.[12]

The scenery and dramatic expression of the theatre were replaced with the key driver of atmosphere in radio—sound effects. Members of the production team produced many of the sounds effects themselves, often with ingenious self-made props:

A Russian orchestra performing at radio station 2CH in Sydney.

> *Thunder was simulated by shaking a large sheet of metal; galloping horses were re-enacted by pounding coconut half shells in a sandbox; and the crunch of footsteps in the snow was created with bags full of corn-starch. Specially designed boxes were created to reproduce the sounds of telephones and doors. Sound engineers kept a large supply of shoes and various floor surfaces on hand to reproduce the sounds of footsteps.*[13]

An incredible array of drama series was developed and broadcast over the period from the 1920s to the 1960s. There were many radio stations throughout the country that required dramatic content as part of their

The main characters of *Dad and Dave*: Dave (John Saul), Mabel (Nell Stirling), Mum (Lois Bingham) and Dad (George Edwards).

programs. Different variety shows were broadcast as well, but regular, dramatic serials were the mainstay of radio.[14]

Radio really did open up a world of information, entertainment and wonder to listeners. The following are some examples from the National Film and Sound Archive of Australia's *Australian Radio Series (1930s to 1970s): A Guide to Holdings*:[15]

Dad and Dave from Snake Gully: This was one of the biggest radio programs on Australian radio, running for 2,276 episodes. The comedy series tells the story of two farming families living at the fictional Snake Gully. It featured as its theme song *On the Road to Gundagai*.

Hester's Diary: A drama about the struggles of life in early nineteenth-century Sydney. Hester Bamford decides to leave England on a perilous sea voyage to marry a man she knows little about.

Hearts in Harmony: Two people come from very different backgrounds, but find a connection in their passion for music. Confronted with a hostile family reaction to their relationship, they strive to start a new life for themselves. It is accompanied with a light musical score.

The Crystal Skull: A group of explorers push far into the jungle of a South Pacific island in search of a mysterious Crystal Skull.

Tempest: An early radio story about the threat of humanity when it gains control of the environment. A group of fanatics develops the power to harness the elements, and then holds the rest of humanity to ransom.

In an interview on ABC radio in 2017 about his history of Australian radio drama, *Drama in Silent Rooms*, author Peter Philp explained that Australian people were so engaged with radio series that when the well-known *Blue Hills* series ended listeners sent presents to the ABC and people cried—the characters had become a part of their lives.[16]

At the peak, there would be 400,000 or 500,000 people listening to a broadcast. An example is the *Caltex Theatre* (an Australian program similar to the American *Lux Radio* and sponsored by the Caltex Oil Company), broadcast on Sunday by up to 50 different radio stations across Australia.[17]

Peter Philp also spoke of the quality of the Australian actors involved in radio, including Peter Finch, Ruth Cracknell, Bud Tingwell and Lyndall Barbour.

Some programs gained an amazing number of followers. In Melbourne, at one stage, a staggering 50 per cent of the radio-listening audience tuned into a well-known police drama called *D24*, produced by the Crawford family. Today a rating of 15 per cent of the audience share is considered very high.[18]

Lyndall Barbour was one of Australia's actors who began her career in radio.

Rural Australia

The ABC Charter, set down by Parliament, requires the Corporation (as it has been since 1983) to provide informative, entertaining and educational services that reflect the breadth of our nation.

In 1945, *Country Hour* was first broadcast and quickly became the ABC's flagship rural affairs program, providing audiences outside of the city centres with vital information such as weather and stock reports and emergency information in times of need. *Country Hour* is still broadcast on local ABC radio stations for one hour each weekday, presenting rural news and issues. It is the ABC's longest-running radio program.[19]

Other rural radio programs include *Country Breakfast* and *Heywire*, which aims to support and foster communication and careers among younger people living in the bush. The ABC also has many regional-based reporters who provide rural-related news reports to both radio and television.

Many cultures, many voices

First Nations broadcasting began when the Townsville Aboriginal and Islander Media Association (TAIMA) was founded in 1972. TAIMA began broadcasting on Mount Stuart, about ten kilometres south of Townsville in Queensland.[20]

In 1985, many remote Indigenous communities had their first access to radio and video broadcasts when Australia's first domestic satellite, AUSSAT, was launched. Making use of this new technology, the Australian Government set up the Broadcasting for Remote Aboriginal Communities Scheme (BRACS), which aimed to give Indigenous people more access to, and control of, media.[21] Over a period of about six years, BRACS units, comprising basic audio and video equipment, were installed in remote Indigenous communities, allowing broadcasting in language, receiving of mainstream programming and broadcasting community-produced content.

The beehive: Australian-manufactured radios

The Kriesler mantel radio was a popular model when released in 1946. It was nicknamed 'the beehive', because of the lapping, wave-like design of its brown-black plastic bakelite casement.

The radio was manufactured by the Kriesler Radio Company, one of Australia's largest radio manufacturing companies at the time. The company was based in Newtown, Sydney, and was named after Fritz Kreisler, the Austrian-born American composer and violin virtuoso, except that the 'i' and 'e' of his name were swapped around.[22]

By 1946, there were over 250 commercial and public (Australian Broadcasting Commission) radio stations across Australia, delivering news, education, sport and culture into households around the country. This is reflected in the complex dial glass of the radio, which is organised by state.

The radio retailed at around £18, the equivalent of about $1,300 today.[23] Although this model was far smaller than the heavier, furniture-like radiograms of the 1930s, it still used the same vacuum-tube technology as its predecessors. Vacuum-tube technology would be largely superseded with the arrival of transistor radio technology from the early 1950s.

A Kriesler mantel radio (model 11-4) from around 1946.

In the cities, radio was growing too. Redfern is an inner-city suburb of Sydney, just past Central station, with densely packed terrace housing rapidly put up in the boom times of the late nineteenth century. It is home to a large First Nations community and has been a place where that community thrives—socially, culturally and politically—for more than half a century; it is 'Australia's Black Capital', according to Koori Radio.[24] Radio Redfern emerged during the 1980s, after the resurgence in Aboriginal activism and what Gary Foley described as 'creative political dissent' of the 1970s[25], and in the lead-up to Australia's Bicentenary in 1988. Radio Redfern gave the community a focal point for their views and information-sharing, broadcasting up to 30 hours each week. Koori Radio, operated by the Gadigal Information Service (GIS) Aboriginal Corporation, grew out of Radio Redfern. GIS founders Cathy Craigie, Matthew Cook and Tim Bishop 'saw the need for an Aboriginal-owned and -operated communication organisation in response to negative stereotypes portrayed by mainstream media'.[26]

A Koori Radio poster from around 1998–1999.

Producer-announcer Vic Kennedy records a Learn Italian program for radio station 3ZZ Melbourne with Anna Maria Sabbione and Laura Bregu.

Indigenous radio has gone from strength to strength since then. Today, Koori Radio broadcasts around the clock and plays 99 per cent Indigenous and Black music. In radio broadcasting, there are currently more than 120 Indigenous broadcast services operating around Australia, with an approximate audience of 100,000 people.[27]

'Ciao!' 'Nǐ hǎo!' Just as many Australians hear their first 'good morning' when they turn on the radio, people from different cultural backgrounds hear the same greeting in their own language on radio stations throughout the country. Radio provides ethnic communities with a vibrant on-air presence across Australia, in a range of languages and formats. Community radio has grown since the 1970s—the result of a demand for access to the airwaves by multicultural communities and criticism of the monocultural broadcasting of the 1960s.[28]

For people immigrating to Australia after World War II, establishing a connection to their own community was a vital part of what they needed to start to feel at home in their new country. Through radio broadcasting, they were able to maintain their language and culture, at the same time learning about their new home.[29]

Radio 5UV in Adelaide was a pioneer in cultural radio, when in 1972 it became Australia's first community radio station.[30] It involved five ethnic groups: Italian, Dutch, Ukrainian, Polish and Greek. The station moved to the FM band, becoming 5EB1-FM Radio in 1978. Another pioneering station was 3ZZ in Melbourne, established in October 1974, initially broadcasting in English and 20 other languages.[31] When it was closed in 1977, 3,000 people rallied at Melbourne's Town Hall.[32] It was reborn in 1989 and is now the largest ethnic community station in Australia.

Today, ethnic community broadcasting is listened to by hundreds of thousands of Australians. It is supported by approximately 4,000 volunteers, and broadcast in over 110 languages.[33] Apart from entertainment, these radio stations provide local news in the community language and information on important issues like discrimination and where to find help. As new groups arrive in the country, new radio stations are set up in response. More than 5,000 people listen to the Somali language show on 3CR 855 AM in Melbourne, with talkback calls coming in 'from the suburbs of North West Melbourne to the east, as well as many roaming calls from taxi drivers'.[34]

Airmail in the interwar years

The first experiments in carrying mail in Australia by air took place before World War I. On 16 July 1914, French aviator Maurice Guillaux set out from Melbourne to Sydney with special mail and 'soared gracefully into the air like a carrier pigeon', according to newspaper reports at the time.[35]

Flying a Blériot aeroplane, Guillaux made the trip in a series of flights, which by today's standards were quite short. The first leg was from Melbourne to Seymour, a town to the north of Melbourne. After refuelling, Guillaux flew to Wangaratta, south-west of Albury–Wodonga.

Maurice Guillaux in his Blériot XI monoplane holding a bag of airmail in advance of his flight to Sydney.

He then flew to Wagga Wagga, then to Harden, north-west of Canberra. From there, Guillaux flew to Goulburn, the flight being 'the worst I have ever experienced in any part'. From Goulburn, he flew to Liverpool and then, finally, Moore Park in Sydney.

Guillaux's plane was preserved and is now on display at the Powerhouse Museum in Sydney. The frame is very light, the wings almost transparent and the landing wheels narrower than a modern-day BMX bike. It is a marvel that Guillaux survived through the storms he encountered.

On 20 July 1914, an article in the *Murrumburrah Signal and County of Harden Advocate* reported a mixed flight, ranging from a glorious view of the Snowy Mountains, which Guillaux said reminded him of Mont Blanc in France, to a more difficult approach to Sydney:

> *He passed over Moss Vale at a height of 7,000 feet, and at a rate of 100 miles an hour, and alighted at Liverpool, not knowing what town it was. His wrists were aching, owing to the hard work at the controller.*

Between Moss Vale and Liverpool he travelled at the rate of 116 miles an hour. The rainstorm between Liverpool and Sydney, added Guillaux, took all the pleasure out of the trip, and he had to wait till the rain steadied before he 'could land at Moore Park.' In the interval he went for a cruise round Parramatta, Manly, and other places.

Kelly Burke writes in her book *The Stamp of Australia*:

Not only had the Frenchman successfully completed Australia's first aerial mail delivery, he had also set a world distance record for the carriage of mail by air. It had taken him two and a half days and a total of nine and a half hours' flying time. In that time, the mail train could have travelled from Melbourne to Sydney and back again, but that wasn't the point.[36]

World War I broke out weeks later, and Australia was soon sending troops to support Britain. The war would last four years, with more than 60,000 Australian volunteers killed in Europe. Guillaux himself was a victim of the war. He volunteered as news of the outbreak of war came through. By early 1915, he was back in France. His role was to test new warplanes, a difficult and dangerous task. In 1918, reports reached friends in Sydney that Guillaux had been killed flying a test model of a new plane.[37]

Many Australians had learned to fly in the war and, as part of the Australian Flying Corps, had participated in the deadly warfare of dogfights and missions over the trenches in Belgium and France. At the end of the war, the Australian prime minister, Billy Hughes, organised a competition for the first plane to travel from England to Australia. The prize was £10,000.

Six Australian crews entered the race. Most of the men had served in the Australian Flying Corps. A seventh, unofficial, entry was made by French aviator Étienne Poulet.[38]

Billy Hughes organised the England to Australia air race in 1919.

The race commenced on 21 October 1919. In the end, only two planes completed it; there were two fatal crashes. On 13 November 1919, Roger Douglas and Leslie Ross were killed when their Alliance P2 Seabird (G-EAOX), named *Endeavour*, spun out of control soon after take-off from the starting point of the race at Hounslow, West London. The next day more tragedy struck when Cedric Howell and George Fraser had to ditch their Martinsyde Type A MkI (G-EAMR) into the sea near the Greek island of Corfu. Both men drowned.

The race was won in the end by the brothers Ross Smith (pilot) and Keith Smith (navigator) with engineers Walter Shiers and James Bennett. They took off from England on 12 November 1919, in a Vickers Vimy twin-engine biplane, and landed at Darwin on 10 December. Darwin's postmaster, E.J. Cook, 'posted' Australia's first official transcontinental airmail. The other plane to complete the race was an AIRC DH9 flown by Ray Parer and his copilot John McIntosh (this plane is on display at the Australian War Memorial).[39]

A range of pioneering flights took place in the 1920s, setting milestones in distance flying. The huge scale of the change brought by flight was evident in one man's experience. In 1922, outback pioneer Alexander Kennedy was a guest on the maiden airmail flight by Qantas in November 1922. The trip from Charleville to Cloncurry took two days. In the 1870s, Alexander had done the same trip by bullock wagon, taking eight months.[40]

Burke writes in *The Stamp of Australia*:

> *Airmail was clearly the way of the future, and in a country as vast as Australia, innovations in aviation were as essential for transcontinental communication as they were internationally. As the pioneers of the Australian skies clocked up countless 'firsts' and further national and world records, their triumphant landings would inevitably culminate in the thud of a mailbag dropping on the landing strip.*[41]

Mail transport by train was still more efficient for most overnight locations, but the plane was going to form an important vehicle for remote and outback areas in Australia.[42] In 1929, Australia's first regular interstate airmail

On 24 April 1931, the *Southern Sun*, piloted by Charles Kingsford Smith, set off from Darwin, laden with the first official airmail sent between Australia and London. The plane carried 17 mail bags filled with more than 25,000 letters from around the nation.

delivery took place between Perth and Adelaide, with Western Australian Airlines carrying the mailbags.[43] By the 1930s, regular routes had been established, particularly in Western Australia.

Airmail is still important for remote areas of Australia. In 2018, an ABC reporter took to the air with an outback mail delivery flight:

> *As the single-engine Cessna touches down, a cloud of red dust billows out behind it. The pilot—an affable 27-year-old named Harvey Salemeh—turns around and grins.*
>
> *'Welcome to Tjuntjuntjara.'*
>
> *Further down the runway, there is no terminal or ground crew waiting on the tarmac, if you could call it that. Instead, there are a handful of parked four-wheel drives waiting for the plane to come to a stop.*
>
> *Although it is equipped to seat 10 including the pilot, this morning's flight is not carrying any passengers. Instead, there is a mix of cardboard boxes, sealed crates and packages in plastic wrapping stowed in its undercarriage.*
>
> *This is how mail is delivered in some of Australia's most remote communities dotted across the outback ...*
>
> *'We're 1,000 miles from Kalgoorlie and 1,000 from Alice Springs,' says* [shire president] *Mr McLean.*
>
> *'It used to be very remote. Now with the internet, TV, phones, it's not nearly as remote as it used to be.'*
>
> *And with a regular airborne delivery through rain, hail or shine, that is unlikely to change.*
>
> *The population serviced by the remote mail program is admittedly very small and unevenly spread across the country.*
>
> *Yet ask anyone who uses it and they will tell you, life would be very different without it.*[44]

6

War in the Pacific

1941–1945: Radio communications in the Pacific theatre in World War II

Telegraph and radio were mainstream technologies when World War II broke out on 1 September 1939. Their use had been integrated into military strategies and tactical responses and protocols.

World War II was a more mobile conflict than its predecessor. World War I was fought in the trenches of the Western Front in Belgium and France, in the restricted areas of the Dardanelles, and in Palestine and Syria. While there were many other battles, particularly at sea, in other parts of the globe, the key area of conflict, which ultimately decided the outcome of the war, was on the Western Front.

By contrast, the campaigns of World War II took place across vast distances. Beginning in Europe with Germany's conquest of Poland and France in 1939 and 1940, *Blitzkrieg*, or lightning war, took place at a far greater pace than the campaigns of World War I.

The war in Europe was to expand across the map even further when Nazi Germany invaded the USSR in June 1941, launching tank and aircraft attacks into the vast reaches of Ukraine and Russia.

All of these rapid movements were supported by wireless communications. Wireless radio was used at both a strategic level (by command centres) and in the field (between ships, aircraft and troops on the ground). Radio and wireless telegraphy enabled the movement of tanks and planes and mobile technology; without it, communications would soon have broken down.

A poster for the home front, urging the public to look after their radios, so production could be focused on the military.

The Golden Age of Radio in the US, an exhibition in the Digital Public Library of America, sets out the key changes by 1941:

> *By the time the United States entered World War II in late 1941, radio technology had vastly improved from the equipment available in the 1910s. Vacuum tube radios, which just thirty years ago were bulky and hard to carry, were now smaller. This paved the way for lighter weight, portable, battery-operated transistor radios, encased in metal, for military field use during World War II. In addition to hand-held use by US soldiers on the ground, radios were now an integral part of airplane, submarine, and tank communications. Transmissions went greater distances and were more reliable, and soon became a staple of the war effort.*[1]

In 1940, Australia sent its first army division to the Middle East to support the British Empire, with a second following later that year. However, Australia's communication systems would soon be required to support the defence of its own coastline.

Japan enters the war

On 7 December 1941, Japanese forces attacked the American naval base at Pearl Harbor in Hawaii, killing more than 2,400 naval personnel and destroying six major ships, including three battleships. The United States, Australia and the United Kingdom were at war with Japan. The Japanese forces struck hard, capturing the Philippines, Malaya (Malaysia), and then, on 15 February 1942, the jewel in the crown of Britain's South-East Asian empire, the island of Singapore. The loss of Singapore was a humiliation for the British Empire and its prime minister, Winston Churchill, and the beginning of a crisis for Australia, which was now faced with a rampant Japanese force looking south, hungry for more conquests.

Although bitter, prolonged fighting took place on the ground across the Pacific, it was navies and air forces that supported, supplied and

Opposite page: The war in the Pacific was a mobile conflict, requiring sea and air transport, and sophisticated radio communications.

Rabaul, Key to Japan's Offense—and Defense—in Pacific

UNDER the personal command of General Douglas MacArthur, Allied troops have captured Buna and Gona on New Guinea, clearing the way to the strong Japanese base at Lae. From this latter point, once it is taken, the Allies can strike at Japs' main operating base, Rabaul, from two directions.

It is from Rabaul, on the island of New Britain, that the Japs have sent ships, planes and men to strike at Guadalcanal and the approaches to Australia.

Once Lae is taken the Allies can move on Rabaul from New Guinea and Guadalcanal.

Rabaul is a natural fortress, supplied from Truk, which has been called the Japanese Singapore. In its landlocked harbor a fleet can anchor, protected by a narrow gateway that can easily be mined. Back of the harbor is a made-to-order airfield, surrounded by jutting heights where artillery and anti-aircraft guns can be placed. Rabaul will not be taken easily.

Meanwhile, the Japs have been reported landing troops on Timor, across from Darwin, vital Allied base on Australia's north coast, a move possibly designed to draw the Allies away from Rabaul.

Japan has thrown great forces against Americans in the Solomons, apparently fearing that the Allies will use the same road the Japs took when they started into the south Pacific. It is a two-way road, and over it the Allies can reach Japan.

After Rabaul, once it is in Allied hands, the great Jap bases of Truk, Palau, Kusaie, Ponape and Jaluit can be attacked. These stand between the Allies and Japan itself.

That is why the Japs are striving desperately to win the battle of the south Pacific.

Arctic Ocean
Beaufort Sea
ALASKA
Bering Sea
Gulf of Alaska
Sea of Okhotsk
ASIA
SOVIET UNION
SIBERIA
MANCHUKUO
CHOSEN
Sea of Japan
Yellow Sea
East China Sea
South China Sea
FRENCH INDOCHINA
PHILIPPINE IS.
CAROLINE ISLANDS
MARSHALL IS.
JAPANESE MANDATED ZONE
EAST INDIES
NETHERLANDS INDIES
BORNEO
HAWAIIAN ISLANDS
North Pacific Ocean
South Pacific Ocean
NORTH AMERICA
VICTORIA ISLAND
Hudson Bay
UNITED STATES
MEXICO
Gulf of Mexico
AUSTRALIA
WESTERN AUSTRALIA
NORTHERN TERRITORY
QUEENSLAND
SOUTH AUSTRALIA
NEW SOUTH WALES
VICTORIA
TASMANIA
Coral Sea
Tasman Sea
NEW ZEALAND
Important U.S. Naval, Military and Air Bases
DON LEE BROADCASTING SYSTEM
THE NATION'S GREATEST REGIONAL NETWORK
1941 INTERNATIONAL RADIO NEWS MAP 2nd Edition
Political Legend
Axis Powers
(Japan non-belligerent in Europe)
Occupied by Germany and Italy
Occupied by Japan
Defeated by Axis Powers but not Occupied
Great Britain and Allies
(China at war with Japan only)
Occupied by Great Britain
Neutral or non-belligerent
Military Legend
Major Foreign Naval Bases
U.S. Naval Operating Bases
U.S. Naval Air Stations
U.S. Navy Yards
U.S. Air Bases acquired from Britain
U.S. Fortified Areas
Possible Wartime Bases
U.S. Army Air Bases and Facilities
(See list on reverse side)
Base Copyright by Rand McNally & Company, Chicago.

reinforced those troops. Fighting occurred in the deep jungles of Papua New Guinea, in Solomon Islands and on the heavily fortified islands of Tarawa and Saipan. These were the spaces on a chessboard, with constant movement across and around them, based on naval deployments, striking distance by air, supply lines and the location's part in a defensive wall (by the Japanese) or offensive stepping stone (on the part of the Americans and Allies).

The Pacific War involved places and names that most people had never heard of—Guadalcanal, Gona, Buna, Tarawa and Iwo Jima. Many of these places were literally dots on the map in a sea of blue, but they were significant. Tarawa, for example, was a tiny atoll, just big enough to build an airport on. These locations would become household names in the United States, Australia and the rest of the world—sometimes overnight.

For Australians, there are also lesser-known stories, including the vital role of the coastwatchers, the desperate SOS messages sent by radio from merchant ships torpedoed off the Australian coast, the scramble to reinforce Darwin after it was bombed by Japanese forces, and the men who escaped from the Japanese in remote areas, hunted and seeking refuge in an occupied land.

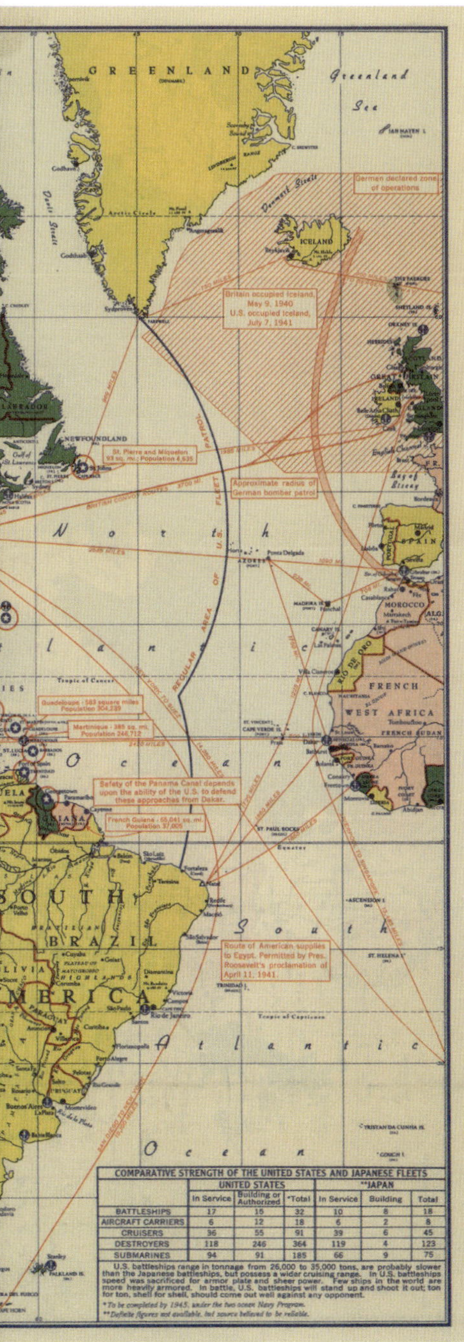

COMPARATIVE STRENGTH OF THE UNITED STATES AND JAPANESE FLEETS						
	UNITED STATES			**JAPAN		
	In Service	Building or Authorized	*Total	In Service	Building	Total
BATTLESHIPS	17	15	32	10	8	18
AIRCRAFT CARRIERS	6	12	18	6	2	8
CRUISERS	36	55	91	39	6	45
DESTROYERS	118	246	364	119	4	123
SUBMARINES	94	91	185	66	9	75

U.S. battleships range in tonnage from 26,000 to 35,000 tons, are probably slower than the Japanese battleships, but possess a wider cruising range. In U.S. battleships speed was sacrificed for armor plate and sheer power. Few ships in the world are more heavily armored. In battle, U.S. battleships will stand up and shoot it out; ton for ton, shell for shell, should come out well against any opponent.

*To be completed by 1945, under the two ocean Navy Program.

**Definite figures not available, but source believed to be reliable.

Some of the vast networks of radio news networks, in the context of World War II, as of 1941.

December 1941: Australia's preparedness and radio communications network

Northern Australia was the front line in the Pacific War for Australia. In parts, northern Australia is dry, arid country. When the wet season comes, many areas are transformed into a vibrant green wetlands. Indigenous people have lived, moved about and flourished in northern Australia for many thousands of years, but it is not an environment Europeans took to easily, if at all, when they arrived. And so, when war came to the Pacific, Darwin was only a small settlement. Originally called Palmerston, and established at the time the Overland Telegraph Line was built, by 1933 it had a population of just over 1,500 and was a centre for pearl traders and shipping.

An airstrip had been built at Parap, a suburb of Darwin, for the England to Australia air race of 1919. This became the home of Australian and American air forces during World War II. Australia is often cast as being ill prepared for a Japanese onslaught, and certainly, in relation to its armed forces, it was. However, Darwin's strategic importance had been recognised, and preparations began fairly early on, as Ted Ling of the National Archives of Australia explains:

> *Construction of the Darwin air base began in 1938, as did the Larrakeyah Barracks for the Army. The Navy began to build base facilities on shore, and construction of an anti-submarine boom across the harbour began in June 1940. It was ultimately 5.59 kilometres long, the longest boom net in the world.*
>
> *By the late 1930s, most Darwin residents obtained their water from wells and storage tanks. Wells were unreliable due to the seasonal nature of the town's rainfall. The need for a dedicated water supply was recognised, particularly given the steadily increasing numbers of defence personnel based in and around Darwin. The construction of Manton Dam, about 65 kilometres south of Darwin, began in September 1939 and was completed in January 1941. For the first time Darwin residents were provided with a reticulated water system.*[2]

Vernon Jones' *A Spitfire at Darwin* highlights the importance of Darwin as a key Australian base for the Allies in the war in the Pacific.

Communications were also part of the process of expanding preparations at Darwin and around the coast.

When Australia joined the war on 3 September 1939, operations of the Coastal and Island Radio Services were transferred to the Royal Australian Navy. Existing staff continued to be paid by AWA. Dedicated lines were established from the key radio stations to the closest Naval Intelligence Centres. A variant of Morse code called 'tiddly Morse code' was used. Dispatch riders were also used to send urgent messages.[3]

A Royal Australian Navy Radio Station for Darwin, at the land base HMAS *Coonawarra*, was commissioned in February 1941. HMAS *Coonawarra* then took over naval communications from the Darwin Coastal Radio Station, which maintained radio services with merchant shipping.[4]

This radio station at Darwin would later receive a direct hit from Japanese bombers in the early hours of 27 August 1942. The two radio operators heard the air raid warning and had just safely left the building when two bombs scored direct hits on the station.[5]

Radar was another new technology installed around Darwin to assist in identifying approaching aircraft.

A new technology: Radar

War, by its nature, thrives on chaos. And it is surprise that causes chaos, and the accompanying panic, uncertainty, crumbling morale, confusion and dissolution of forces. Once the element of surprise has been achieved, one of the key causes of defeat is the loss of effective communications. At a strategic level, the need to coordinate and concentrate forces is critical, and any way of disrupting these functions will result in maximum impact. As well, knowing what the enemy is planning to do is a decisive advantage.

During the Battle of Britain, in August–October 1940, the use of a new technology, radar, which communicated the location of objects moving through the air, was made famous when the network of radar stations along the south-eastern coast of England was able to pick up approaching German planes. Supported by spotters on the ground, this gave Fighter Command early warning of German movements, which meant the RAF did not have to mount exhausting standing patrols, but instead could be scrambled to directly intercept German attackers.

In faraway Darwin, radar equipment arrived in the first week of February 1942. But, despite the best efforts of RAAF personnel, it was not operational when the Japanese launched their first, and most devastating, raid on Darwin. The raid came on 19 February 1942, just days after the British Army, including an Australian division, had surrendered to the Japanese at Singapore.

The radar was set up at Dripstone Cliffs. A second was installed at Charles Point on the western approaches to Darwin Harbour. Three more stations became operational in June. Radar towers at Cape Fourcroy (on the south-western coast of Bathurst Island) and Melville Island provided the potential for advance warning at a range of 60 miles (nearly 100 kilometres). Advance warning was essential if Allied planes were to be scrambled in time to gain enough altitude to engage with the Japanese formations, which flew very high over mainland Australia.

There was an Allied air presence at Darwin in early 1942. At the time of the first Japanese raids, the RAAF had two squadrons of Hudson bombers, one squadron of Wirraway fighters (technically outdated compared with the Japanese Zero fighter) and two USAAF squadrons equipped with the Douglas A-24. The number of Allied planes continued to grow.

The fall of Singapore and raids on Darwin

British forces at Singapore surrendered to the Japanese Imperial Army on 15 February 1942. It was a terrible blow to Britain, and also to Australia, which, with New Zealand, was now the last bastion of resistance to Japanese forces in the region. In the same month, the Japanese also took over much of the Dutch East Indies (now Indonesia).

The Japanese launched their first devastating raid on Darwin on 19 February from four aircraft carriers, *Akagi*, *Kaga*, *Soryu* and *Hiryu*, which were positioned 350 kilometres north-west of Darwin. In total, 188 aircraft, known as Nagumo Force, were launched to attack the outpost on which the Allies now pinned so much importance.[6]

The force was first seen by a naval reservist at HMAS *Coonawarra*, nine kilometres from Darwin. Father John McGrath, on Bathurst Island, radioed his sighting to Darwin, just as six fighters dived low and strafed the area. The reports were unfortunately lost in the system, and Darwin had no time to prepare for the attack to come.[7] Without radar warning, the planes of the RAAF could not get into the air in time to form an effective screening resistance.

A heavy focus of the attack was on the shipping in Darwin's port, with a second part of the force attacking installations in the town. The anti-aircraft stations mounted a furious volley of fire, but the Japanese attack was overwhelming. Parap airfield was put out of action. Captain Mitsuo Fuchida reported that 'The job of attacking Darwin seemed hardly worthy of Nagumo Force ... We quickly accomplished our objectives'.[8]

Official figures were 243 killed and 300 wounded in the Darwin raid. Convinced an invasion would soon follow, many people fled.

Things would get worse before they got better. On 9 March, Australian, British and Dutch forces surrendered to the Japanese on the island of Java. However, more American troops were beginning to arrive, particularly in Perth. The United States built a number of aerodromes outside Corunna Downs and Marble Bar.[9]

With the Japanese intent on taking Port Moresby—so as to have the capacity to attack significant parts of the eastern coast of Australia—a battle was looming. The Japanese forces were on the rampage. Their attack on Pearl Harbor on 7 December 1941 was carefully coordinated with other attacks in the Philippines, Hong Kong and Malaya. With hindsight, we can see their forward movement would eventually be halted by the growing military strength of the United States, but that was nowhere near obvious in the early days of 1942. And if the Japanese had taken Port Moresby, they would have been in bombing range of Brisbane.

Opposite page: Oil storage tanks burn after being hit during the first Japanese air raid on Darwin in 1942.

Cable 'wars'

It was at this time that a remarkable dispute took place via telegram between the British prime minister, Winston Churchill, and the Australian prime minister, John Curtin. The bombing of Darwin had the effect of galvanising Australia into action. Curtin confronted Churchill via telegram in the 'battle of the cables', insisting on the return of two of Australia's army divisions to Australia from service in the Middle East.[10] The government was also lobbying for more American troops, knowing that Britain was not in a position to send reinforcements. Churchill, an avid defender of the British Empire, was incensed at Curtin's appeal to the United States for assistance. Although on the other side of the world, he had direct control over the orders being given. Curtin had to convey the force of the Australian Government's decision through a series of agonising cables: it was a battle of wills.

Churchill wanted the two divisions to go to Rangoon (now Yangon), the capital of Burma (now Myanmar), to try and save the city from the Japanese forces advancing on it. He argued that only the Australian divisions could save Rangoon from being lost to the Japanese. Curtin insisted on the troops coming back to Australia.

Churchill cabled Curtin on 20 February 1942:

> *I suppose you realise that your leading division, the head of which is sailing south of Colombo to N.E.I.* [Netherlands East Indies] *at this moment in our scanty British and American shipping, is the only force that can reach Rangoon in time to prevent its loss and the severance of communication with China.*[11]

Churchill, unbeknown to Curtin, had already instructed the Admiralty to turn the troopships carrying the Australians north to Rangoon.

On 22 February, Curtin sent what he thought would be his last telegram to Churchill on the subject: the government could see no reason to change its mind. It was a long cable, and it was 'probably one of the most important messages ever sent by a Prime Minister', according to historian Michael McKernon.[12]

English Prime Minister Winston Churchill's and Australian Prime Minister John Curtin's cable exchanges over Curtin's request for two Australian divisions to return from overseas to defend the continent were tense, and strained diplomatic relations between the two countries.

Faced with Churchill's wrath, Curtin stood his ground—the troops would return to Australia.

The soldiers arrived safely in Adelaide on 23 and 27 March 1942. The troops who returned to Australia undertook jungle training and were then sent to Papua New Guinea, where they were engaged in bitter and deadly fighting with the Japanese at several locations—Milne Bay (on the Kokoda Trail), Gona, Buna and beyond. They were a key part of the force that turned the Japanese around, with Milne Bay being recognised by many as the first land-based defeat of the Japanese.

Winston Churchill later recalled the incident as a 'painful episode' in which Australia had not come to Britain's aid.[13] But Curtin had judged correctly. He was right to look to the United States (which recognised the strategic importance of Australia) to carry on the fight with Japan, to push northwards and roll back the Japanese conquests over the next three years. Curtin was also right to insist on the return of the Australian divisions; doing so boosted Australia's defences and morale enormously.

Again, the power and importance of communications were at the fore. In this case it was an issue of control—Curtin had to use his cables to wrest a decision out of Churchill in a hard-won battle of wills.

The management of the war effort required intense and constant commitment, which ultimately wore Curtin out, contributing to his untimely death in 1945, aged 60. He is regarded by many as one of Australia's greatest prime ministers.

The Battle of the Coral Sea

The Japanese wished to cut off Australia from its supplies by capturing a range of islands around it, such as Fiji, Samoa and New Caledonia. They also aimed to take Port Moresby on Papua's southern coast. They could then look at the option of invading Australia.

The United States Navy, with intelligence from their codebreakers that Japan had plans for Port Moresby and the Pacific islands, moved to cut off any attack, ordering two naval taskforces to steam for the area.[14]

An Australian coastwatcher on Bougainville Island in the Solomon Sea provided the first news of Japanese movements. Watching the Japanese anchorage at Shortland Islands from his vantage point near Buin, Paul Mason, who had grown up in Solomon Islands, observed a group of ships weighing anchor.[15] He advised on 2 May 1942 that a large contingent of enemy ships was sailing southwards. Another coastwatcher, on the island of New Georgia, reported on the ship movement later the same day. Both coastwatchers sent their sightings to headquarters at Port Moresby, and the messages were then relayed.

The Japanese force heading for the administrative capital of the Solomons, Tulagi, was spotted by aircraft and, also on 2 May, by the coastwatcher D.G. Kennedy, who was stationed on Ysabel Island. The Australian garrison stationed at Tulagi was evacuated the same day.[16]

The Battle of the Coral Sea took place between 4 and 8 May 1942. It was a remarkable battle, demonstrating the way naval warfare would now take place. The two forces never saw each other, but operated through the use of reconnaissance and radio communications to launch airpower from aircraft carriers. The battle was like a complex game of chess, with often confusing events. The United States sank the Japanese aircraft carrier *Shokaku*; the Japanese sank the American aircraft carrier *Lexington*.

The result was a tactical draw—in the sense that the United States and the Japanese each lost an aircraft carrier—but a strategic victory for the Allies, as the battle and the loss of a covering carrier for the troops on their way to Port Moresby meant the Japanese had to turn back.

The ability to break codes became critical in World War II. It assisted in two key American victories at the Battle of Midway in June 1942. When

The Japanese aircraft carrier *Shokaku* under attack by American aircraft.

Japan attacked America's naval fleet at Pearl Harbor in December 1941, early radar warnings were dismissed; surprise was complete. However, before the Battle of Midway, the Americans believed they had cracked the Japanese naval code. They decided to test it out. They sent an innocuous message about the water tower being broken at the United States-held Midway Island. When the Americans saw this information repeated in intercepted Japanese messages, they knew they were right. Based on this, Admiral Chester W. Nimitz, commander-in-chief of the United States Pacific fleet, determined to send his aircraft carriers to Midway. The subsequent battle was the key naval victory for the United States against Japan during World War II.

Keeping POWs informed

Warrant Officer Kevin Healey enlisted in the Second AIF in Sydney on January 1940. He was wounded and captured by the Germans in Greece, and transferred to Stalag XXA in Torun in central Poland. Here, Healey began the process of trying to assemble a radio. Once completed, he managed to trade 100 cigarettes with a German pilot for an earpiece, making it possible to listen to the BBC. He kept his fellow prisoners updated on the war news.[17]

In Gravina, in southern Italy, British Prisoners of War (POWs) were able to smuggle in radio parts and construct a radio, but would it actually work? After several unsuccessful attempts, they gathered around the radio. Suddenly, they heard the sound of Scottish regional. The men were transfixed with excitement. From this moment on, they were able to tune in every second evening to hear the overseas broadcast.[18]

Prisoners of war, seen here in Stalag XXA, often had no knowledge of the progress of the war: in a number of cases, POWs secretly constructed radios which gave them access to news.

In the nerve centre

A radio room in a ship was a sparse-looking arrangement. There was a simple desk, a filing cabinet and a radio, normally very solid in build, next to the desk. A set of headphones was kept on the desk, as listening without them was sometimes difficult. A clock hung on the wall. A lamp complemented the harsh light bulb that illuminated the room, which may, or may not, have had a porthole.

During the war, very few messages were actually sent by ships as radio silence was required. Ships, however, constantly received incoming messages from shore stations about weather, submarine movements or other information. The Canadian Navy used a system when receiving and passing on messages:

> *Using a pencil, the operator would copy broadcast messages from shore authorities onto a naval message form, which, in the short form, consisted of 50 blocks or 100 blocks in the longer form. At the top of the form, the operator entered the coded, lettered address delivery groups while into the blocks went four figured cipher groups. At the bottom were spaces for logging the time of receipt, the operator's name, the frequency and other particulars. Without a doubt, the broadcast operator was kept fairly busy filling in these forms, especially with long messages pertaining to convoy dispositions and U-boat situation reports.*[19]

Bad weather presented challenges:

> *The single worst cause of discomfort and danger to any crew member is a rolling, pitching ship. For many, this resulted in terrible bouts of seasickness. A few of those who did not succumb to this malady would find a suitable spot on the ship to watch the sea in its full torment. Sometimes, it was like standing on a hill and looking down into a valley of grey and white immensity. The ship, heading into one of these watery valleys, would hit with a violent thump. To those in the radio office, it sounded like a thunderstorm manifesting its fury directly on the outside of the hull. It wasn't really that menacing, because crew members had sublime confidence in the seaworthiness of their ships. Great, green*

coloured waves, were always breaking over the bow of the ship. This made it hazardous for anyone going aft or coming forward. Because of this, no one was permitted on the upper deck after dark. During inclement weather, radio operators sometimes kept double watches if they were located in the secondary wireless office as it was simply too hazardous to leave that area to walk on deck. Sometimes, the ship rolled for long stretches at a time and ended up chafing the nerves of the whole crew. From time to time, it was necessary to transit an icy deck while the ship steamed through mountainous seas. To execute this manoeuvre, one would judge the roll of the ship and, at the opportune moment, go skiing across to grab a stanchion on the other side. Losing your equilibrium could be very dangerous or deadly.[20]

A radio officer knew that his role was critical. They were at the nerve centre of the ship. They received essential messages and updated the captain and crew. In the radio room, they would have an ashtray, as on long shifts they would sometimes need to light a cigarette and allow it to burn down to their fingers to wake them up if they had fallen asleep. Many would carry the scars for the rest of their lives.

In 1942, the Japanese navy sent submarines down the eastern coast of Australia, to harass shipping and to launch the famous mini-submarine attack on Sydney Harbour on 31 May 1942.

On the night of 3 June 1942, one of BHP's fleet of merchant ships, *Iron Chieftain*, left Newcastle, New South Wales, bound for Whyalla in South Australia with a load of coal and building materials. Just before 11pm, the ship was torpedoed by Japanese submarine *I-24*. *Iron Chieftain*'s captain, Lionel Haddelsey, had seen the submarine, and tried to take evasive action, also calling to the radio officer to send out a distress signal. Even as the ship sank, wireless operator Sidney Francis 'Sparks' Stafford stayed at his station, sending out signals. He was lost, along with 11 other crew, including the captain.[21]

On the morning of 5 June, the coastal town of The Entrance, a small fishing village and holiday destination on the Central Coast of New South Wales, was stirring. It had been a cold, rainy night. As the *Newcastle Sun* reported that day:

Telegraphist W.G. McCartney aboard HMAS *Vendetta*, contacts Rabaul by radio in 1945.

Twenty-five more men from the cargo steamer sunk 35 miles east of Sydney on Wednesday night by an enemy submarine are safe. They appeared off a small fishing village on the eastern coast of New South Wales before daylight to-day in a ship's lifeboat. Weary and suffering from 30 hours' exposure to rain and bitter cold, some of them clad only in pyjamas and drenched to the skin, the men rowed their boat slowly ashore, landing about 6.30 a.m. Thirty-seven members of the crew of 49 have now been saved, a ship having picked up three rafts with 12 men yesterday.

Ongoing operations, 1942–1945

The tide began to turn against the Japanese forces halfway through 1942. Japan's aggressive expansion was halted with important battle victories by the United States at Midway Island (June 1942) and Guadalcanal (August 1942–February 1943). Australian actions at Milne Bay and along the Kokoda Trail (and later at Gona, Buna and Sanananda) in Papua were also key turning points.

American naval commanders next set their sights on an island-hopping campaign across the central Pacific. They intended to take the Marshall Islands followed by the Mariana Islands, then advance on Japan. General Douglas MacArthur, who in 1942 had been appointed Supreme Commander of Allied Forces of the Southwest Pacific operations, was determined to take his land forces back through to the Philippines, from where he had been evacuated when the Japanese forces invaded in early 1942. For much of the war, MacArthur was based in Australia, in Brisbane.

In Darwin, radio continued to be critical in supporting campaigns. Timor had been invaded by the Japanese in February 1942. Many Allied soldiers were evacuated, but remnants of the British, Dutch and Australian forces had retreated further inland and lost contact. In April 1942, at the height of the Japanese push southwards, a faint signal was received at HMAS *Coonawarra*. It was from the Australian Army's 2/40th Battalion (Sparrow Force) in Timor. They had been joined by the 2/2 Independent Company and were still fighting. The message, sent from a scratch-built radio, read: 'Force intact. Still fighting. Badly need boots, money, quinine, Tommy gun ammunition'.

The *Coonawarra* replied to the signal and arranged a rendezvous. On 27 May 1942, HMAS *Kuru*, a 23-metre wooden boat, met up with the force at Betano Bay on the Timor coast. *Kuru* resupplied the force; another vessel, HMAS *Vigilant*, an ex-customs launch, made three trips to Timor under cover of darkness.[22]

The RAN sent HMAS *Voyager*, a destroyer of 320 crew, with reinforcements for the forces on Timor. It had already been in the thick of the action in the Mediterranean, notably during 1941 when the British expeditionary force was sent to Greece and Crete and then later had to be

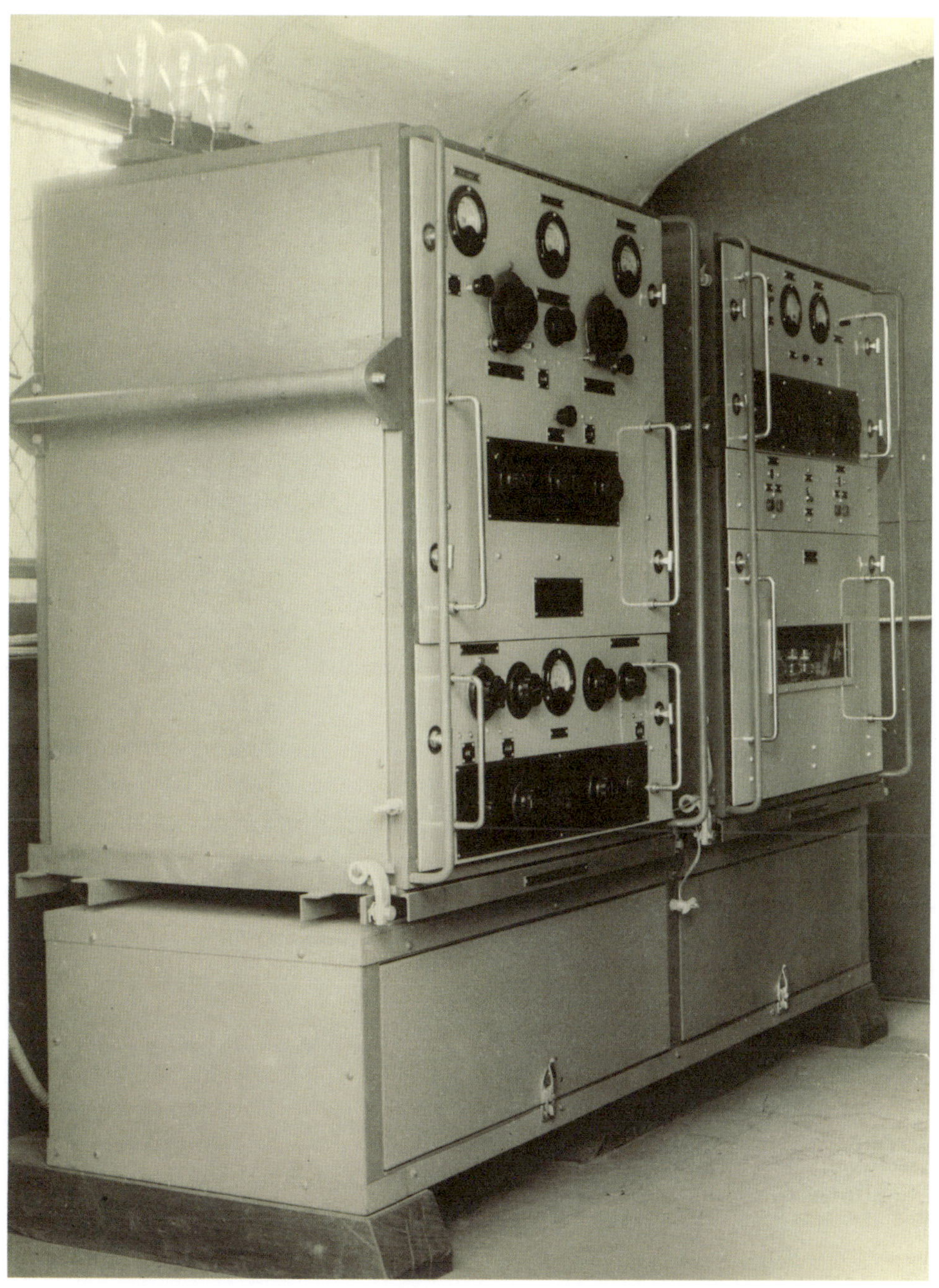

A radio transmitter unit used in Darwin in 1944.

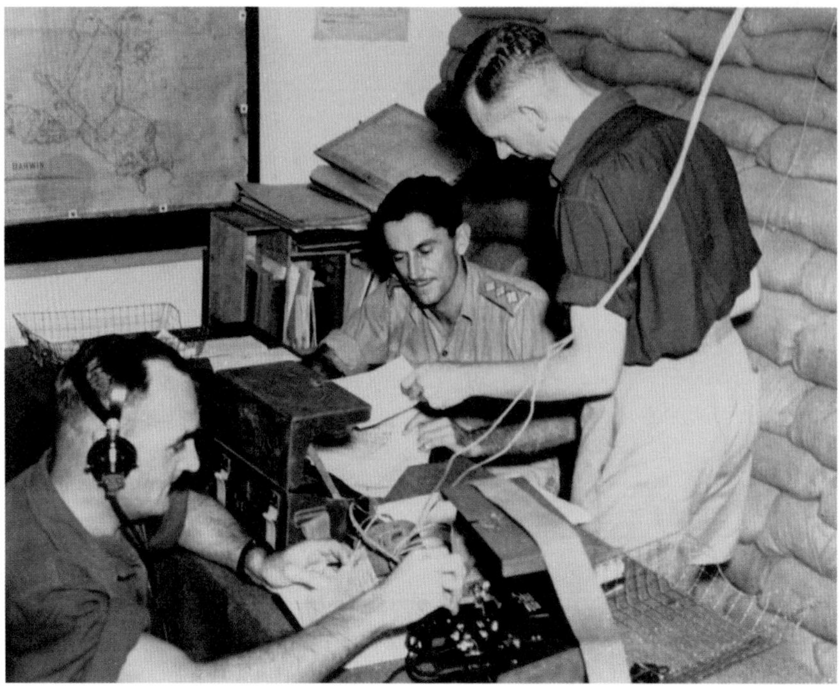

Communications required specialised staff.

evacuated. In September 1942, the destroyer hit a reef at Betano Bay.[23] The Japanese soon spotted the ship, launching bombers to sink it and attack the crew. The *Voyager* sent a distress message.

Tommy Baulk, a *Coonawarra* leading telegraphist, used his technical skill to interpret and receive the message in full. On 25 September, HMAS *Kalgoorlie* and HMAS *Warrnambool* safely evacuated the *Voyager*'s company and brought them back to Darwin.[24]

The Japanese conducted over 50 raids in the Northern Territory (Darwin), Queensland (Townsville) and Western Australia (Broome) over the next two years. Darwin continued to grow and became a major base for air and naval operations.

But it was still, to many, a remote place. When the United States Chief of Staff, General George C. Marshall, visited American airmen at Fenton airbase near Darwin, he called it 'the loneliest and most isolated base he'd seen in a long while'.[25] What would he make of modern Darwin?

The coastwatchers

The coastwatchers were members of a voluntary organisation set up before World War II to monitor movements around Australia's north and coastline. Coastwatchers were provided with an AWA 3B Tele-radio. It was of rugged design, able to withstand heat and wet conditions but very heavy. Their lives were in great danger, as many continued to work in Japanese-occupied territories from 1942. One of the most important contributions coastwatchers made, using their precious radio sets, was during the campaign at Guadalcanal:

> *The network on the Solomons, which uniquely included a female, Honorary Third Officer Ruby Boye, WRANS, continued to provide intelligence even as the Japanese occupied the islands, including information about the construction of a strategically important airstrip near Lunga Point on the north coast. Native Solomon Islanders took work in the Japanese camps and later related what they had seen to the coast watchers. This intelligence was used in maps of Lunga, Tulagi and Gavutu, identifying the position of Japanese guns, defence works and other installations. Following the landing on 7 August 1942, coastwatchers on Buka, Bougainville and New Georgia Islands alerted the Allied forces on Guadalcanal to incoming Japanese air raids allowing them to prepare for, and repel, the enemy aircraft.*[26]

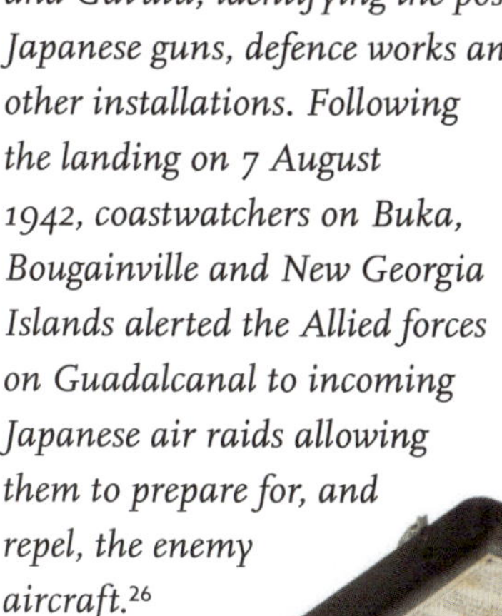

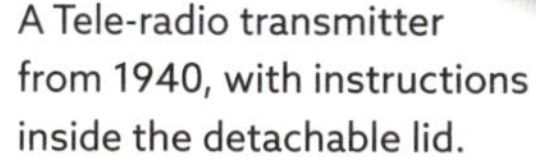

A Tele-radio transmitter from 1940, with instructions inside the detachable lid.

The intelligence provided by the coastwatchers contributed significantly to the success of the Allied campaign:

> *Such was the coastwatchers' contribution to the campaign that Admiral of the Fleet, William F. Halsey, USN, later said 'The coastwatchers saved Guadalcanal, and Guadalcanal saved the South Pacific'.*[27]

Apart from surveillance, coastwatchers also saved many lives—civilians, downed airmen, and lost soldiers and sailors who had survived shipwreck, including the future American president, John F. Kennedy, and the crew of his torpedo boat, *PT-109*.

On 1 August 1943, Lieutenant Kennedy's patrol boat was rammed by a Japanese destroyer and cut in half. Two crew members were lost, but 11 survived, all wearing life vests, and managed to clamber back on board what was left of *PT-109*. One had been badly burned. Lieutenant Kennedy, who had suffered a ruptured spinal disc in the collision, supported him in the water and helped him to the boat.[28]

They made it to a tiny coral island, and Kennedy went in search of food and possible help. He encountered two islanders. He wrote a message on a coconut shell and gave it to them: 'Nauru Isl commander / native knows posit / he can pilot / 11 alive need small boat / Kennedy'. (The coconut shell is now on display at the Kennedy Library in Boston.) The next day, eight islanders appeared on Kennedy's island with a message from an Australian coastwatcher, Reginald Evans, a lookout posted on another island to whom they had shown the coconut. Evans radioed Rendova, an island in Solomon Islands that the United States had recently recaptured from the Japanese, and the survivors were picked up by patrol boat.[29] Years later, when Kennedy was President of the United States, he hosted Reginald Evans at the White House.

On 2 September 1945, following the United States' action to drop atomic bombs on Hiroshima and Nagasaki, Japan surrendered. It had been a bitter, bloody and long-fought campaign. The world had been turned upside down, and for many people it was hard to comprehend they had survived when so many others had perished.

Violet McKenzie: Australia's first female electrical engineer

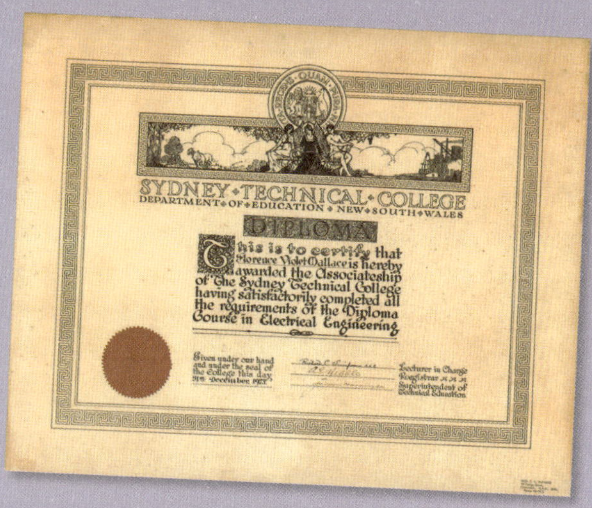

SYDNEY • TECHNICAL • COLLEGE
DEPARTMENT • OF • EDUCATION • NEW • SOUTH • WALES

DIPLOMA

This is to certify that Florence Violet Wallace is hereby awarded the Associateship of The Sydney Technical College having satisfactorily completed all the requirements of the Diploma Course in Electrical Engineering

Given under our hand and under the seal of the College this day 9th December 1923

Lecturer in Charge

Registrar

Superintendent of Technical Education

Florence Violet McKenzie (nee Wallace) was born in Melbourne on 28 September 1890. Her family moved to Austinmer, south of Sydney, when she was still an infant. Violet was an excellent student, winning a bursary to study at Sydney Girls High School. Her passion was electrics and she had a great interest in new radio technologies. After studying at the University of Sydney in 1915, she approached Sydney Technical College to inquire about studying engineering. In an oral history interview, Violet would later recall:

> *I went down to Technical College and saw the Head there, and he said, 'Oh, you can't come here and do engineering unless you're working at it' ... I said, 'Well now, suppose I had an electrical engineering business and I'm working at it; would that be all right?' He said, 'Yes, if you produce proof.' So, I went back and I had some cards printed with my name on, and electrical work, and got the paper and wrote down the ads, and read that a house ... way out beyond Marrickville somewhere, was asking for prices for putting in electric light and power ... I went out there and nobody else was silly enough to go, so they gave me the job. It was about a mile from the end of the tram line ... I went back to Tech and took my card down and showed them the contract for the job, and they said, 'All right, you can start.'*[30]

A woman of great intelligence and energy, Violet went on to start her own wireless shop in the Royal Arcade in Sydney. She set up an Electrical Association for Women and championed training for women in the electrical industry. In World War II, she established the Women's Emergency Signalling Corps (WESC), which trained approximately 12,000 service men and women in the use of radio and Morse code. The service was provided on a voluntary basis.

Above: Violet McKenzie's diploma of electrical engineering, awarded in 1923.

7

Post World War II: TV and the space race

1960–1970: Television comes to Australia, and the 'Dish' helps televise man on the Moon

The late 1940s and early 1950s saw vast social and technological change. The United States, in particular, went through a postwar period of prosperity and growth. It was from the United States that the next big thing in communications, television, was to emerge.

The early days of television

Philo Farnsworth was born in Utah, in the United States, in 1906. As a teenager, he learned about science and technology by reading science magazines. He became interested in communicating and projecting moving images electronically—television. He conceived the view that an electronic system could scan and then connect images to make this happen.

By the early 1920s, Farnsworth had developed the key concepts of television. He continued to refine the invention, despite setbacks, and conducted his first television transmissions in 1927.

In 1930, Farnsworth rejected an offer from the Radio Corporation of America (RCA), which had its own television system, for the purchase of his invention, which led to a series of court cases as RCA sought to challenge Farnsworth's patents. Farnsworth eventually set up his own television manufacturing company, but RCA was a much bigger player in the field. His work, however, had helped make television a reality.

In Australia, the Menzies government decided in 1950 to introduce television.

An Australian-made AWA television receiver, Radiola 'Deep Image', manufactured in 1956.

This decision was followed by a protracted period of doing nothing as the country pondered the pros and cons—there was a royal commission, no less—but the Melbourne Olympics of 1956 provided the final prod that pushed the broadcast beast over the line.[1]

At the end of 1956, by which time the ABC and channels Seven and Nine had been launched, only 1 per cent of Sydney residents and 5 per cent of Melbourne residents owned a television set, a luxury that cost six to ten times the average weekly wage.[2]

Large towers are required for television transmission, and in Sydney the 'Artarmon Triangle'—the television towers for the ABC, Channel Nine and Channel Seven—have been a landmark in the North Shore suburb of Artarmon since their construction:

> *Paris is a long way from Sydney, but there are plenty of Eiffel Towers in the Sydney suburbs. On the lower north shore there are three—the television transmission towers collectively known as the Artarmon Triangle. These tall, red and white pyramids at Gore Hill, Artarmon and Willoughby have been sending out TV signals since their construction in the 1950s and 60s.*
>
> *It stands out from its surroundings now, so it must have been even more striking when it was built in the 1950s. This was long before the neighbouring dark brick colossus of Royal North Shore Hospital was constructed and the highway was still mostly lined with houses. Sydney's first official television broadcast—which began with Bruce Gyngell in front of a map of the world saying 'Good evening and welcome to television'—aired in 1956. The towers were a symbol of this new era of technology.*[3]

Television was to also have probably its most famous moment, in June 1969, when the lunar module *Eagle* landed on the surface of the Moon. Farnsworth was in Utah, watching. His wife later recounted the moment in a Television Academy Foundation interview:

> *Interviewer: The image dissector* [Farnsworth's invention] *was used to send shots back from the Moon to Earth.*
>
> *Elma Farnsworth: Right.*

Television manufacturing at Richardson Television in Victoria in 1958.

Interviewer: And what did Phil think about this?

Elma Farnsworth: All right, we were watching it, and when Neil Armstrong landed on the moon, Phil turned to me and says, 'Pem, this has made it all worthwhile.' Before then, he wasn't too sure.[4]

This was the culmination of the space race, in which Australia played a part in bringing visual communications from the Moon back to Earth.

Television and the space race

The 1950s and 1960s saw significant change across the globe. Many countries that had been part of the British, Dutch or French empires became independent nations—such as India, Indonesia and Vietnam. The United States had turned, during the course of World War II, from a protectionist, non-interventionist nation to an undisputed world power, and was engaged in a Cold War with the USSR that threatened prosperity and growth post World War II.

The space race was a direct consequence of the Cold War. The two superpowers were competing to get the most advanced technology into space and be the first to reach the Moon. Australia was going to find itself, once again, involved in the implementation of cutting-edge communications as satellites were launched.

The space race seized the imagination of science-fiction writers and filmmakers around the globe. Writers had already considered the possibility of landing on the Moon. The plot of both *The War of the Worlds* (1898) and *The First Men in the Moon* (1901) by British novelist H.G. Wells involved encounters with alien beings, which made for a dramatic story, but both books used sound scientific principles to describe space travel.[5] The mechanics of making it happen, however, were very, very difficult, and the USSR and America poured huge amounts of money into their projects.

A keen student of flight beyond the Earth's atmosphere was the Russian schoolteacher and mathematician Konstantin Tsiolkovsky. In 1903, he set out the key principles of space flight in his publication *Exploration of Cosmic Space by Means of Reaction Devices*.

The 1950s saw a fascination with space travel and what lay beyond.

Sputnik 1, on display at the Russian Memorial Museum of Cosmonautics, was the first satellite to orbit Earth, launching the space age.

By the start of the twentieth century, the technology of rockets had advanced to the point where it was reasonable to consider an object could be launched away from Earth and against the pull of gravity.

The first artificial Earth satellite was launched by the USSR on 4 October 1957. The satellite, called *Sputnik* (roughly translated as 'fellow traveller'), was placed into orbit by a rocket, a superb scientific feat. The metal sphere was 58 centimetres wide and weighed 83 kilograms. It carried two long antennas and emitted a distinctive 'beep' back to Earth.

In Australia, the satellite was first spotted over Hobart on Sunday 6 October. *The Canberra Times* of 7 October 1957 reported on *Sputnik*'s significance from a Cold War political perspective:

> *Senator Jackson, chairman of a Senator sub-committee on military applications of atomic energy, said the Russian triumph was 'a devastating blow to America's scientific, industrial and technical prestige in the world'. He said the Defence Department should now restore cuts made in funds for developing missiles and producing B-52 bombers.*

Despite the military concerns, many scientists saw this as a significant technological advance. The United States responded with its ambitious space program, leading to the Moon landing in 1969.

The Russian dog Laika returned from space on *Sputnik 2* in November 1957, but died soon after. The first human to go into space, Yuri Gagarin, successfully completed an orbit around the Earth on 12 April 1961.

Yuri Gagarin was born on 9 March 1934 near a village called Gzhatsk (renamed Gagarin in 1968), which is roughly 170 kilometres from Moscow. He joined the Soviet Air Force Cadet School and completed his studies in 1957. He was chosen as one of the cosmonaut candidates for the USSR space program, and became the pilot of the *Vostok 1* spacecraft.

Just after 9am on 12 April 1961, *Vostok 1* lifted off from Baikonur cosmodrome in Soviet Kazakhstan. 'Poyekhali!' ('Let's go', or 'off we go!') said Gagarin, which immediately became a famous phrase. His flight, a single orbit around the Earth, went off without a hitch. The orbit was completed in one hour 29 minutes at a maximum altitude of 301 kilometres. On return, however, the cables joining the *Vostok*'s descent module and service module failed to separate properly. This caused the spacecraft to shake uncontrollably on re-entering Earth's atmosphere. Gagarin ejected before landing, parachuting down safely near the Volga River.

Gagarin was a national hero and toured the world as a representative of the USSR. But the fame affected him, and he began to drink. Gagarin and one other pilot were killed in 1968 in the crash of a two-seater jet aircraft.

The American Apollo space program, however, was not far behind. Alan Shepard became the first American in space when the *Freedom 7* spacecraft left Cape Canaveral, Florida, on 5 May 1961.

Australia was also participating in a small way. The Woomera Rocket Range in South Australia was used for upper atmosphere research. Australia's first satellite, *WRESAT 1*, was launched from Woomera on 29 November 1967, carrying atmospheric composition and solar radiation experiments.

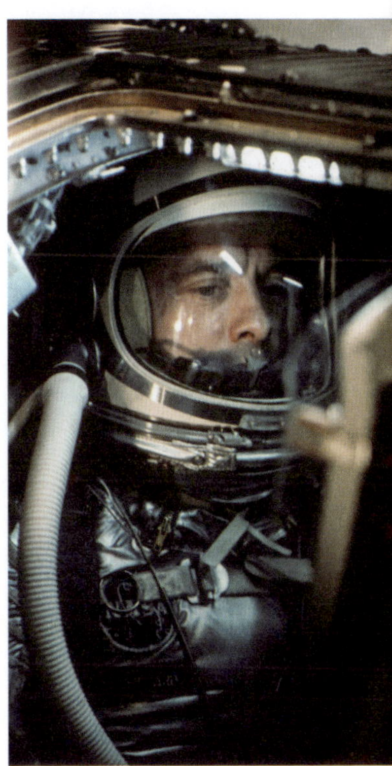

Alan Shepard inside the *Freedom 7* spacecraft awaiting launch.

From 18 to 26 May 1969, *Apollo 10* lay a path for what the Americans hoped would be the ultimate, successful mission. On board the spacecraft, Thomas Stafford, John Young and Eugene Cernan orbited the Moon. Stafford and Young descended to within nine miles (14.5 kilometres) of the Moon's surface in the lunar module *Snoopy*, while Young flew the main craft, *Charlie Brown*. The crew also surveyed and photographed the landing sites for *Apollo 11*.

The landing on the Moon

History was made from 16 to 24 July 1969, when *Apollo 11* travelled into space and orbited the Moon several times before separating from the lunar module *Eagle*. On 20 July, Neil Armstrong made the historic first landing on the Moon, followed about 16 minutes later by Edwin 'Buzz' Aldrin.

The separation of the lunar module from the main craft, *Columbia*, was the most suspenseful and climactic event of the trip. At 7 metres tall and 4 metres wide, the *Eagle* was a tiny speck of a craft to carry out humanity's first landing in space.

The command module pilot, Michael Collins, inspected the lunar module, after which Aldrin and Armstrong departed in the *Eagle* and headed for the lunar surface, leaving Collins to orbit the Moon. This powered descent was the most dangerous part of the flight. For two hours, Aldrin and Armstrong descended towards the Moon's surface. As they got closer, with fuel supplies running very low, Armstrong realised that the computer's auto-landing program was taking them towards a boulder-strewn crater.

In what has become a famous moment, Armstrong took over manual control and steered the *Eagle* towards a clear spot beyond the crater. Armstrong was a veteran test pilot, and remained calm even as warning alarms blared in the cramped cabin and Mission Control announced that there was only 30 seconds of fuel left in the reserves.

The landing module came to a gentle rest and Armstrong cut the engines. 'The Eagle has landed,' said Armstrong to Mission Control. The reply was also famous: 'Roger, Tranquillity. We copy you on the ground', responded fellow astronaut Charlie Duke in Houston. 'You got a bunch of guys about to turn blue. We're breathing again. Thanks a lot.'

The televised shots came from a camera rigged to the outside of the lunar module, which Aldrin and Armstrong turned on as the Moon walk commenced. As he stepped onto the surface, Armstrong radioed back to Earth, 'That's one small step for [a] man, one giant leap for mankind'.

Australia played an essential role in helping NASA broadcast television images of the landing around the globe. Three stations were receiving signals: Goldstone in California, Honeysuckle Creek in the Australian Capital Territory and Parkes radio telescope in New South Wales. Initially, NASA shifted its TV feed between Goldstone and Honeysuckle Creek, but the images from Goldstone were of such poor quality that they switched to Honeysuckle Creek just as Armstrong set foot on the Moon. The Honeysuckle Creek Tracking Station, which had been built specifically to support the Apollo crewed missions, also had two-way voice contact with the lunar module.

Like the Parkes station, Honeysuckle Creek Tracking Station received and relayed broadcast of the Moon landing.

The Honeysuckle Creek images were grainy and low-resolution, due to a low signal strength and small bandwith (Honeysuckle Creek's was the smallest of the three dishes). Nonetheless, they were the first images that appeared when Neil Armstrong stepped onto the surface of the Moon.[6]

Houston then switched its feed to the Parkes signal for the remainder of the broadcast. By this time, Parkes was getting good images. The Moon had risen sufficiently for the chief detector to pick up the signal clearly. When strong winds hit Parkes, staff there continued to operate the dish beyond safety limits for high-wind conditions, as seen in the movie *The Dish* (2000). Relayed to NASA in Houston, the vision from the Moon was broadcast to a worldwide TV audience of perhaps 600 million—an unforgettable experience for those lucky enough to see it.

Newspaper interviews from the time reflected the general euphoria:

> *'It's marvellous', a grey-haired woman nearing 70, said as she stood on a window sill craning her neck to catch a glimpse of the Apollo-11 moon walk. Supported by her slightly younger companion the elderly lady, 4ft above Pitt Street, in the city, was trying to see a television set in a small electrical store. 'It's just like being there when Columbus or some other explorer landed', she said. Lunch-time crowds in Sydney spilled out of their offices and ran to the nearest TV set. All major retail and electrical shops were filled to capacity from 12pm to 3pm.*[7]

Neil Armstrong captured this moment with his 35mm camera. The Moon landing was seen live by millions as TV images were received from the lunar module by tracking stations in Australia.

Armstrong was the first human to walk on the Moon. He was followed by Aldrin. The pair brought home the first rock samples from another celestial body. The headline in *The Sydney Morning Herald* of Monday 21 July 1969, simply stated, 'Men on Moon':

> *Man has landed on the moon. The U.S. spacecraft, Eagle, carrying Neil Armstrong and Edwin Aldrin, touched down on the lunar surface early today (Sydney time). It followed a perfectly executed 250,000-mile flight from the earth and a series of lunar orbits by the main Apollo spacecraft, Columbia.*

This was an astonishing event. The world had not long come out of a world war. Many people had been through two world wars. They had suffered much, despite the great technical advances of the century. The war and destruction across the globe weighed heavily. An event like this captured the imagination of the world; it created a genuine euphoria. And the world got to see the first steps on the Moon in real time on television.

The Parkes dish and the *Apollo 13* rescue

The *Apollo 13* spacecraft blasted off from the Kennedy Space Center in Florida on 11 April 1970. Its destination was the Moon. It was expected that the mission would be 'routine', if there could be such a thing for a space flight to the Moon.

When an explosion occurred in the service module of the spacecraft on the third day of the mission, the lives of the three astronauts—mission commander Jim Lovell, lunar module pilot Fred Haise and command module pilot Jim Swigert—were in grave danger. The mission to land on the Moon was abandoned. The only aim now was to try and get the astronauts back to Earth alive.

Newspaper reports from the time showed the fluctuating emotions and concerns about the fate of the mission.

Opposite page: Parkes also played an important role in the salvage mission to bring the crew of the stricken *Apollo 13* safely back to earth.

The news travelled everywhere. The *Papua New Guinea Post Courier* of 16 April 1970 reported:

> *The stricken Apollo 13 spaceship is slightly off course and its astronauts will miss the earth by 104 miles and soar off into a distant, fatal orbit if a steering correction is not made. 'If the descent engine does not burn, we cannot bring them back,' said retro officer Thomas Weichel at Mission Control ... To successfully re-enter earth's atmosphere, the astronauts must fire the big engine on their lunar module briefly to put their ship into the narrow, imaginary corridor in space leading to a safe touchdown.*

A successful burn of the rockets on the lunar module (the service module being disabled) was achieved, but the communication between the astronauts and NASA was critical to achieving key steps. It was here that the Parkes dish came in. In a detailed presentation in 2020, John Sarkissian, Commonwealth Scientific Industrial Research Organisation (CSIRO), Parkes Radio Observatory, told the story.[8] As early as eight minutes after the explosion, legendary NASA flight director Gene Kranz raised the need to start using the '210s' (210-foot/64-metre antennas), of which there were only two in the world: Goldstone (California, Northern Hemisphere) and Parkes (New South Wales, Southern Hemisphere).

The larger dishes could more clearly and accurately receive the signals being sent by *Apollo 13* using a much weaker transmitter, due to the need to preserve power. The Parkes dish had not been brought online for the *Apollo 13* mission because other, smaller dishes, such as the one at Honeysuckle Creek, were to receive the signals. But with power so critical, it was imperative that it be up and running.

The importance of preserving power was emphasised in the 1995 film of *Apollo 13*. With the service module severely damaged, much of their power was lost. In the movie, John Aaron (played by actor Loren Dean), the flight controller responsible for electrics, says to an assembled group, 'Power is everything. Without it they don't talk to us, they don't correct their trajectory, they don't turn the heat shield around'.

Goldstone was receiving the signals when the explosion occurred on *Apollo 13*. However, it was due to lose the signal in a few hours. Chris

Kraft of NASA in Florida quickly got on the phone to Tom Reid, the director at Honeysuckle Creek, to advise that NASA needed the Parkes dish up and running.

Parkes had been fully geared up to receive transmissions from *Apollo 11* in 1969, including receiving the famed Moon walk TV pictures. The only trouble now was that the infrastructure was not in place for *Apollo 13* at Parkes. A lot had to happen in a very short space of time.

In order to communicate the full signal from Parkes back to Sydney and onto Houston, a series of temporary microwave links had to be constructed. Equipment was brought in by NASA, and the Postmaster General's Department (PMG) flew specialists from Sydney to provide a radio link between the telescope and the tower at Mount Coonambro (about 28 kilometres from Parkes), the closest link to the PMG's existing infrastructure of microwave towers.[9] Workers toiled through the night to erect six aerials over the 28-kilometre distance. When complete, the radio link enabled the full range of data to be passed through to Sydney, then on to NASA in the United States.

Hope began to grow that the astronauts could make it back. The world rejoiced when they re-entered the Earth's atmosphere on 17 April 1970 and splashed down safely in the South Pacific Ocean.

Less than 200 years after Governor Phillip sat in his tent at Sydney Cove writing a letter to England that he knew would take up to eight months to arrive, television pictures were being sent in real time from the Moon to Earth and then around the world. It was a remarkable event.

Australian space tracking and communications stations

Australian stations were built to support of America's space programs. In 1957, Australia's Weapons Research Establishment constructed a tracking station near Woomera in South Australia. Stations were then established in Western Australia and the Australian Capital Territory. There were other key stations used during America's Moon-landing program:

Woomera deep space tracking station was located 43 kilometres north of the small town of Woomera. It is a remote area, and was used by the

Woomera was used for rocket testing by the British and Americans during the 1950s.

Australian and British governments for rocket testing in the 1950s. In 1957–1958, planning commenced to build a tracking station at the existing base for the first space-tracking network to support the Vanguard project, the first rocket built by the United States designed to launch satellites. The antenna was 26 metres in diameter.

Muchea tracking station, near Perth, was built to support Project Mercury, phase one of America's plan to land a person on the Moon. A plaque on the site reads: 'This plaque is to mark the spot where an Australian first spoke to a space traveller'. This was Gerry O'Connor, a communications technician at Muchea, and the astronaut was John Glenn aboard *Friendship 7*. The station was shut in 1964.[10]

Carnarvon tracking station was located 10 kilometres south of the Western Australian town of Carnarvon, which is 900 kilometres north of Perth. Carnarvon sits on the other side of the Earth to NASA's launch site at Cape Canaveral, Florida. The station was built to support NASA's Gemini, Apollo and Skylab programs. It was commissioned in 1964 and operated for 11 years, with more than 220 staff at the height of its operations.

Carnarvon had an important role in the *Apollo 11* mission, transmitting to the astronauts the all-clear message to proceed to the Moon after the spacecraft's first orbit of the Earth. *Apollo 11* would send 'hundreds of pieces of telemetry data—the pressure and temperature inside the craft, astronauts' heartbeats and respiratory rates, and available fuel and oxygen'.[11] These were relayed to Mission Control in Houston as an essential check on the crew's wellbeing before the final thrust into space.

Carnarvon also had an important role in the extraordinary rescue of *Apollo 13* in April 1970 when it was crippled by an explosion on board. Jim Gregg was one of the technicians working at Carnarvon at the time:

> *'The chances of getting the crew back were very low.' Mr Gregg says technicians and engineers worked day and night to bring the crew back alive. He says the station provided the spaceship with the critical command data to turn on the power in the capsule that would bring it back to Earth ... 'It's entirely remarkable that they got themselves back,' Mr Gregg says. 'When we realised that they were coming back alive, the whole place just went ape.'*[12]

Locals have fond memories of the station. One of them, Laurie Glocke, applied for a job as an equipment operator at the station. 'I used to be a waitress and used to serve those guys [from NASA] ... and I had made a lot of money from their tips because they were American,' she said. She was initially unsuccessful in her job application because she did not have her junior certificate, having left high school before she completed Year 10. But she challenged the interviewer and promised she could do the job without the certificate. She soon proved herself right and loved working at the site.[13]

Keeping track of space probes

Australian space stations have continued to receive data from NASA space probes. On 20 August 1977, over 40 years ago, NASA launched the *Voyager 2* spacecraft from Cape Canaveral aboard a Titan-Centaur rocket. A few weeks later, on 5 September, *Voyager 1* launched, also from

Cape Canaveral. Their main mission was to study the planets Jupiter and Saturn. Reaching Jupiter, they found active volcanoes on the giant planet; at Saturn, they provided close-up views of the planet's rings.

These probes continue to transmit data back to Earth. At the NASA's Jet Propulsion Laboratory in Pasadena, California, there is an Australian flag positioned next to a monitor which shows data coming back from NASA's deep space network. Beside the flag, the symbol for the Australian relay flashes as data comes in from spacecraft travelling both within and beyond the solar system.[14]

The *Voyager* spacecraft went beyond the scope of current tracking capabilities, so NASA worked with the CSIRO to boost *Voyager 2*'s weak radio signal.

In 1989, NASA expanded the diameter of the largest 'dish' at the Canberra Deep Space Communication Complex to increase its ability to pick up data from *Voyager 2*. This allowed the Canberra dish to continue to receive data as the spacecraft continued past Neptune. The tracking station continues to receive data from both *Voyager* craft.[15]

Australian tracking stations continue to receive data from the *Voyager* journeys.

Apollo 11: Sophisticated communications equipment from Scottsdale

The Apollo missions were highly complicated operations, and their communications equipment was essential to their success. The equipment had to be designed to function in cold, heat and radiation. *Apollo 11* also needed to transmit more data than in previous NASA missions, including as television signals.

Hundreds of employees in Scottsdale, Arizona, began developing the 'Unified S-Band Transponder' for *Apollo 11* in 1962, a new system that would track the Apollo spacecraft, transmit and receive signals, communicate between ground stations and the spacecraft, and, hopefully, provide a link for the TV broadcast from the surface of the Moon. The contract was awarded to Motorola Inc.

Motorola's Government Electronics Division built key communication devices for the *Apollo 11* mission. Design engineer Scotty Miller, who remembers working long hours in the months before the mission was launched, summed up the challenges:

> *If something's on the ground and it fails, you can repair it and make it work properly. With space hardware, you don't have that luxury. If it fails, the whole mission is gone.*[16]

NASA's Mission Control Center was a busy scene during the Moon landings.

8

Search, rescue, respond

Communicating in a crisis:
Finding and helping shipwrecked sailors,
lost airmen and bushfire victims

The word 'telegram' derives from the Greek word *tele*, which means 'at a distance' or 'to a distance'. The ability to reach across long distances with a message in times of distress has saved many lives at sea, on land and in the air. For a country as large as Australia, this capacity to communicate across vast distances has been essential in search, rescue and emergencies.

Before the advent of radio communications, accounts of maritime history are littered with ships that were lost, destroyed or shipwrecked, with no trace left of their fate except from survivors, eyewitnesses or the melancholy arrival of flotsam and jetsam. Those on land might have been able to see a ship in distress if it was close to shore, or they might have become concerned if a ship was late returning to port. Ships themselves had to rely on flags or lights to signal their distress.

So common is the availability of communications in today's world, we tend to assume there will always be a way to track the movement of a vessel or a party of people (unless a conscious decision is made not to be tracked). But up until the advent of radio communications, it was easy to get lost, to disappear off the map. If you were in distress, how would you get word out?

Those fortunate enough to survive shipwrecks were often lost or marooned.

On 10 November 1796, the *Sydney Cove*, under Captain Guy Hamilton, left Bengal with a range of goods for the settlement at Port Jackson. During the journey a leak sprung up, causing concern to the captain and crew.

They tried to slow or stop the leak by passing a heavy sail, greased and tarred, under the ship where the leak was—this is called fothering or thrumming the ship. The process worked to an extent, but the ship was still leaking. On 4 February, *Sydney Cove* passed Maria Island off the eastern coast of Tasmania. A gale sprung up, increasing in intensity to a hurricane, with a 'dreadful sea'. At 3.30pm a new leak appeared in the hull:

> [It] *gained so fast on the pumps as rendered it necessary to bear up for land to save the lives of the people, and, if possible, to get the ship into a place of security. Bore in accordingly for the land and made more sail, Cape Barras by accounts W. ½N. or W. and by N., distant by accounts 90 miles. The cargo was thrown overboard; but notwithstanding every exertion to keep the leak under, at 5 p.m. there were 2½ feet water in the well, and hourly gaining. At 8 p.m. the water had increased to 5 feet.*[1]

Hamilton decided they could go no further, and ran the ship aground on a shoal near a group of islands. The people were all landed safely on what is now called Preservation Island, and a well was sunk to obtain water. How would the survivors get word to Sydney, 700 kilometres away?

On 10 February, Captain Hamilton started to prepare the ship's longboat for a journey to Port Jackson with an account of the loss of the ship. The longboat was dispatched on 27 February in the charge of Hugh Thompson, the chief mate, with W. Clark as assistant supercargo and 15 crewmen.

The longboat travelled north, across Bass Strait, then ran into a storm. In 'Narrative of the Shipwreck of Captain Hamilton and the Crew of the *Sydney Cove*', the author writes:

> *Being unable to land, the only chance of preservation was to come to with both anchors, which was accordingly done. The boat lay in the most imminent danger from being often almost entirely filled with water by the heavy sea, which during the night continued to break over her. In this perilous situation they remained till daylight, when they cut both cables and set the foresail; but the boat at this time suddenly filling,*

Shipwrecks were a difficult fact of life in 19th century travel and transport.

it was not without the utmost difficulty that they got her through the surf, when she went to pieces a few minutes after the people had gained the beach.[2]

Unable to shelter, the boat was wrecked on a beach in what is now Victoria. With the longboat destroyed, they were faced with only one choice: to try and walk more than 600 kilometres to Port Jackson.

The 'Narrative' continues:

Imagination cannot picture a situation more melancholy than that to which the unfortunate crew was reduced—wrecked a second time on the inhospitable shore of New South Wales; cut off from all hopes of rejoining their companions; without provisions, without arms, or any probable means either of subsistence or defence, they seemed doomed to all the horrors of a lingering death, with all their misfortunes unknown and unpitied. In this trying situation they did not abandon themselves to despair; they determined to proceed to the northward in the hopes of reaching Port Jackson.

They marched on. In places they were helped by local First Nations people, who often guided them on the best paths to progress northwards. They began to suffer terribly from hunger. A number, too weak to carry on, had to be left behind, and these were never heard from again:

> *Had a fatiguing march over very high bluffs, sharp rocks, and afterwards through very thick brushwood, interspersed with stumps of trees and other sharp substances, by which our feet were so much bruised and wounded that some of the party remained lame for some time afterwards; and to aggravate our sufferings we were now living upon a quarter of a pint of dry rice per diem. As we got out of this harassing thicket we missed two of our unhappy fellow-travellers. At 4 p.m. we provided ourselves a lodging for the night, having walked, or rather crawled, 10 miles, over the ground above described.*

The men averaged between 10 and 14 miles (16 to 22 kilometres) per day, but they soon began to suffer from fatigue and hunger. Again, they were helped by First Nations people, who offered fresh fish and guided them for some of their way. Their reception was less welcoming as they approached Port Jackson, crossing into land belonging to those First Nations groups who had been the first to experience the effects of British colonisation.[3]

They trudged along the coast, across coves and beaches, headlands and bluffs, keeping the sounds of the waves always in their hearing. Exhausted, they crept closer to Sydney. On the evening of 16 May, they reached the cove of Wattamolla, in the current-day Royal National Park.[4] There was a fishing vessel there from Sydney; they hailed the fisherman and were taken the final leg of the journey by boat.

Governor Hunter immediately dispatched a rescue party to look for those who had been left along the way. He also sent two ships to Preservation Island. The ships reached the island on 9 June, and most of the party returned to Sydney Cove with what cargo they could salvage. A party volunteered to stay behind with the rest of the cargo, and a further ship was sent to their aid.

It is easy to forget how vast the oceans are. In the early European history of Australia, a ship could easily completely disappear. A week after the First

Finding a path towards help was a dreadful experience for many shipwreck survivors.

Fleet arrived at Botany Bay, two European ships made anchor, becoming witnesses to the British settlement of the continent. They were two French ships, *L'Astrolabe* and *La Boussole*, under the command of Jean-François de Galaup La Pérouse. La Pérouse had been sent to explore the Pacific in the footsteps of James Cook.

L'Astrolabe sinking on the reef at Vanikoro, in Solomon Islands.

Relations between La Pérouse and the British were good. La Pérouse established a camp on the northern shore of Botany Bay, at the place now named after him. The British moved north to Port Jackson to establish the penal settlement at Sydney Cove. The British, however, visited the French camp on a number of occasions during the French explorer's six-week stay. La Pérouse and his men sailed on 10 March and were not heard of again. The ships had disappeared altogether.

The disappearance of La Pérouse caught the imagination of the European public.[5] In 1791, the French Government sent ships under Rear-Admiral Bruni d'Entrecasteaux in search of the expedition, but it was not until 40 years later that traces were found.

In 1826, a sea captain, Peter Dillon, bought a number of swords from local people in the Santa Cruz Islands (part of present-day Solomon Islands). He suspected that they may have belonged to the members of the La Pérouse expedition. The locals took him to the island of Vanikoro, where Dillon saw the remains of the wreck of *L'Astrolabe*.

In 1964, the wreck of *La Boussole* was found on the reef off Vanikoro, confirming that this was the area where La Pérouse's expedition had come to grief.

L'Astrolabe and *La Boussole* were just two of the many ships lost or wrecked in the seas around Australia in the first decades of settlement. It would not be until the introduction of wireless telegraph systems in 1899 that a way to communicate distress at sea became possible. Radio communication quickly evolved into an indispensable safety aid for mariners. By the early twentieth century, ships were able to communicate with each other as well as with shore-based stations.

Marconi's wireless invention transformed communication at sea.

In 1904, the Marconi Company released information about a Morse code signal for distress at sea known as 'CQD'. It was replaced by the better known 'SOS' just two years later.

The use of wireless radio to call for help became part of history's great tragedies when the luxury transatlantic liner and mail ship RMS *Titanic* struck an iceberg on its maiden voyage in 1912. By this time, the majority of passenger ships crossing the Atlantic had a Marconi radio installation, which was operated by one of the Marconi Company's trained operators.[6]

The wireless equipment used in ships of that era could transmit messages for 300 miles (nearly 500 kilometres) during the day, but at night messages could travel much further, due to the refraction of long-wave radiation in the ionosphere.[7] This is because a radio wave deviates from its original course when it encounters a different atmosphere or object. For certain frequencies of radio waves, at night the waves bounce between the ground and the ionosphere and thus travel further around the planet.

There was no guarantee in the early days of wireless radio that there would be radio operators on duty at night, as many ships carried only one operator. When the *Titanic* collided with an iceberg in calm seas on the night of 14 April 1912, Harold Cottam, operator on the nearby Cunard liner *Carpathia*, was still awake. He received the first distress signals from the *Titanic*, sent by senior wireless operators Harold Bride and Jack Phillips. *Carpathia* immediately turned and steamed the 60 miles (nearly

100 kilometres) towards *Titanic's* given position, a journey of almost four hours. Many ships, however, lacking a 24-hour radio watch, did not receive the signals.

When dawn broke, *Carpathia* arrived at the location transmitted by the *Titanic*. The *Titanic* had sunk about two hours earlier. Those passengers who reached lifeboats were the only ones from *Titanic* left alive. Many had gone down with the ship, and those in the water had long since succumbed to the freezing conditions.

Carpathia's crew rescued all the survivors they could find, retrieved 300 bodies from the water and set course for New York.[8] Without the wireless telegraph, it is probable there would have been far fewer survivors. Both Harold Bride and Jack Phillips made it off the *Titanic*, but Phillips did not survive.

In the aftermath of *Titanic's* sinking, a range of new regulations were put in place to ensure there was a stronger radio presence on all major ships.

In Australian and other waters, the advent of wireless was being used to great advantage in averting disaster in the everyday passage of ships, in sometimes difficult conditions. On 14 April 1914, this article appeared in the Adelaide *Register*:

> *Disabled steamer towed to Port*
>
> *After having become disabled at sea by the sudden loss of her propeller on Saturday night, the cargo steamer Largolaw, bound to Newcastle from Batavia, Java, in ballast, had the good fortune to receive a response to her signal of distress only two and a half hours later from the well-known collier Prophet, which was on her way to Newcastle from Port Pirie. The Prophet* [responded] *to her signal of distress. The collier subsequently started for Hobson's Bay with her charge in tow, and both vessels arrived safely and anchored off Williamstown at half-past 10 o'clock this morning. The accident happened a few minutes after 8 o'clock on Saturday night midway between Cape Otway and the Port Phillip Heads. Without the least warning the propeller, 'boss and blades complete,' dropped to the bottom of the sea, the tail shaft having snapped asunder apparently through some vital fracture.*

HMAS *Parramatta* was required to radio for help in a dreadful storm in the Bay of Biscay, cutting their engine power. Fortunately the ship and crew (the authors grandfather included) made it safely back to port.

HMAS Parramatta: Bay of Biscay, 1919

In the depth of war, ships are still subject to the dangers of the sea, as well as the lurking enemy. In 1919, the destroyer HMAS *Parramatta* (on which the author's grandfather was a crew member) had been at war for five gruelling years of patrolling and convoy duty in the South China Sea and the Mediterranean. The *Parramatta* had sunk a U-boat, chased off other submarines and watched torpedoes plough past just metres below the ship. But there was one last danger the crew didn't see coming: the hands of the sea. As the records of the *Parramatta* show, on 4 January 1919, the ship and another destroyer, the *Yarra*, ran into the full fury of the Atlantic at its worst.

Off Cape St Vincent, southern Portugal, early on 5 January, the ships became separated and were soon in trouble. For three days they battled the worst weather the Bay of Biscay could produce. On board the *Parramatta*, conditions were chaotic. A crew member wrote:

> *She steamed out into the Bay of Biscay into the teeth of a cyclone, and snored away from it, head to sea, until the fuel ran low. Then she had to turn about and run back to port for shelter. A fearful sea caught her beam when she was halfway round and rolled her over at an angle never contemplated by her designers. Another ship may have kept on rolling and never seen port again; but she was always a lucky one, and got off with 13 bottom plates stove-in and every breakable object on board smashed.*[9]

After this incident, Lieutenant Commander Gerald Hill realised his ship was in danger of foundering and radioed for help. A number of tugs were sent but did not find her. *Parramatta* eventually joined HMAS *Huon* and together they made port.

The war wasn't quite over for the *Parramatta*. She was sent to run as a dispatch ship between Sevastopol and Constantinople (Istanbul) when the British forces supported the White Army against the Bolsheviks in Russia following the Russian Revolution. The *Parramatta* arrived back at its home port of Sydney on 20 May 1919.[10]

Lost flights

From the first flight of the Wright brothers until the end of 1930s, flying was a dangerous business. The pilots knew this, but continued to take the risks. In the boom days of aerial expansion immediately after World War I, many pilots had seen action during the war. Perhaps this influenced their views: they were used to taking deadly risks. With pioneering flights there was a specific goal in mind; it was a free decision.

Keith and Ross Smith were the winners of the England to Australia air race in 1919.

In Australia, there were only about ten recorded flights prior to the beginning of World War I. The end of the war in late 1918 brought a huge impetus to expand aerial services. In 1919, the Australian Government announced its financial support for an air race from England to Australia. The competition was won by Keith and Ross Smith, when they landed in

Darwin on 10 December 1919. The journey involved landings at a range of aerodromes, some of them only recently built, and took a total of 27 days and 20 hours. Ross Smith was killed in a flying accident three years later.

The first flight from Tasmania (Stanley) across Bass Strait to the Australian mainland (Torquay, Victoria) took place on 16 December 1919. The flight was completed by Lieutenant Arthur Long, a Tasmanian airman.

The first attempt to fly across the Tasman was undertaken by two New Zealand pilots, John Moncrieff and George Hood, in a Ryan monoplane. The two World War I veterans set out from Victoria on 10 January 1928. They sent out signals from the radio transmitter on their plane for about 12 hours, then the signals suddenly stopped. Despite searches, the wreckage of the plane has never been found.

The Coffee Royal affair: Kingsford Smith goes missing

The Coffee Royal affair hinged around a missing radio receiver and the quirks of a transmitter design.

Sir Charles Edward Kingsford Smith is Australia's best known aviator. Born in Brisbane, Kingsford Smith joined the Australian Imperial Force in 1914 when World War I broke out. He was at Gallipoli as a signaller (sapper) and dispatch rider. He joined the Australian Flying Corps in 1916, and after completing his training as a pilot, was transferred to Number 23 Squadron in France. He was shot down and wounded, but survived the war.

In 1919, Kingsford Smith and his friend Cyril Maddocks flew joy flights around England. Kingsford Smith had ambitions of completing the first trans-Pacific flight from the United States to Australia, but he could not raise sponsors. On his return to Australia, he flew for Western Australian Airways, but always had an eye on conducting pioneering flights.[11]

In early 1928, Kingsford Smith and fellow pilot Charles Ulm flew around Australia in just over ten days, an achievement that gained them a lot of media attention. Following this remarkable feat, they were able to secure funding for an attempt at a trans-Pacific flight.

The plane that Ulm and Kingsford Smith chose for the attempt was a three-engine aircraft made by Fokker, named the *Southern Cross*. With two American crew members, Kingsford Smith and Ulm took off in the *Southern Cross* from Oakland, California, on 31 May 1928. They flew via Hawaii and Suva to Brisbane, completing the historic crossing of the Pacific Ocean in 83 hours and 38 minutes of flying time.

It was the first flight across the Pacific, and it made headlines around the world. Kingsford Smith was famous.

Kingsford Smith's next venture was an around-the-world flight. He and his crew of three (copilot Charles Ulm, radio operator Thomas McWilliam and navigator Harold Litchfield) took off in the *Southern Cross* from Richmond, north of Sydney, on 31 March 1929. They were bound for Wyndham, on the northern coast of Western Australia. An hour into the flight, Litchfield, who was taking navigational measurements with a sextant out of the stern window, accidentally dislodged one of the aeroplane's two radio aerials. They decided to continue but did not receive messages from Sydney about bad weather developing in the Wyndham area.[12]

On reaching the area around Wyndham, they became lost, bad weather was closing in and the plane was running very low on fuel. Kingsford Smith decided to bring the plane down on the only open land he could see, a mud flat on a broad tidal inlet on the Glenelg River. Although they had been able to transmit in flight, the power needed to transmit could not be generated when not flying. They were lost.

A major search soon got underway to find the missing airmen. They had limited rations, and were soon facing hunger, although they had a flask of Coffee Royal—coffee with brandy mixed in—which later gave the incident its name.

Kingsford Smith's flight across the Pacific inspired the nation.

Supplies next to the aeroplane de Havilland DH61 Giant Moth biplane airliner G-AUHW *Canberra*, which located the lost *Southern Cross*.

They were found by the aeroplane *Canberra* after 12 days, and supplies were dropped before they were rescued by an overland party. But before help reached the stranded men on 13 April, tragedy struck: pilot Keith Anderson and mechanic Robert Hitchcock, friends of Kingsford Smith, perished on their way to help in the search when their plane crash-landed in the Tanami Desert. Unable to restart the plane, and having only a small amount of water on board, they died of dehydration.

When their bodies were recovered, there was national mourning. The memorial service for Anderson was particularly memorable, drawing a crowd of many thousands in his home suburb of Mosman in Sydney, his coffin carried on a gun carriage with a military escort. Aeroplanes flew low overhead, dropping wreaths along the way to the burial site.[13]

The deaths of the two men caused a public outcry. Many sections of the press accused Kingsford Smith of staging the disappearance of *Southern Cross* for publicity purposes. Feelings ran high. An official inquiry exonerated Kingsford Smith and Ulm from a charge of having staged the incident for publicity, but Kingsford Smith's reputation in Australia had been damaged.

Kingsford Smith went missing when flying across the Andaman Sea on 8 November 1935 and was never seen again. It was a tragic end to a brave man's endeavours.

There was no question that radio helped improve rescue and communications for both ships and aeroplanes. Reliable radio signals helped many people in the coming years. But radio signals sometimes do strange things, as this article from the South Australian *Victor Harbor*

Times, on 29 April 1976, attests:

> *During local rescue operations on Sunday freak radio conditions enabled the Victor Harbour Yacht Club to receive a distress signal from a disabled boat 900 kilometres away. The disabled boat, registered number K.J. 21. reported its position off Port Albert which is 200 kilometres east of Melbourne. It had broken down and requested assistance. The message was received at the VHYC Bridge at 12.45 p.m. and it was passed on to police who in turn notified Marine Rescue Operations in Canberra. Information was later received from Marine Operations via Adelaide Police Operations that the vessel had been taken in tow and its crew were safe. It is understood the craft was a fishing trawler and the trouble had been a broken propeller shaft.*

Beacon of hope

Personal locator beacons are now widely available for purchase through adventure, marine and outdoor retailers. These systems can alert search and rescue teams to the position of anyone lost on land or at sea.

When an emergency signal is received by satellite, the information is sent to the nearest station back on Earth. The location of the transmitter is calculated based on the signal, and information is passed on to the appropriate emergency response area for search and rescue.

In January 2021, a solo yachtsman was rescued when he activated his personal locator beacon on his life jacket. He had fallen overboard from his yacht in the Arafura Sea in deteriorating weather conditions.[14]

Personal locator beacons have helped locate sailors washed overboard or shipwrecked.

The rescue of Tony Bullimore, Southern Ocean, 1997

There was a time when if a yacht capsized in the lonely Southern Ocean 2,500 kilometres from the Australian coast, there was no chance of being found. However, during the 1960s, NASA realised the possibilities of using space satellites to help track locations on Earth. This technology was developed to the point where, today, global positioning systems (GPSs) are used in countless instances worldwide.

It was fortunate that, in 1996, a tracking system was used for the Vendée Globe round-the-world yacht race. Vendée Globe used the well-established ARGOS system, which was developed in the late 1970s by NASA, the United States National Oceanic and Atmospheric Administration and the French Space Agency, as a scientific tool for collecting and relaying meteorological and oceanographic data around the world. It was often used to track wildlife such as turtles, birds and sharks.

The Vendée Globe is a solo international yacht race, which is held every four years. In January 1997, the yachts participating in the race were located far south in the Southern Ocean. At latitude 55 degrees, they were even further south than the remote subantarctic Macquarie Island.

The weather was bad and two boats were lagging behind the fleet. One was the *Exide Challenger*, sailed by Tony Bullimore, a 57-year-old British businessman. The other was the *Pour Amnesty International*, captained by Thierry Dubois. Each participant carried an ARGOS beacon, allowing the boat to be tracked by the race headquarters.

Author John Roberson describes what happened in the race:

> *For more than a day, Philippe Jeantot at race headquarters had been monitoring with concern the extremely slow progress indicated by their ARGOS positioning beacons transmitting in 'normal' mode. Progress was so slow that Jeantot surmised they had capsized. Then Bullimore's ARGOS switched to 'distress' mode.*
>
> *The next morning, Monday, January 6, a Royal Australian Air Force PC-3 plane was dispatched on a sortie, flying 1,400 miles from southwest Australia. Dubois had only just turned on his EPIRB but they found him first, perched on the bottom of Pour Amnesty International in his survival suit, holding on to a rudder. They dropped him a life raft. A few hours later another plane discovered Bullimore's Exide Challenger with its keel snapped off. But the sailor was nowhere to be seen.*[15]

Tony Bullimore first hit trouble when winds lifted to about 60 knots during a severe storm that whipped waves up to frightening levels. After a lull, Bullimore thought he was through the worst of it. But the wind picked up again, and the keel of his yacht shattered. The boat flipped upside down, one of the windows stove in and Bullimore was trapped inside the hull.

It was feared that Bullimore may have drowned. The Australian Government made the decision to dispatch HMAS *Adelaide* southwards to conduct a search and rescue. The captain,

The rescue of Tony Bullimore in the Southern Ocean was a dramatic moment in 1997.

Raydon Gates, was woken by a telephone call at 1am on 6 January and gave the orders to prepare to sail. After recalling men and getting stores on board, *Adelaide* left Fremantle in Western Australia at 4pm.

At 4.30am on 9 January, *HMAS Adelaide* launched its Seahawk Helicopter to find Dubois. He was located, taken off the life raft he had launched, and brought successfully back to the ship. The *Adelaide* then sailed on to find Bullimore, guided by the ARGOS beacon on board his boat. The Royal Australian Navy continues the story:

> *As Adelaide neared the stricken Exide Challenger, the Seahawk was again launched to conduct a photographic search of the hull, remaining in a low hover for approximately ten minutes. There was no response to the helicopter's presence. Adelaide then circled the Exide Challenger, sounding her siren—again no response.*
>
> *With only one option left, Captain Gates ordered the sea boat be launched with the task of closely examining the hull of Exide Challenger prior to attempting to cut through the hull. To the surprise and relief of those there, Tony Bullimore responded to loud tapping on the hull, and appeared on the surface moments later. Leading Seaman Clearance Diver Alan Rub then proceeded to help Bullimore towards Adelaide's sea boat, where he was hauled in by Chief Petty Officer Peter Wicker. Images of Bullimore kissing the unsuspecting, bearded Wicker were later seen around the world.*[16]

The *Adelaide* berthed in Fremantle on 13 January to a rapturous welcome. The rescue was a tribute to the RAN and the resilience of the two yachtsmen. They had both suffered hypothermia and frostbite. Bullimore had lost part of one finger, but he was alive—surviving in an air pocket in a makeshift hammock, suspended above the water.

Tragically, race organisers lost contact with a third competitor, Canadian Gerry Roufs, who was reported lost on 8 January, more than 2,500 kilometres west of Cape Horn. Six months later, his yacht was seen drifting off the coast of Chile, and in September 1998, wreckage was found in the Straits of Magellan.[17]

Bushfires: Warning!

Bushfires are a part of life for many people in Australia, becoming increasingly so due to the effects of climate change. Anyone who has grown up in Australia is familiar with regular summer news reports about bushfires. But watching television, you are removed from the reality of the sights, sounds and smells of what is happening—the injured animals and the consuming walls of fire.

Australia has experienced bushfires for many thousands of years. The First Nations people used—and continue to use—fire as a land-management tool. Its uses include: fuel and hazard reduction; regeneration of habitat; generation and management of particular sources of food, fibre and medicines; facilitation of access and movement; protection of cultural and natural assets; and healing Country's spirit.[18]

With colonial expansion, and ignorant of First Nations land management practices, many farmers and pastoralists were putting themselves in the way of danger.

On 6 February 1851, a day that came to be called The Black Thursday, terrible fires burned through five million hectares of land—almost a quarter of modern-day Victoria. It was one of the largest bushfires to occur in Australia's history. Fifteen people died and 1,300 buildings were destroyed.[19] Fire outstripped any warning that could be carried by a messenger on horseback.

An article in *The Argus* of 11 February 1851 stated:

> *As distance allows the various accounts to reach Melbourne, news of destruction, devastation, and ruin come pouring in upon us, until our very heart sickens at the fearful nature of our duty. The excitement which this terrible event has earned is without parallel in our colony.*

Another contemporary account tells of the speed and devastation of the fire:

> *The work of years has been swept away from those industrious families and severe sufferers. Their fences, their crops, and their homes have been annihilated at a stroke. Just at the same hour the Bush Tavern, which*

The scale and devastation of the 1851 Black Thursday bushfires shocked colonial Australia.

has stood ... for many years in the midst of a dense forest, and proved so often a place of shelter, to the forlorn traveller from the pitiless storm of winter and the scorching heat of summer, is now a heap of ashes. The fire reached the buildings without warning; and the few articles which were saved from the wreck ignited afterwards with the excessive heat which burning houses created. The bridge across the Fitzroy has shared a similar fate with the house.[20]

The phrase 'without warning' was true enough. In the twenty-first century it is difficult enough to communicate ahead of a fire in an emergency; in the mid-nineteenth century it was barely possible. Telegraphy was in its infancy, a horse-rider might perhaps ride ahead, but in catastrophic conditions the fire travels faster than any horse.

Bushfires continue to be a difficult and sometimes tragic part of Australian life. The Black Tuesday fires took place in south-eastern Tasmania on 7 February 1967. The fires caused the deaths of 64 people and led to widespread property damage. The 2009 Black Saturday bushfires in Victoria caused the greatest loss of life from fire since colonisation: 173 people lost their lives, 414 were injured, more than a million wild and domesticated animals were lost and 450,000 hectares of land were burned.[21] In recent years, the impact of climate change and warming temperatures has made the situation worse—the bushfires of 2019–2020 were deadly in scale and stretched the resources of the nation.

For people who have not experienced a bushfire, it is almost impossible to imagine what it is like. Communication is critical, and it is one of the

The 1967 bushfires in Tasmania devastated communities, including that of Sorell.

most difficult issues: how to warn people that fire is coming, and how to communicate whether they should stay put or evacuate. In the worst conditions, even the best managed communications systems start to break down.

In 2020, emergency agencies across Australia worked hard on communications through online presence, text messaging, fire tracking and observation. Even so, communications remained an issue. On 30 June 2020, in the aftermath of the 2020 bushfires, *The Canberra Times* wrote:

> *Many areas lost communications during the 2019–2020 bushfires, with residents of a small town on the New South Wales/Victorian border having to drive to warn others of impending danger, the bushfires royal commission has been told 'Many in the community expressed*

John Flynn and the Australian Inland Mission

Australia's Royal Flying Doctor Service began with the vision of a young man from Moliagul in central Victoria. In 1911, John Flynn was working as a young Presbyterian minister in the northern Flinders Ranges in South Australia. He was interested in the physical, emotional and spiritual wellbeing of people in the outback—both Indigenous and non-Indigenous. In 1912, he undertook a survey of missionary needs in the Northern Territory, and the Presbyterian church appointed him superintendent of the newly formed Australian Inland Mission.[23]

Over the next few years, Flynn expanded the support to remote communities, providing nursing homes and hospital care. He then began to work on the concept of a flying doctor service. But how would people communicate with the service, and vice versa, across such vast distances? Flynn began to experiment. In 1925, with radio technician George Towns, he took a Dodge Duckboard wireless system on the road to Alice Springs, testing it at different towns along the way, using a generator connected to the back wheel of the car.

Flynn realised that a barrier to the use of radio in the outback was the lack of electrical power. He called on the support of engineer and inventor *their frustration with interruptions and loss of service from fixed line telephones, mobile phone service and loss of power and the length of time these services remained unavailable,' senior counsel assisting the commission Dominique Hogan-Doran SC said on Tuesday. She said firefighters also rely on services delivered by mobile systems, including critical communication between teams in the field and between fire management and brigades.*

The importance of communications was recognised in the Royal Commission into National Natural Disaster Arrangements in October 2020. Recommendations included introducing an all-hazard emergency warning app—a twenty-first century form of communication that will provide another tool for getting word and warnings out.[22]

Alfred (Alf) Traeger, who overcame this barrier by inventing a pedal-operated generator to provide power for a radio transceiver (that is, with the ability to both send and receive messages).[24] The Aerial Medical Service began with its first aeroplane, the *Victory*, in May 1928, when Dr Vincent Welch answered the first call. It was renamed the Flying Doctor Service in 1942, with 'Royal' added by Queen Elizabeth II in 1955.

Flynn continued to support the establishment of effective communication networks across the outback. In time, a vital network was built, using wireless transceivers from the base of the Australian Inland Mission at Cloncurry, in Queensland. Today, the Royal Flying Doctor Service provides a 24-hour emergency service for people across 7.69 million square kilometres in the outback of Australia.[25]

The pedal powered transceiver allowed people to communicate with the Inland Mission and Flying Doctor Service.

Radio as a lifeline during times of crisis

The value of community radio for First Nations people was shown during 2020 and 2021, when the coronavirus (COVID-19) pandemic arrived in Australia. Two radio stations operating in Groote Eylandt and East Arnhem Land were able to customise messages coming out about COVID-19 to assist local communities, where English was often not the

Natalie Davey (left) and Bullen Rogers, hosts of Danggujarra—Good Language, Wangki Yupurnanupurru Radio's breakfast show, with guest host Caroyln Davey.

first language. By listening to familiar and trusted voices, people were better able to understand the virus and act on public health advice.[26]

The approach of these radio stations was to talk about COVID-19 in a more conversational way, and follow up broadcasted content with online discussions with their listeners. They answered key questions and explained terms like 'social distancing' and 'self-isolating'. Messages and conversations about COVID-19 were included throughout the day among the normal radio programs and announcer schedules.[27]

Community radio also plays an important role in debunking fake news. On remote Milingimbi Island, off the coast of Arnhem Land, information was spreading that a vital barge providing supplies to the community wasn't coming in due to COVID-19. Yolŋu Radio presenters spoke to government staff and were able to reassure the community that the barge was indeed on its way.[28]

In early 2023, communities along the Fitzroy River dealt with a catastrophic flooding event, caused by torrential rain in the aftermath of a tropical cyclone. Fitzroy Crossing's Wangki Yupurnanupurru Radio has served the region for more than 25 years[29], but in January 2023 it became a lifeline to isolated riverside communities, broadcasting emergency information, and then switching to social media when other technology failed.[30] Its transmitter, located on the other side of the river, 20 kilometres out of Fitzroy Crossing, was hit by lightning during the storms; with the bridge broken, servicing the transmitter had to be carried out via helicopter.[31] On 14 January 2023, they advised:

> *Remember to stay long way from powerlines because they might be dangerous ... Doctors and nurses at Rec Hall and hospital, and remember to tell the doctor and get help if you're feeling no good ... In some communities, you might need to boil tap water to get rid of germs for one minute if water mob tell you. Don't drink rainwater until it's been checked. Cover up from mosquitos and use your mosquito cream. Look out for spiders and snakes and crocs*[32]

9

The daily news

The unique history and distinctive content of Australian newspapers

For much of human history, people have received news by word of mouth. First-hand information from those who had witnessed important events was particularly important and valued. For larger communities, news might be conveyed by drama or song.[1]

When printing became available in Europe, with Johannes Gutenberg's invention of moveable type in the mid-fifteenth century, written accounts were not always trusted because the writer was not usually available for cross-questioning (an early version of 'don't believe everything you read'). You could not sit with the writer and ask questions to help verify, in your own mind, if this person was telling the truth.

Despite Gutenberg's invention, the development of newspapers was slow. The first commercial news services, which emerged in sixteenth-century Italy, were handwritten briefings, known as *avvisi*, sent to subscribers including many of Europe's rulers.[2] These were still common in the Italian news market in the early seventeenth century.

Gradually, newspapers gained in popularity, but censorship was often an issue. English monarchs, for example, claimed a privilege over affairs of state and intensely disliked discussion of domestic or foreign policy. In 1620, King James I ordered writers to cease the act of 'intermeddle by Penne, or Speech' in relation to state affairs.[3]

By the late eighteenth century, the business and culture of news had changed. Local news still travelled by word of mouth, and pamphlets were often used for political matters. But now newspapers were printed and distributed regularly.

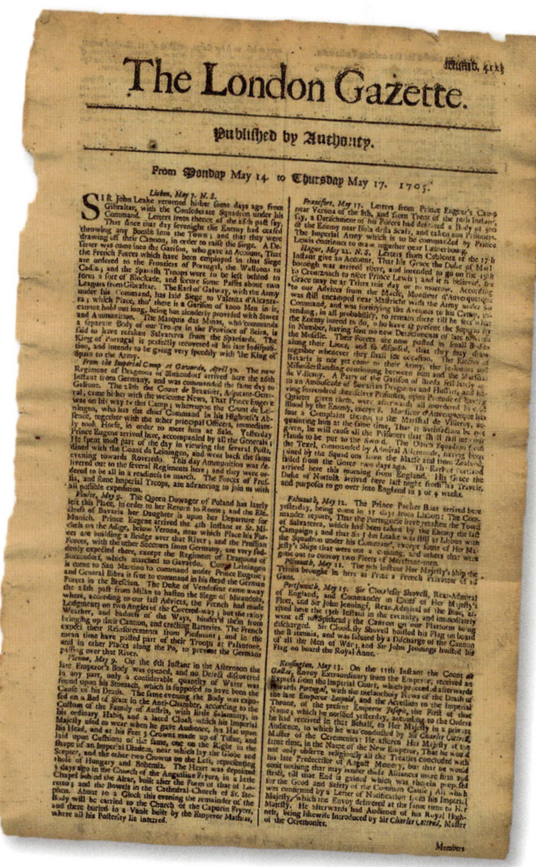

The London Gazette.

Published by Authority.

From Monday May 14. to Thursday May 17. 1705.

Lisbon, May 7. N. S.

SIR John Leake returned hither some days ago from Gibraltar, with the Confederate Squadron under his Command. Letters from thence of the 25th past say, That since that day sevenight the Enemy had ceased throwing any Bombs into the Town; and that they were drawing off their Cannon, in order to raise the Siege. A Deserter was come into the Garison, who gave an Account, That the French Forces which have been employed in that Siege are ordered to the Frontiers of Portugal, the Walloons to Cadiz; and the Spanish Troops were to be left behind to form a sort of Blockade, and secure some Passes about two Leagues from Gibraltar. The Earl of Galway, with the Army under his Command, has laid Siege to Valenza d'Alcantara; which Place, tho' there is a Garison of 1000 Men in it, cannot hold out long, being but slenderly provided with Stores and Ammunition. The Marquis das Minas, who commands a separate Body of our Troops in the Province of Beira, is said to have retaken Salvaterra from the Spaniards. The King of Portugal is perfectly recovered of his late Indisposition, and intends to be going very speedily with the King of Spain to the Army.

From the Imperial Camp at Gavardo, April 30. The new Regiment of Dragoons of Sinzendorf arrived here the 26th Instant from Germany, and was commanded the same day to Galione. The 28th the Count de Beaufort, Adjutant-General, came hither with the welcome News, That Prince Eugene was on his way to this Camp; whereupon the Count de Leiningen, who has the chief Command in his Highness's Absence, together with the other principal Officers, immediately took Horse, in order to meet him at Salo. Yesterday Prince Eugene arrived here, accompanied by all the Generals; He spent most part of the day in viewing the several Posts, dined with the Count de Leiningen, and went back the same evening towards Roveredo. This day Ammunition was delivered out to the several Regiments here; and they were ordered to be all in a readiness to march. The Forces of Prussia, and some Imperial Troops, are advancing to join us with all possible expedition.

Venice, May 9. The Queen Dowager of Poland has lately left this Place, in order to her Return to Rome; and the Electress of Bavaria her Daughter is upon her Departure for Munich. Prince Eugene arrived the 4th Instant at St. Michels on the Adige, below Verona, near which Place his Forces are building a Bridge over that River; and the Prussian Forces, with the other Succours from Germany, are very suddenly expected there, except the Regiment of Dragoons of Sinzendorf, which marched to Gavardo. Count Leiningen is come to San Martino to command under Prince Eugene; and General Bibra is sent to command in his stead the German Forces in the Bressian. The Duke of Vendosme came away the 28th past from Milan to hasten the Siege of Mirandola, where, according to our last Advices, the French had made Lodgments on two Angles of the Covered-way; but the rainy Weather, and badness of the Ways, hinder'd them from bringing up their Cannon, and erecting Batteries. The French expect their Reinforcements from Piedmont; and in the mean time have posted part of their Troops at Palantone, and in other Places along the Po, to prevent the Germans passing over that River.

Vienna, May 9. On the 6th Instant in the Afternoon the late Emperor's Body was opened, and no Defect discovered in any part, only a considerable quantity of Water was found upon his Stomach, which is supposed to have been the Cause of his Death. The same evening the Body was exposed on a Bed of State in the Anti-Chamber, according to the Custom of the Family of Austria, with little Solemnity, in his ordinary Habit, and a laced Cloak which his Imperial Majesty used to wear when he gave Audience, his Hat upon his Head, and at his Feet 3 Crowns made up of Tissue, and laid upon Cushions of the same, one on the Right in the shape of an Imperial Diadem, near which lay the Globe and Scepter, and the other two Crowns on the Left, representing those of Hungary and Bohemia. The Heart was deposited 3 days ago in the Church of the Augustine Fryers, in a little Chapel behind the Altar, built after the Form of that of Loretto; and the Bowels in the Cathedral Church of St. Stephen. About 10 a Clock this evening the remainder of the Body will be carried to the Church of the Capucin Fryers, and there buried in a Vault built by the Emperor Mathias, where all his Posterity lie interred.

The London Gazette, 17 May 1705.

They were available in cities in Britain and North America, and in the West Indies. They were also starting to make substantial amounts of money. In eight months, from January to August 1707, *The London Gazette* made £1,135 in sales of the newspaper to the public, of which £790 (70 per cent) was advertising revenue.[4] This equates to about £457,000 in today's values.

Newspapers in early colonial times

Arthur Phillip brought a basic wooden screw printing press out to Botany Bay in 1788, but no-one had time to print orders, let alone newspapers, in the early years of the colony—it was struggling for survival. It was also, at that stage, first and foremost a penal colony, focused on the incarceration of convicts.

At Sydney Cove in 1797, a young man by the name of George Hughes dusted off the same printing press brought by Phillip and began to print government orders. He also printed several broadsheets and a few playbills. One of the playbills, printed in March 1800, was for *The Recruiting Officer*, a play in which he was a performer.[5]

By the 1800s, the colony had changed. A trickle of free settlers had arrived, many convicts had received their ticket of leave and had begun farming, the original settlement had expanded to the Hawkesbury River area, and the settlement of Newcastle had been established to the north (1804). Sydney's population had grown to the size of a large English town and a newspaper would now be viable.

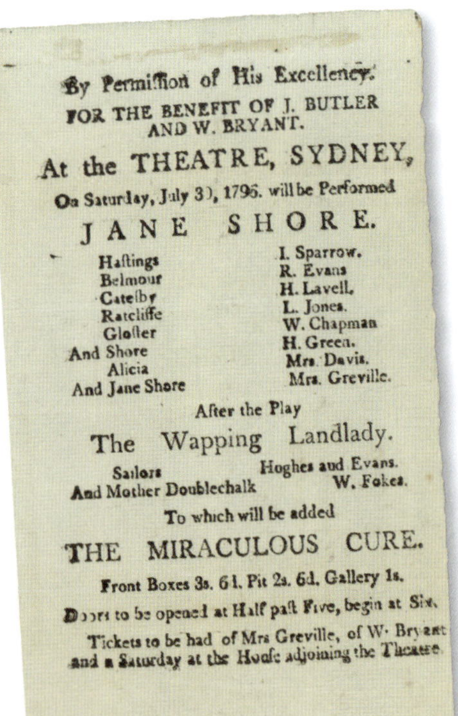

By Permiſſion of His Excellency.
FOR THE BENEFIT OF J. BUTLER
AND W. BRYANT.
At the THEATRE, SYDNEY,
On Saturday, July 30, 1796. will be Performed
JANE SHORE.

Haſtings	I. Sparrow.
Belmour	R. Evans
Cateſby	H. Lavell.
Ratcliffe	L. Jones.
Gloſter	W. Chapman
And Shore	H. Green.
Alicia	Mrs. Davis.
And Jane Shore	Mrs. Greville.

After the Play
The Wapping Landlady.

Sailors	Hoghes and Evans.
And Mother Doublechalk	W. Fokes.

To which will be added
THE MIRACULOUS CURE.
Front Boxes 3s. 6d. Pit 2s. 6d. Gallery 1s.
Doors to be opened at Half paſt Five, begin at Six.
Tickets to be had of Mrs Greville, of W. Bryant
and a Saturday at the Houſe adjoining the Theatre

The earliest surviving document printed in Australia is this 1796 playbill, advertising a performance at the Theatre, Sydney.

At this point, George Howe arrived in the colony. Howe was born on the island of St Kitts in the West Indies, the son of Thomas Howe, the government printer. George and his brother were both apprenticed to the printing trade. In 1790, Howe went to London and worked on *The Times* and other newspapers. In March 1799, he was tried at the Warwick Assizes for shoplifting; his death sentence was commuted to transportation for life. He arrived at Sydney in November 1800, although his wife died on the voyage. He soon became the colony's government printer, succeeding Hughes.[6]

In 1802, Howe published the first book in Australia, *New South Wales General Standing Orders*. In March 1803, he began to publish *The Sydney Gazette and New South Wales Advertiser,* the first newspaper in Australia, contending with a shortage of paper and ink, along with recalcitrant subscribers.[7]

The Sydney Gazette was essentially a mouthpiece for the government. It was censored and never raised contentious views. The first alternative and independent newspaper was *The Australian* (1824–1828) published by businessman and politician W.C. Wentworth, which was often critical of the government administration. *The Sydney Herald* (now *The Sydney Morning Herald*) first appeared as a weekly paper in 1831, then as a daily newspaper from 1840.

Newspapers communicated different points of view in the colony. Some views were confronting, exposing the prejudices and self-justification of the country's brutal racism in the nineteenth century. The Myall Creek Massacre of 1838 was an example of the prejudice of many colonists. On 10 June, the colonists detained a group of Wirrayaraay people who were camped near the the Myall Creek station, chained them and then proceeded to murder the entire group with swords or guns (except for one woman). They then dismembered and burned the bodies of their victims. The owner of the station, William Hobbs, on returning, found the bodies and reported the atrocity to the authorities in Sydney.[8]

Ten settlers were put on trial and were initially found not guilty. They were found guilty in a second trial, and seven of them were sentenced to hang and subsequently executed.

THE

SYDNEY GAZETTE,

And New South Wales Advertiſer.

PUBLISHED BY AUTHORITY.

Vol. I. SATURDAY, MARCH 5, 1803. Number 1.

It is hereby ordered, that all Advertiſements, Orders, &c. which appear under the Official Signature of the Secretary of this Colony, or of any other Officer of Government, properly authoriſed to publiſh them in the SYDNEY GAZETTE, AND NEW SOUTH WALES ADVERTISER, are meant, and muſt be deemed to convey official and ſufficient Notifications, in the ſame Manner as if they were particularly ſpecified to any ONE Individual, or Others, to whom ſuch may have a Reference.

By Command of His Excellency the Governor and Commander in Chief, WILLIAM NEATE CHAPMAN, Secretary.

Sydney, March 5th, 1803.

General Orders.

REPEATED Complaints having been made of the great loſſes ſuſtained by the Settlers at Hawkeſbury, from the vexatious conduct of the Boatmen by whom they ſend their Grain to Sydney, the following Regulations are to be obſerved.

Every perſon ſending grain from the Hawkeſbury to Sydney in an open boat, or a boat that is not truſt-worthy, the Magiſtrates are directed to take no notice thereof.

If on proof it appears that the Maſter of a Boat receives more grain than the veſſel ought to take with ſafety, the Maſter ſhall make good any quantity he may throw overboard, or otherwiſe damage, loſe the freight of that part, and, on conviction before two Magiſtrates, forfeit 5l. to the Orphan Fund.

If it ſhall appear to the Magiſtrates that grain coming round to Sydney has been wetted that it might weigh heavier or meaſure more than the quantity put on board, the Maſter will, on conviction, forfeit 5l. to the Orphan Fund.

The Commanding Officer of the New South Wales Corps will direct the Corporal of the Guard on board the Caſtle of Good Hope to read the General Orders that are marked off in the Extracts he is furniſhed with, to the Corporal, and the Party that relieves him; the ſaid Orders are alſo to be read to the Guard on board the Supply Hulk.

By Command of His Excellency W. N. CHAPMAN, Sec.

Government Houſe, Feb. 21, 1803.

THE Receiving Granaries at Parramatta and Hawkeſbury, being filled with Wheat which is ſpoiling, no more can be taken in at thoſe places until further Orders, except in payment for Government Debts, and the Whalers Inveſtments lodged in the Public Stores.

Wheat will continue to be received into the Stores at Sydney, until further Orders.

Wheat will be iſſued to the Civil, Military, &c. until further Orders; except to the detachments and labouring people at Caſtle-Hill, Seven-Hills, and other Out Poſts, who will receive Flour, as they have not the convenience of Mills.

By Command, &c. W. N. CHAPMAN, Sec.

Government Houſe, Feb. 24, 1803.

THE GOVERNOR having permitted Mr. Robert Campbell to land 4000 Gallons of Spirits for the domeſtic uſe of the Inhabitants, from the Caſtle of Good Hope, it will be divided in the following proportion, viz.

For the Officers on the Civil Eſtabliſhment, (including Superintendants and Storekeepers), 1000 Gallons;

For Naval and Military Commiſſioned Officers, 1000 Gallons;

For the Licenſed People, 1000 Gallons;

To be diſtributed to ſuch Perſons as the GOVERNOR may think proper to grant Permits to, 1000 Gallons.

The above to include the Civil and Military Officers at Norfolk Iſland.

By Command, &c. W. N. CHAPMAN, Sec.

Government Houſe, March 4, 1803.

ADDRESS.

Innumerable as the Obſtacles were which threatened to oppoſe our Undertaking, yet we are happy to affirm that they were not inſurmountable, however difficult the taſk before us.

The utility of a PAPER in the COLONY, as it muſt open a ſource of ſolid information, will, we hope, be univerſally felt and acknowledged. We have courted the aſſiſtance of the INGENIOUS and INTELLIGENT:--- We open no channel to Political Diſcuſſion, or Perſonal Animadverſion:---Information is our only Purpoſe; that accompliſhed, we ſhall conſider that we have done our duty, in an exertion to merit the Approbation of the PUBLIC, and to ſecure a liberal Patronage to the SYDNEY GAZETTE.

Contemporary newspaper reports held a stark mirror up to the settlers. Some writers justified the actions of the colonists and argued against the judicial process. But other newspapers identified the appalling nature of the crimes and applauded the actions of the government and the judiciary to try and bring some justice.[9]

One article from the short-lived Sydney weekly *The Colonist*, dated 12 December 1838, included stark condemnation of the perpetrators and some remarkable criticism of British colonisation—alongside outdated and offensive race theories. After describing the court verdict and the details of the massacre, the author asks:

> *What human being can contemplate this frightful tragedy unmoved by horror and dismay? What man, whose heart is not dead to every feeling of humanity, can attempt to palliate the conduct of its diabolical perpetrators.*[10]

A newspaper boom

The colonies continued to grow, and in the nineteenth century newspapers proliferated. Tasmania's first two official newspapers were founded: *The Derwent Star and Van Diemen's Land Intelligencer* (1810) and *The Mercury* (1854), today Tasmania's largest newspaper. And in South Australia, Victoria, Western Australia and Queensland, newspapers grew in number as the century progressed:

Left: By the mid 19th century, newspapers were readily available through an active press in the Australian colonies.

Right: *The Sydney Gazette and New South Wales Advertiser* was Australia's first newspaper.

> [In Victoria] *over five hundred newspapers have come and gone in the Melbourne CBD alone since 1838. The sheer number of examples shows that the survival of The Age and Herald Sun papers is the exception rather than the rule.*[11]

In Western Australia, there was a boom in newspapers during the 1890s gold rush, with the *Kalgoorlie Miner* (1895) a current-day survivor.

These newspapers give us a unique insight into the life and times of people that are, by necessity, lost in the generalisations that form over time. They also show us how history as it emerges is not always as clear cut as we might later take it to be. They provide a valuable primary source for researchers, as they reflect eyewitness accounts, social customs and beliefs, and the details of everyday life.

The local flavour of newspapers also gives us the human stories beyond the headlines, providing direct reporting of details that we would not have found elsewhere. The following report is on the life of bushranger Ben Hall before he became infamous for his crimes—a life which ended when he and his gang were shot dead by police in 1865. The extract is from *The Australasian*, Saturday 27 May 1865:

> *The Forbes correspondent of the Western Examiner (Orange), of May 13, furnishes the following not unfriendly biography of Ben Hall ... Two children were born to him by this marriage; the youngest, Henry, is still living, and about six years old. It was not far from twelve months after the birth of this child, and while he was yet in arms, that his wife eloped with a Mr. James Taylor, with whom she has continued to live since. They reside somewhere on the Fish River. Shortly after his marriage, he, in company with Mr. John Maguire, obtained a lease of a run adjoining Wheogo; called Sandy Creek, which they stocked with cattle and horses. Sandy Creek, Wheogo, and Bandaburra are estimated to be among the very best runs In the Lachlan district. Up to this period Ben Hall was held in high esteem by the settlers throughout the district, not only for his generous, open-hearted qualities—always showing a disposition to assist his neighbours—but for the enterprise and energy he displayed in conducting his business affairs. Very shortly after the elopement of his wife with Taylor ... he was arrested by Sir Frederick Pottinger at the*

Wowingragong racecourse, charged with highway robbery under arms. The surprise that was expressed by the residents of this district that such a charge should be made against Ben Hall is well remembered. However, after lying in the lock up four or five weeks, and being taken to Orange, and undergoing trial, the jury acquitted him without leaving their seats. He then returned to his station, Sandy Creek.

Newspapers also captured the small but dramatic events, ephemeral moments had they not been committed to newsprint. From the Melbourne *Weekly Times* of 19 August 1939:

Dog Rescued! From Tentacles of an octopus

A 9ft. octopus seized and overpowered a heavy Airedale dog in 18 inches of water at Mordialloc (a beachside suburb of Melbourne). The dog was rescued by its owner, Mr Harry Leah, an elderly man, who fought the octopus with a garden fork. He dragged the octopus ashore, still wrapped around the dog, and killed it.

Fishermen said the octopus, which weighed 40 lb, was the biggest they had seen in the Bay for years. They had never found one in such shallow water.

The *Richmond River Express and Casino Kyogle Advertiser* of 13 September 1929 reported:

All hands to the cat's rescue

This is the story of Tim, the ship's cat, of the Grimsby steam trawler Witham (as told in the London 'Daily Chronicle').

Whilst Tim was running along the ship's rail, out in the North Sea, a huge wave engulfed the trawler and swept the cat overboard.

At once the alarm was raised, and Skipper Howard brought the vessel about, the crew springing to their stations as if the alarm had been 'man overboard'.

Baskets and boats were flung over the side to the struggling cat, who, paddling like a dog, was making a brave effort to keep his head above water.

Fifteen minutes elapsed before the vessel, hampered by her fishing gear, could be manoeuvred into a position from which a basket secured to a boathook could be extended to Tim, who, making a last effort, drove his claws into the wicker work and held on grimly until he was dragged on deck.

Tim was for three hours too exhausted to move, but later he recovered completely.

The manoeuvre of the Witham was seen by a Dutch trawler whose master assumed that a man had fallen overboard.

He hurried at full speed to the spot, and was speechless with amazement when he learnt the cause of the excitement.

Newspapers communicated, entertained and informed. In Australia, as elsewhere in the world, local and international news sat side by side. The news of many significant events first came to people by newspaper, although the full story was not always immediately available. Early news of significant events can be traced back through our newspapers, such as the World War I Gallipoli landings reported in *The Argus*, 26 April 1915:

Dardanelles—Bombardment Resumed—Allies' Troops Landed

A decisive action, according to official reports from Athens, has begun in the Dardanelles. The Allies' squadrons bombarded the Straits at various points west of Gallipoli, and troops have been landed at three places, namely, at Suvla, on the Gallipoli peninsula; at Enos, the seaport on the Aegean coast of European Turkey; and at Bulair, a fortified town on the narrow neck of the Gallipoli peninsula.

Selling newspapers on the street was a flourishing business.

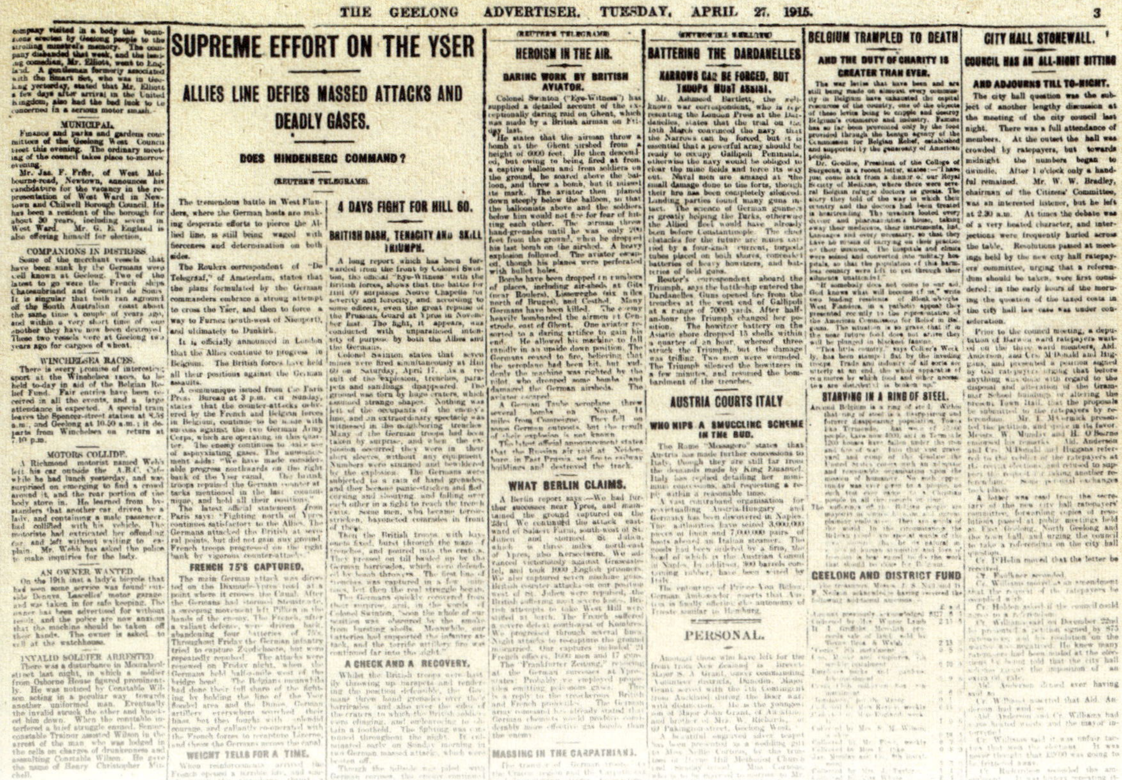

THE GEELONG ADVERTISER. TUESDAY, APRIL 27, 1915. 3

SUPREME EFFORT ON THE YSER

ALLIES LINE DEFIES MASSED ATTACKS AND DEADLY GASES.

DOES HINDENBERG COMMAND?

4 DAYS FIGHT FOR HILL 60.

BRITISH DASH, TENACITY AND SKILL TRIUMPH.

FRENCH 75'S CAPTURED.

WEIGHT TELLS FOR A TIME.

HEROISM IN THE AIR.

DARING WORK BY BRITISH AVIATOR.

WHAT BERLIN CLAIMS.

A CHECK AND A RECOVERY.

MASSING IN THE CARPATHIANS.

BATTERING THE DARDANELLES

NARROWS CAN BE FORCED, BUT TROOPS MUST ASSIST.

AUSTRIA COURTS ITALY

WHO NIPS A SMUGGLING SCHEME IN THE BUD.

PERSONAL.

BELGIUM TRAMPLED TO DEATH

AND THE DUTY OF CHARITY IS GREATER THAN EVER.

STARVING IN A RING OF STEEL.

GEELONG AND DISTRICT FUND

CITY HALL STONEWALL.

COUNCIL HAS AN ALL-NIGHT SITTING AND ADJOURNS TILL TO-NIGHT.

MUNICIPAL.

COMPANIONS IN DISTRESS.

WINCHELSEA RACES.

MOTORS COLLIDE.

AN OWNER WANTED.

INVALID SOLDIER ARRESTED.

The *Geelong Advertiser* reports on the challenges of penetrating the Dardanelles.

By 27 April, *The Geelong Advertiser* was identifying issues with the naval attack that flagged the fact, even then, that the element of surprise had been lost:

> *Battering the Dardanelles*
>
> *Narrows can be forced, but troops must assist*
>
> *Mr. Ashmead Bartlett, the well-known war correspondent, who is representing the London press at the Dardanelles, states that the trial on the 18th March convinced the navy that the Narrows can be forced, but it is essential that a powerful army should be ready to occupy Gallipoli Peninsula, otherwise the navy would be obliged to clear the mine fields and force its way out. Naval men are amazed at the small damage done to the forts, though their fire has been completely silenced. Landing parties found many guns intact. The science of German gunners is greatly helping the Turks, otherwise the Allied fleet would have already been before Constantinople.*

'ASPRO'
Smashes HEADACHES
BREAK-THROUGH TOWARD BERLIN
Germans Say Zhukov Only 45 Miles Away
LAST BARRIER REACHED

Twenty-nine years later, in June 1944, the World War II landing of Allied forces in Europe to liberate occupied countries from Axis occupation had begun. Australians read about the great events happening on the other side of the world. Some had relatives in the battle, particularly Australian pilots serving in the Royal Air Force. Here is how the *Army News*, of Friday 23 June 1944, reported events:

> *Peasant casualty on D-Day*
>
> *A Norman peasant is in Britain today because he drank too many toasts on D-Day. When he heard the Allies had landed, he went down to the cellar and brought out a bottle of brandy he had hidden away.*
>
> *He drank the whole bottle, then roamed the fields singing patriotic songs.*
>
> *When he woke, he was on board a landing craft filled with wounded in a British port.*
>
> *British stretcher-bearers had evacuated the peasant as a 'casualty'.*

Meanwhile, in the Pacific theatre, *The Argus* war correspondent found a touching subject for a story, which was published on 16 October 1942:

> *Anton Ringel leaves his eyrie—Epilogue to Strange New Guinea Drama*
>
> *From GEORGE H. JOHNSTON, 'Argus' War Correspondent, Somewhere in New Guinea*
>
> *Thurs: Few theatres of this war have produced such a spate of human stories of adventure as New Guinea has, but few stories are as moving as the strange drama of Anton Ringel, 82-year-old Czech miner, which has just ended after 45 years. It ended when an unkempt figure in torn grey trousers and a stained felt hat barely covering a great mane of uncut silver hair walked barefooted into Port Moresby to board a ship that would take him out of the land that had given him nothing but hardship and sorrow for almost half a century.*
>
> *War had done what personal tragedy, uncivilised natives, hunger, and disease had failed to do—drive the old man away from the primitive shack on the top of New Guinea's towering mountains. Ringel first came to New Guinea in 1897 after having failed to find gold in the Louisiade Islands.*

Opposite page: A busy newsagency in Drouin, Victoria, around 1944.

Alone, except for native carriers, he fought this way through hostile tribes to the top slopes of 13,000-foot Mount Albert Edward, where he set up his prospecting plant and made his home. He made one fortune and lost the gold on the trip to the coast. He made a second fortune, and this time went on a visit to Austria. But the Great War broke out. Ringel lost all his money, and was conscripted for an Austrian labour gang. He was married soon after arriving in Austria, and raised a family, but the call of New Guinea was too strong. In 1924, with his 14-year old son, he returned to the island and to his tumbledown shack up in the mists and rains of Mount Albert Edward. The field was almost worked out, but Ringel would not leave ... The son died 6 years ago. Ringel stayed on in his mountain eyrie. When he needed stores, he walked barefoot through mountain jungles to Ioma, 40 miles away. The Japanese landed at Gona and moved up the Kokoda track; the old miner was cut off. At first, he refused to leave, but eventually he was persuaded to come to safety. Travelling barefooted over the mountain summit and through jungle, he reached a coastal village, where he immediately marched up to the military officer in charge to ask permission to return to his mine. His request was refused gently, and he was advised to go to the mainland for a while. Ringel quietly accepted the decision, lifted his few belongings wrapped in soiled calico on to his thin shoulders and marched up the wharf with the sunshine gleaming on his great mop of silver hair. Then he turned round and called out: 'I'll be back soon.' And Anton Ringel left the territory. Those who watched him go wondered whether he would come back again.

From *Die Deutsche Post* to *La Fiamma*: Foreign-language newspapers in Australia

At the start of the 1966 film *They're a Weird Mob*, Italian journalist Nino Culotta arrives in Sydney from Italy to take up the job of sportswriter on his uncle's new Italian-language newspaper. Nino finds his uncle has gone broke and left the country, leaving him to find work as a labourer instead. In reality, foreign-language newspapers have flourished in Australia for almost 175 years.

The first was *Die Deutsche Post*—appearing in Adelaide from 1848—with stories in both German and English.[12] The contents list from the 21 June 1849 edition includes: General News; The Mormons; Shipwreck and Wonderful Rescue; The Ship *Nourmuhul*; Criminal Court Session; The Natives of South Australia; 'I Want to Seek Revenge!' (A Poem) and Advertisements. During the twentieth century, the Greek newspaper *Okeanis* was founded in 1913[13], and the Italian *Il Giornale Italiano* was published from 1932 to 1940.[14] The French publication *Le Courrier Australien* is one of the longest running foreign-language newspapers, appearing from 1892 to 2011 and then from 2016 to the present, 'unit[ing] francophones and francophiles across the vast Australian territory'.[15]

What do foreign-language newspapers give the people who read them? A bit like ethnic community radio, they share views, information, entertainment and news that connect people with their culture, while at the same time discussing Australian issues from the community's perspective. The Italian newspaper *La Fiamma* (the flame) is an example. Founded in 1947, the newspaper is still going strong today. It contains Italian, Australian and world news, sport from Italy, Australia and around the world, magazine sections and a TV guide. It also contains opinion pieces; in short, it is 'the hub of a great Australian community'.[16]

Going digital

In 1977, Australians bought more than four-and-a-half million newspapers each day, and three million on Sunday.[17] News Limited, John Fairfax and Sons, and the Herald and Weekly Times Ltd made huge profits from sales and advertising, and these groups also expanded into television and other media outlets.

The rise of the internet and the digital economy brought extensive change to the media landscape across the world, but the newspaper survives today. It is still found in print form in newsagents and on doorsteps, but much of its content is digital, using paywalls and online advertising for revenue.

And they're off!

Australians love a race and, in 1913, a typesetter made headlines—at least in his own newspaper—for a typesetting record. In 1913, typesetting was still completed through the laborious process of hand-setting each character on each page, in preparation for printing—a process requiring great skill and accuracy. *The Cairns Post* of 11 October 1913 was clearly proud of its gun-typesetter:

> *A feat worthy of publication in the newspaper trade of North Queensland was achieved at the Cairns 'Post' monoline composing department on Friday morning, when Messrs A.G. Lawson and W.G. Gairdner gave the remarkably good return of 2½ columns of type in 43 minutes. This feat is all the more meritorious since it must be remembered that the operators put up this fine performance at the latter end of a heavy shift, and our expert (Mr. Lawson), who has a knowledge of all noteworthy records in the South, and also worked in several of the leading offices where records are forthcoming, at frequent intervals, informs us that this record, so far as his experience … is concerned, has 'never been equalled—or approached'.*

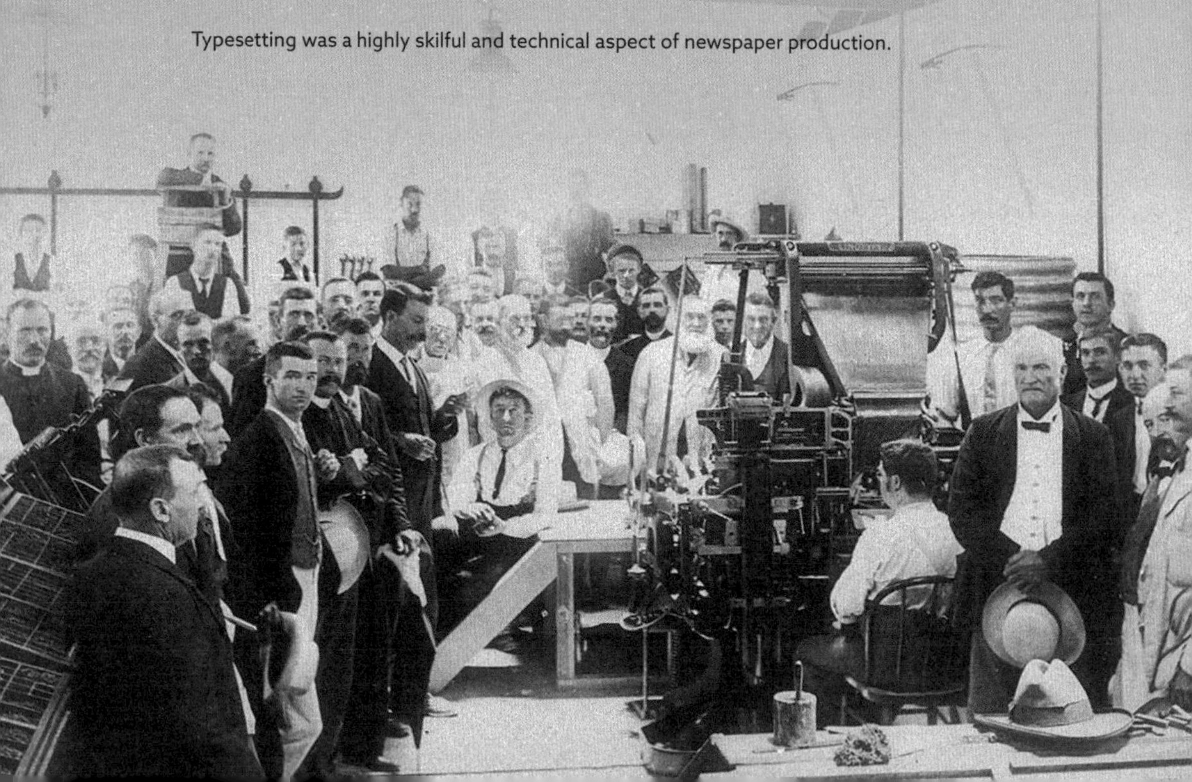

Typesetting was a highly skilful and technical aspect of newspaper production.

Right: Newspapers helped remote communities stay connected before the advent of the internet.

Below right: A worker sorts loose papers at the Chullora, New South Wales, printworks in 2000.

The loss of print versions of some of Australia's favourite newspapers was the breaking news many readers across regional Australia did not want delivered. An ABC report in 2020 highlighted the impact of the rationalisation:

> *Regional communities are reeling after the announcement that more than 125 News Corp newspapers will be closed or become digital only, and hundreds of jobs will be slashed.*
>
> *Papers that have been providing a voice for their local communities since the late 1800s are among the long list of publications to be shuttered or moved online.*
>
> *Queensland's oldest regional newspaper, The Queensland Times, in Ipswich, which started in 1859, will stop printing at the end of June, along with the Rockhampton Morning Bulletin (1860), The Daily Mercury in Mackay (1867), and the Northern Star in Lismore (1876). They will all become digital-only paid subscription news outlets along with 25 other regional titles and nearly sixty community titles across Australia.*[18]

People now source news from multiple media platforms, but there is still an important place for the print newspaper in the twenty-first century.

10

Screen time

1990–2010: Australia and the internet

The arrival of the World Wide Web in the 1990s brought yet another revolution in communications across the globe. Consistent with earlier inventions and innovations, a series of incremental developments occurred, which were essential stepping stones before a final 'breakthrough'. In this case, the personal computer and the internet came together to bring worldwide access to the office and home.

In a textbook display of the 'diffusion of innovation' theory, the World Wide Web jumped from obscurity to being one of the most dominant forces in our lives today.

The internet's story goes back to the late 1950s when the United States Government created the Advanced Research Projects Agency (ARPA), an arm of the Defense Department, whose aim was to create a method of communication that did not depend on phone lines. In 1962, J.C.R. Licklider, the first head of the computer research program at ARPA, wrote a paper about the potential for information sharing through interconnected computers worldwide. The question was: how?

Later in the 1960s, developers Lawrence Roberts and Thomas Merrill at the Massachusetts Institute of Technology began working on the concept of sending packets, small parts of a larger message, that could then be recombined by the receiving computer. In 1965, Roberts and Merrill were able to connect computers in California and Massachusetts using a dial-up telephone, but more work was needed to be able to transfer the information packets. The first message using packet-switching technology was sent between four computers in the United States in October 1969.

Early computers took up a lot of space and were the domain of specialists.

This established the ARPA network, or ARPANET, which soon expanded.[1] The network was first used for file sharing in the British and American military, then universities also began to use the technology. This was on a relatively small scale, among selected groups.

In Australia by the late 1970s, personal computers, manufactured by companies such as IBM and Apple, were becoming increasingly popular, but they were standalone machines needing floppy discs to transfer data. They could not communicate directly with one another.

By the late 1980s, personal computers were common. But there were still restrictions. The author recalls computer rooms at the University of New England in 1989, where they were mainly used for word processing and games, and had to be booked.

In 1990, British scientist Tim Berners-Lee, with assistance from his colleagues at CERN (the European Organization for Nuclear Research), developed hypertext mark-up language (HTML), which underpins how we navigate and view the internet today. He recognised the broad application of the internet and began to champion its application.

Newspaper articles are often useful starting points to identify that a trend or technological change may be expanding. Some new technologies fade into obscurity, some evolve. On 11 October 1993, *The Canberra Times* published an article that shows how something, which dominates our daily communications today, began to expand:

> *Funky Internet to Rule the Roost*
>
> *Now, in the '90s, it's happening again. The latest upstart, redolent with youthful funk, is a global computer network of 17 million people in 20 countries, including Australia. It's unruly and cutting-edge. It's called the Internet. And history is just around the corner. The Internet is absorbing souls at the prodigious rate of a million a month, its growth fuelled in part by legions of high-school and university students addicted to cyberspace. Until relatively recently, the Internet was traversed nearly exclusively by students and academics; access, which is free to the university-affiliated, was available outside only through expensive commercial on-line services. Over the past year and half, however, more entrepreneurs have found a niche marketing more affordable commercial access to the Internet.*[2]

The internet's arrival prompted a transition for people who grew up without computers.

A similar article, from the same newspaper on 26 July 1993, shows the increase in interest in the internet by the American Government:

Congress Hearing Kicks Off Today

The United States House of Representatives will be host from today for the first Congressional hearing to be held over a computer network. Appropriately, the topic is The Role of Government in Cyberspace.

The hearing will be held in the National Press Club in Washington, DC, and is open to the public.

The room will be equipped with 30 Sun SPARC Stations [computers with workstations and servers, developed and sold by Sun Microsystems], *providing congressmen and others with access to the world's electronic networks.*

Some witnesses for the hearing will testify remotely, sending sound and video images over the Internet. The event is being staged by Congress's Subcommittee on Telecommunications and Finance, which says:

'One of the primary points that we are hoping to demonstrate is the diversity and size of the Internet. We have therefore established an electronic mail address by which people can communicate with the subcommittee before and during the hearing.

'We encourage you to send your comments on what the role of government should be in the information age to this address. Your comments will be made part of the public record of the hearing.'[3]

Universities were the first users of the internet in Australia—effectively pioneers. The first Australian web server was at the Australian National University in Canberra. The server software was installed by Gaby Hoffmann, and the site's content was established by David Green in mid-1992. It was among the first 20 sites in the world.

IT consultant and academic Roger Clarke's website about the history of the internet in Australia also identifies computer scientist Rik Harris as an early pioneer. Harris stated:

I set up my first web server in August 1992 when Tim Berners-Lee asked me to do a hypertext version of my Computer Science Technical Reports archive at daneel.rdt.monash.edu.au (which doesn't exist anymore).

Computers and the internet were about to transform many workplaces.

> *I was discussing the format of search term URLs (can you have two ?s in a URL?) with Marc Andreessen in February 1993 when x-Mosaic* [an early web browser] *wasn't able to properly access my databases. I definitely had the Victorian Institute of Forensic Medicine* [VIFP] *web server then.*[4]

VIFP was the second of two Australian URLs in a list of 100 worldwide.

An astrophysicist from Sydney, Ray Norris, another Australian pioneer of internet use, visited the National Center for Supercomputing Applications at the University of Illinois in the United States in October 1992. There he was shown a beta version of the web browser Mosaic, which Microsoft licensed to create Internet Explorer in 1995. Norris says he 'got very excited about it, and on my return home we installed a web server at the [CSIRO] Radio physics Lab ... in Sydney'.[5]

Government and the private sector soon caught on to the possibilities of the internet. Websites were beginning to be listed in packaging and brochures by the mid-1990s. By 2000, they were commonplace, and Australians were beginning to get used to wi-fi.

The CSIRO worked on a microchip that was small but could transmit radio signals at high speed.

Wi-fi, an Australian invention

Initially, the internet was accessed via a dial-up connection through a fixed cable. However, in the 1990s, Australia's CSIRO invented WLAN, or wi-fi, which allowed remote, wireless access.

Wi-fi is now the most popular way of accessing the internet. Patented in 1996, it is now installed on an estimated five billion devices, such as laptops, phones, cameras and games consoles. The CSIRO team, comprising John O'Sullivan, Terry Percival, Diet Ostry, Graham Daniels and John Deane, worked out how to maintain data speed while also maintaining a regular signal. They developed a fast chip that reduced the 'echo' effect that would otherwise distort the radio signal.[6]

As seems to have been the case with many innovations, the invention was soon copied and accessed by others for commercial gain. The CSIRO had to bring legal action to effectively stop a range of large commercial companies from using the technology without royalties. Eventually, settlement was reached. On 24 November 2013, however, the CSIRO confirmed all of their wi-fi patents had expired.

The National Broadband Network

The construction of telegraph lines and radio and TV broadcasting towers are infrastructure milestones in our communications history. Perhaps the National Broadband Network (NBN), a national infrastructure project with the goal of providing consistent broadband services across the country, is not seen in the same way, as it is such recent (and controversial) history. The NBN is, however, a major work of infrastructure, and one that has not been without its problems.

In 2011, the government passed the *National Broadband Network Companies Act 2011*. Rollout of the broadband began that year, with the aim of having NBN completed in ten years. The initial rollout in Tasmania had many issues, from substandard installation to concerns about contract performance and timing.[7]

One of the key issues was that the rollout proposed by the previous government in 2007 used a single technology, Fibre to the Premises (FTTP), in which fibre-optic cables connect a home directly to the NBN network. This was changed to a Multi Technology Mix (MTM), which uses a mixture of technologies, especially Fibre to the Node (FTTN), in which the cables go to a central point that then serves a cluster of residences connected to the node using existing copper wires. MTM was seen as the most pragmatic approach to rolling out the infrastructure across a big country, with the aim of getting the infrastructure in place quickly, so that it could also start generating revenue.[8] FTTN is far more cost effective to install, but is a less powerful form of broadband than FTTP.

In 2020, at the peaceful location of Scotland Island, in Pittwater, north of Sydney, work was taking place to install the NBN. The island was one of the last identified locations in Australia for the NBN to be put in place. Despite some criticism of the rollout, the NBN passed a crucial test during 2020 with a high level of demand on the service due to COVID-19 restrictions. The system coped well.

From 'the brick' to our daily lives—the arrival of the mobile phone in Australia

We use our mobile phones for many things; we pay our bills, surf the web, send texts and emails, listen to music, and take photos and videos. Occasionally we even make phone calls from them!

Australia's first mobile phone network, designed for car phones, was launched in 1981.[9] In 1987, the handheld 'brick' phone arrived, so called for its block-like shape and heftiness, and costing over $4,000 at the time. These models were intended for cars or briefcases.[10] They used the 800 megahertz band, in a similar way to radio transmission. Each mobile phone tower—of which there were far fewer at the time—could handle about 300 calls at any one time. By 1990, stakeholders were conjecturing

Right: The mobile phone: our modern go-to multitasking communication system.

Below: The 1987 Telecom Walkabout was one of the earliest mobile phones in Australia.

that, in the future, mobile phones would be available to almost everyone.[11]

In 1993, Telstra launched the digital network in Australia, and mobile phones began to be more recognisable and more popular; text messaging was enabled, operating from a 2G model. As technology improved, a vast range of phones—smartphones and Androids—began to appear on the market.

In the meantime, telecommunication companies were building the networks to support mobile coverage across Australian cities and regional areas.

Mobile phones have now been part of our lives for more than 20 years. We are shocked if we are in a location where we find ourselves without network coverage. There are currently 31.9 million registered mobile phones in Australia.[12]

Communications are constantly evolving and developing in ways that we do not always predict. We look back—with some nostalgia—at communications methods of the past, such as Morse code or early radio. It would have been hard, in 1980, to imagine the full capacity of today's mobile phone, for example. Given the exponential curve of technological development we have seen since the beginning of the nineteenth century, it may well be that in a few decades' time, another technology will make what we use now seem quaintly obsolete.

Appetite for gigabytes

During the 1990s, the internet was provided in the home through telephone dial-up access, initially through a 56-kilobyte modem. This allowed for access to simple internet sites and the ability to download some data. Today we can download a one-gigabyte file (a short video for example) in about 32 seconds. In the 1990s, this would have taken around three-and-a-half days.

Increased download speeds became possible due to the introduction of broadband. Through advances in transmission technology, broadband became available at a lower price. It was provided through a separate communication line, which operated simultaneously to the telephone line.[13] These advances, combined with wi-fi, have allowed us to stream and download the huge data files that we take for granted today.

Two men using computers in 1997 at a local library in Sydney to play chess and access the internet.

11

An uncertain future

2020 onwards: Communications and data—opportunities and risks in a time of uncertainty

What will the internet look like by 2040 or 2050? Experts in the field can make predictions on the capacities we already know are feasible, but which need further development.

At the same time, in recent years, the rise of 'cyber wars' and privacy concerns have created uncertainty and unease for both individuals and governments. We can guess what technological progress might look like, but how will it affect us?

If we think the internet is a big part of our lives now, it will only get bigger, as computer scientist and entrepreneur Zaryn Dentzel notes:

> *The future of social communications will be shaped by an always-online culture. Always online is already here and will set the trend going forward. Total connectivity, the Internet you can take with you wherever you go, is growing unstoppably. There is no turning back for global digitalization.*[1]

Eye implants may be a feature, and we've already seen the forerunners of this technology in various smart and augmented reality (AR) glasses. Some of these devices feature the ability to make calls and take photos, others integrate with existing voice assistant programs. These early examples are a 'stepping-stone to more fully realised forms of wearable AR'[2], which may one day in the not-too-distant future include eye implants that allow us to overlay the real world with the digital.

This integration, essentially of our smart phones with our bodies, promises much: not only swift communication through various channels, but also instant information about the world around us; directions laid out before us in pulsating arrows; starred reviews on restaurant windows; or historic information about the statue we're staring up at. The potential implication for education and travel are significant. We could be physically here in our home, yet standing on a lookout in the Serengeti, or atop the *Endeavour* with Shackleton and his men.

The way we are perceived in another person's digital display can also be manipulated with this technology. Further even than the option to 'touch up my appearance' offered by the video conferencing program Zoom, we could be using digital avatars to represent ourselves and our identities in other ways than our physical bodies.

Another area of advancement is language. Already, internet applications have translation facilities that can get simple messages across quite quickly. What is still missing, of course, are the nuances of language—tone, cultural meaning, the slight changes in pronunciation, expression and context that are so essential. The world's most powerful computers can't perform accurate real-time interpreting of one language to another. Yet, human interpreters are able to use the subtle understanding of language and differences to interpret quickly and—if done well—take in the nuance of language differences.

In 20 years' time, will the risk be not being able to communicate when we need to or, worse, not being able to opt out of communication? That we will progress technologically is probable, but what if this progress becomes a self-destructive advance by humanity?

The first two decades of the twenty-first century have seen the rise of the 'cyber war', a cold war between national interests. This has included attempts to access secure and confidential data. In September 2022, data hackers accessed the personal data of up to nine million Australian Optus customers, prompting a major mitigation response from both Optus and the federal government. In a further event in October 2022, hackers accessed personal data of customers of the Medibank Private health fund. While society has grown used to the convenience of instant communication and online transactions, security risks have increased. Cyber-hacking and data and privacy breaches are everyday issues at national and social levels. In 2020, the ABC reported:

Foreign government cyber-attacks on Australia have increased further since June, when Prime Minister Scott Morrison revealed Australian organisations were under sustained digital assault.

Defence Minister Linda Reynolds says the alarming 'new normal' of persistent cyber-attacks on Australia is blurring the difference between 'peace and war'.

'We're now facing an environment where cyber-enabled activities have the potential to drive disinformation, and also directly support interference in our economy, interference in our political system, and also in what we see as critical infrastructure,' Senator Reynolds said.[3]

Our ability to advance communications even further presents both opportunity and risk.

The cyber age has helped us progress in different ways but, ultimately, we are creating a tool that can be used for good or ill. This is part of the constant arm wrestle that humanity has with itself. The same can be said for countless inventions: the power of flight, industrial capacity, even the ability to publish or send telegrams.

Although we can predict there will be technological improvement, we do not know yet if it will help us address our present concerns: global warming, food security, armed conflict or any of our other major challenges. In the end, government policy and directions will guide the progress and use of emerging technologies. This is particularly the case with artificial intelligence and privacy issues.

Australia has come a long way in terms of communications, along with the rest of the world. The key issue for the twenty-first century is to make communications systems a help, not a hindrance, to our progress.

Acknowledgements

I would like to begin by thanking an entire cohort of fellow students for helping me with this book. I began writing *Southern Signals* in mid-2020 when I was studying the Masters in Creative Writing course at the University of Technology Sydney. It was the staff and students involved with this course who inspired me to see that I could realise my goal of writing a non-fiction history book, one step at a time. The course itself was a motivation, as we kept each other going through the tough times of COVID during 2020 and early 2021, meeting face to face when we could, but mostly online.

I would like to thank the staff at libraries throughout Australia who have supported me with my research enquiries, especially the staff at the Library of South Australia, the State Library of New South Wales, Stanton Library and my 'local', Marrickville Library.

Many thanks go to Peter Vaughan-Reid, for his thorough and professional edit of the very first draft of the book. I would also like to express my gratitude to my brother Guy for his review of the manuscript; an archivist with the Australian Broadcasting Corporation (ABC) for over 30 years, Guy brought his detailed knowledge of all things Australian, and the ABC especially, to his comments on the book.

My heartfelt thanks go to the publishing team at the National Library of Australia who have made this book happen. Their editorial and publishing professionalism was fundamental in getting the book to publication. I learned a great deal about writing non-fiction history from their input.

I would like to also acknowledge the many historians who contribute their enthusiasm to researching the byways of Australian history, such as radio and the internet. In these publications and articles, you find forgotten worlds brought back to life.

Thank you to my wife, Amanda, and our sons, Hamish and Jack, for their ongoing support of my writing. Lastly, I thank my late parents, Peter and Robin, both authors and historians, whose encouragement in life and writing stays with me always.

Notes

1. 'The ships sail tomorrow'

1 'Advertisements and Notices,' *World*, 20 April 1789, Seventeenth and Eighteenth Century Burney Newspapers Collection, gale.com/intl/c/17th-and-18th-century-burney-newspapers-collection.
2 G.B. Barton, *History of NSW from the Records*, Sydney: Charles Potter, Government Printer, 1889.
3 Ibid.
4 A number of countries are lobbying the British Museum to return artefacts taken from them during the eighteenth and nineteenth centuries.
5 David S. Macmillan, 'Ross, Robert (1740–1794)', *Australian Dictionary of Biography*, adb.anu.edu.au/biography/ross-robert-2608.
6 Frederick Watson (ed.), *Historical Records of Australia. Series I., Governors' Despatches to and from England*, Melbourne: Library Committee of the Commonwealth Parliament, 1914, Despatch no.1, 15 May 1788.
7 David Andrew Roberts, '26 January 1788: The Arrival of the First Fleet and the "Foundation of Australia"', in Martin Crotty and David Andrew Roberts (eds), *Turning Points in Australian History*, Sydney: UNSW Press, 2009, p.36.
8 'Who Was Sir Joseph Banks (1743–1820), State Library of New South Wales, sl.nsw.gov.au/research-and-collections-significant-collections-sir-joseph-banks-papers-1767-1822/sir-joseph.
9 See Ruth Campbell, 'NSW and the *Gloucester Journal*, 1787–1790', *Journal of the Royal Australian Historical Society*, vol.68, December 1982.
10 F.M. Bladen, Alexander Britton and James Cook, *Historical Records of New South Wales*, Government Printer: 1892, pp.746–747.
11 Colin Steele and Michael Richards, 'Bound for Botany Bay: What Books Did the First Fleeters Read and Where Are They Now?', Canberra: Friends of the ANU Library, 1988, openresearch-repository.anu.edu.au/bitstream/1885/41047/3/Steele.pdf.
12 Watkin Tench, *A Complete Account of the Settlement at Port Jackson*, London: Nicol & Sewell, 1793, chapter 7.
13 Geoffrey Blainey, *The Tyranny of Distance: How Distance Shaped Australia's History*, Melbourne: Sun Books, 1966, p.47.
14 David Collins, *An Account of the English Colony of NSW*, vol.1, London: T. Cadell and W. Davies, 1798, chapter 10.
15 The author proposed in a paper, 'Pathways to the Press', that the recipient was Lord George Gordon. See sydney.academia.edu/HughTranter.
16 'Advertisements and Notices', *The Diary, or, Woodfall's Register*, 3 August 1791, Seventeenth and Eighteenth Century Burney Newspapers Collection, *op. cit.*
17 It was common for British newspapers simply to cut and paste each other's articles. This letter appeared in *The Diary, or, Woodfall's Register* on 3 August 1791 and the *Morning Chronicle* on 4 August 1791. The quotation is from *The Diary, or, Woodfall's Register*.
18 'Advertisements and Notices', *The Diary, or, Woodfall's Register*, 3 August 1791, Seventeenth and Eighteenth Century Burney Newspapers Collection, *op. cit.*
19 'News', *Public Advertiser*, 23 July 1791, Seventeenth and Eighteenth Century Burney Newspapers Collection, *op. cit.*
20 John Nicol, *The Life and Adventures of John Nicol, Mariner*, Edinburgh: William Blackwood, and London: T. Caddell, 1822, chapter 9.
21 'Lord George Gordon', *Encyclopaedia Britannica*, britannica.com/biography/Lord-George-Gordon.

22 Robert Watson, *The Life of Lord George Gordon*, London: H.D. Symonds and D.I. Eaton, 1795, p.109.
23 Hannah Wills, 'Adventures in Eighteenth-century Papermaking', University College London, blogs.ucl.ac.uk/researchers-in-museums/2017/07/21/adventures-in-eighteenth-century-papermaking/.
24 Anisha Gupta, 'The Ins & Outs of Iron Gall Ink', American Philosophical Society, amphilsoc.org/blog/ins-outs-iron-gall-ink.
25 *Letters from the Rev. Richard Johnson to Henry Fricker, 30 May 1787–10 August 1797, with Associated Items*, Collection 18, Letter of 21 August 1790, State Library of New South Wales.
26 See, for example, Michael Flynn, *The Second Fleet: Britain's Grim Convict Armada of 1790*, Sydney: Library of Australian History, 1993, p.49; and Kelly Burke, *The Stamp of Australia: The Story of Our Mail—From Second Fleet to Twenty-first Century*, Sydney: Allen & Unwin, p.11.
27 Ibid, Flynn, pp.76–82. There were other letters that alerted social reformers to the appalling death rate on the Second Fleet, such as a letter from Captain Hill to his friend Samuel Wathen, friend of William Wilberforce, the anti-slavery campaigner (see David Hill, *1788: The Brutal Truth of the First Fleet*, Sydney: William Heinemann, 2008, p.283).
28 Australian Bureau of Statistics, 3105.0.65.001—Australian Historical Population Statistics, 2006.
29 David Hill, *Convict Colony*, Sydney: Allen & Unwin, 2019, p.149. The cost of return to England was about £50 in 1804, but many men could work as crew. For women, the cost was beyond most of them.
30 'Passenger Ships to Australia', Australian National Maritime Museum, sea.museum/collections/library/research-guides/passenger-ships-to-australia.
31 Hill, *Convict Colony*, *op. cit.*, p.255.
32 Matthew Flinders, *A Voyage to Terra Australis*, London: G. & W. Nicol, London, 1814.
33 David Mackay, 'Far-flung Empire: A Neglected Imperial Outpost at Botany Bay 1788–1801', *Journal of Imperial and Commonwealth History*, 1981, vol.9, no.2, pp.125–145.
34 A.G.L. Shore, 'Bligh, William (1754–1817)', *Australian Dictionary of Biography*, adb.anu.edu.au/biography/bligh-william-1797.
35 Ibid.
36 *Further Copy of a Letter Received by William Wellesley-Pole of the Admiralty from William Bligh*, Series 40.090, 30 April 1808, State Library of New South Wales.
37 Hill, *Convict Colony*, *op. cit.*, p.266.
38 Proceedings of a general court-martial, 7 May 1811, at Chelsea Hospital for the trial of Lieutenant-Colonel George Johnston (on a charge of mutiny for deposing the Governor of NSW, William Bligh), accessed from: 'Mutiny; and the Trial of Lt. Col. Johnston', gutenberg.net.au/ebooks13/1300731h.html.
39 A.T. Yarwood, 'Johnston, George (1764–1823)', *Australian Dictionary of Biography*, adb.anu.edu.au/biography/johnston-george-2277.
40 Kelly Burke, *The Stamp of Australia: The Story of Our Mail—From Second Fleet to Twenty-first Century*, Sydney: Allen & Unwin, 2009, p.14.
41 Ibid.
42 Ibid, p.19.
43 'First Post Office', National Museum of Australia, nma.gov.au/defining-moments/resources/first-post-office.
44 '200 Year of Australia Post', postalheritage.wordpress.com/tag/isaac-nichols.
45 Jeremy Black, *The English Press in the Eighteenth Century*, London: Crook Helm, p.143.
46 Dean Boyce, 'Defending Colonial Sydney', *Dictionary of Sydney*, 2008, dictionaryofsydney.org/entry/defending_colonial_sydney.
47 Ibid.
48 For example, the inner Sydney suburb of Waterloo was named after the battle (see monumentaustralia.org.au/themes/conflict/colonial/display/97283-battle-of-waterloo). Wellington Valley and the town of Wellington were named by the explorer John Oxley in 1817.

49 'Ode for His Majesty's Birthday 1816', *Sydney Gazette and NSW Advertiser*, 8 June 1816, nla.gov.au/nla.news-article2176691.
50 Hill, *Convict Colony*, *op. cit.*, pp.295–296.
51 See, for example, the free online facilities provided by Trove or through the State Library of New South Wales.
52 *Bury and Norwich Post, or Suffolk, Norfolk, Essex, Cambridge and Ely Advertiser*, 15 January 1817.
53 *Asiatic Journal*, 1 February 1821.
54 *Caledonian Mercury*, Edinburgh, 31 July 1820.
55 Burke, *op. cit.*, p.220.
56 'Gold', in Bruce Pratt (ed.), *Australian Encyclopaedia*, 3rd edition, Sydney: Grolier, 1977.
57 *Daily Alta California*, 29 May 1852.
58 *Shasta Courier*, 21 May 1853.
59 Henry Lawson, *Selected Poems of Henry Lawson*, Sydney: Angus & Robertson, 1918.
60 Kathy Riley, 'Cobb & Co Coaches: Historical Transport', *Australian Geographic*, 18 October 2011, australiangeographic.com.au/topics/history-culture/2011/10/cobb-co-coaches-historical-transport.
61 'Population', in Bruce Pratt (ed.), *Australian Encyclopaedia*, 3rd edition, Sydney: Grolier, 1977.
62 Margaret Caldwell, 'Henning, Rachel Biddulph (1826–1914)', *Australian Dictionary of Biography*, adb.anu.edu.au/biography/henning-rachel-biddulph-3753.
63 *Stand Easy: After the Defeat of Japan*, Canberra: Australian War Memorial, 1945, p.52.
64 Charlotte Higgins, 'The Lost Art of Letter Writing', *The Guardian*, 23 October 2012, theguardian.com/culture/charlottehigginsblog/2012/oct/23/lost-art-letter-writing.
65 David Whitley, 'The River Postman, Hawkesbury River', *Traveller*, 9 July 2017, traveller.com.au/the-river-postman-hawkesbury-river-this-is-the-worlds-best-postal-route-gxdjjt.

2. Connecting to the world

1 The colonies were, in order of their white settlement, New South Wales (1788), Tasmania [Van Diemen's Land up to 1856] (1803), Queensland (1824), Western Australia (1829), South Australia (1836) and Victoria (1837).
2 Peter Tranter, *Sydney*, Lane Cove: Nelson Doubleday, 1968, p.14.
3 'Overland Telegraph Line', in Bruce Pratt (ed.), *Australian Encyclopaedia*, 3rd edition, Sydney: Grolier, 1977.
4 David Hill, *The Making of Australia*, Sydney: William Heinemann, 2014, p.230.
5 'Overland Telegraph', National Museum of Australia, nma.gov.au/defining-moments/resources/overland-telegraph.
6 Jean Gittins, 'McGowan, Samuel Walker (1829–1887)', *Australian Dictionary of Biography*, adb.anu.edu.au/biography/mcgowan-samuel-walker-4094.
7 Ibid.
8 'The Telegraph: A Wire around the World', ABC Science Show, 26 November 2005, abc.net.au/radionational/programs/scienceshow/the-telegraph---a-wire-around-the-world/3314488.
9 Pratt, 'Overland Telegraph Line', *op. cit.*
10 'Expedition Six', John McDouall Stuart Society, johnmcdouallstuart.org.au/729-2.
11 NMA, 'Overland Telegraph', *op. cit.*
12 Burke, *op. cit*, p.73.
13 G.W. Symes, 'Todd, Sir Charles (1826–1910)', *Australian Dictionary of Biography*, adb.anu.edu.au/biography/todd-sir-charles-4727.
14 'Loading Camels with Wool, Euston District, New South Wales, circa 1900', Museum Victoria Collections, collections.museumsvictoria.com.au/items/769194.
15 Pratt, 'Overland Telegraph Line', *op. cit.*
16 ABC Science Show, 'The Telegraph ...', *op. cit.*
17 *Diary Kept by Walter Rutt, Overseer of the Overland Telegraph Construction Party*, section 1, State Library of South Australia, digital.collections.slsa.sa.gov.au/nodes/

view/2520#idx17493. The Foelsche referred to in the 5 November entry is likely to be Sub-Inspector Paul Heinrich Matthias Foelsche (1831–1914), a police inspector, who was a long-standing police officer in the Northern Territory. Foelsche was German by birth and also worked as a dentist, lawyer, photographer, botanist, anthropologist, diplomat and detective.

18 Charles Todd, *Report by C. Todd, Esquire, C.M.G., On the Construction and Completion of the Adelaide and Port Darwin Line of Telegraph*, 1 January 1873, telegramsaustralia.com/Assets/Overseas/OLT/Reports/1873%20OLT%20by%20Todd%20-%20Construction%20and%20Completion.pdf.

19 'Joining Point of the Overland Telegraph, 22 August 1872', Engineers Australia, portal.engineersaustralia.org.au/system/files/engineering-heritage-australia/panel-title/Overland%20Telegraph%20Joining%20Point%20Interpretation%20Panel.pdf.

20 'Overland Telegraph', National Museum of Australia.

21 'Joining Point of the Overland Telegraph', Engineers Australia.

22 'Australian Telegraph', *The Australasian*, 19 October 1872, nla.gov.au/nla.news-article137575092.

23 'English News Twenty-four Hours Old', *South Australian Register* (Adelaide), 23 October 1872, nla.gov.au/nla.news-article39264247.

24 Bill Bryson, *Made in America*, London: Secker & Warburg, 1994, p.113.

25 Ibid, p.106.

26 'History of the Telephone in Australia and Worldwide', vintagephones.com.au/ccpo-display/history-of-the-telephone-in-australia.html.

27 'When and How Did Telephones Come to Victoria?', Museums Victoria, collections.museumsvictoria.com.au/articles/16334.

28 'Telephone', *The West Australian*, 11 June 1886, p.3, nla.gov.au/nla.news-page732650.

29 'The Telephone in Queensland', Queensland Historical Atlas, qhatlas.com.au/content/telephone-queensland.

30 Ibid.

31 'Eucla', Nullarbor Net, nullarbornet.com.au/towns/eucla.html.

32 Robert Virtue, 'Significant Moment in History to Be Re-enacted', ABC News, 13 December 2012, abc.net.au/news/2012-12-13/telegram/4425620.

33 'Last Australian Telegram', eHive, 1993, ehive.com/collections/9664/objects/1073719/last-australian-telegram.

34 'SOS, RIP', *The Economist*, 21 January 1999, economist.com/science-and-technology/1999/01/21/------sos-rip.

35 J.L. Heilbron, *Electricity in the 17th and 18th Centuries: A Study of Early Modern Physics*, Berkeley: University of California Press, 1979 (ebook 2020), ch.III.

36 'Invention of the Leyden Jar', Encyclopaedia Britannica, britannica.com/science/electromagnetism/Invention-of-the-Leyden-jar.

3. 'Seeking Awarua Station'

1 Australian Bureau of Statistics, 3105.0.65.001—Australian Historical Population Statistics, 2006.

2 F.J. Jacka, 'Mawson, Sir Douglas (1882–1958)', *Australian Dictionary of Biography*, adb.anu.edu.au/biography/mawson-sir-douglas-7531.

3 Reginald Leslie Smith-Rose, 'Guglielmo Marconi', *Encyclopaedia Britannica*, britannica.com/biography/Guglielmo-Marconi.

4 'Pioneering Antarctic Communications', Australian Antarctic Program, antarctica.gov.au/about-antarctica/history/communications/the-wireless-of-wireless-hill.

5 Douglas Mawson, *The Home of the Blizzard*, London: Hodder & Stoughton, 1938, abridged edition, p.34.

6 Ibid, p.40.

7 Ibid, p.78.

8 Ibid, chapter 9.
9 Ibid, p.116.
10 Ibid, p.164
11 Ibid, p.34.
12 Ibid, p.304.
13 Ibid.
14 Ibid, p.305.
15 Ibid.
16 Australian Antarctic Program, 'Pioneering Antarctic Communications', *op. cit.*
17 Mawson's relationship with Jeffryes has been closely critiqued. See, for example, Elizabeth Leane, Ben Maddison and Kimberley Norris, 'Beyond the Heroic Stereotype: Sidney Jeffryes and the Mythologising of Australian Antarctic History', *Australian Humanities Review*, issue 64, May 2019, pp.1–23.
18 'Mawson Radio Operator Finally Recognised', *Nambucca Guardian*, 12 October 2018, nambuccaguardian.com.au/story/5698832/mawson-radio-operator-finally-recognised.
19 Mawson, *op. cit.*, p.321.
20 Peter Yates, 'Information and Community Technology in Antarctica', *Journal of Telecommunications and the Digital Economy*, December 2015, telsoc.org/journal/ajtde-v3-n4/a29.
21 John L. Fuhring, 'Shackleton's "Missing" Radio Equipment', geojohn.org/Radios/MyRadios/Shackleton/Shackleton.html.
22 Kelly Tyler-Lewis, *The Lost Men: The Harrowing Story of Shackleton's Ross Sea Party*, London: Bloomsbury, 2006, p.32.
23 Ibid, pp.31–32.
24 Ibid, p.57.
25 Ibid.
26 Ibid, pp.57–58.
27 Ibid, p.127.
28 Ibid, p.57.
29 David McGonigal, 'Ernest Shackleton: The Ross Sea Party (1915–17)', Antarctic Guide, antarcticguide.com/about-antarctica/antarctic-history/heroic-age/ernest-shackleton-the-ross-sea-party-1915–17/.
30 Tyler-Lewis, *op. cit.*, p.205.
31 Ibid, p.210.
32 Ibid.
33 Ibid, p.2.
34 *Nambucca Guardian*, 'Mawson Radio Operator Finally Recognised', *op. cit.*
35 Chris Turney, *1912: The Year the World Discovered Antarctica*, Melbourne: Text Publishing, 2012, p.124.
36 Ibid, p.133.
37 Ibid; Tim Bowden, 'Antarctica's Links with Tasmania', The Companion to Tasmanian History, utas.edu.au/library/companion_to_tasmanian_history/A/Antarctica%27s%20links%20with%20Tasmania.htm.
38 'Interview with Armundsen', *The Mercury* (Hobart), 8 March 1912, nla.gov.au/nla.news-article10209491.
39 Turney, *op. cit.*, p.133.
40 Daina Fletcher, 'Lessons from the Arctic: How Roald Amundsen Won the Race to the South Pole', Australian National Maritime Museum, sea.museum/2017/03/21/lessons-from-the-arctic-how-roald-amundsen-won-the-race-to-the-south-pole.

4. Running the line

1 'Victory at Trafalgar—How the News Was Delivered', Naval Historical Society of Australia, navyhistory.org.au/victory-at-trafalgar-how-the-news-was-delivered.

2 George Back and George Thompson, 'The Advent of Electrical Signaling', *Encyclopedia Britannica,* britannica.com/technology/military-communication/The-advent-of-electrical-signaling.
3 Ibid.
4 Desmond Lambley, *The Australian Imperial Signal Force in World War One: Jack the Rooster*, Doncaster, Vic.: Royal Australian Corps of Signals, 2015, chapter 4, 'Signals at War'.
5 Humphrey Carpenter, *J.R.R. Tolkien: A Biography*, London: George Allen & Unwin, 1977, p.117.
6 Lambley, *op. cit.*, p.14.
7 Ibid.
8 Ibid, foreword.
9 Department of Veterans' Affairs, 'Technology and Equipment Developed During World War I', *DVA Anzac Portal*, anzacportal.dva.gov.au/wars-and-missions/ww1/military-organisation/technology-and-equipment.
10 'Signaller Silas the ANZAC, Artist and Adventurer in Gallipoli', Defence Health, healthhq.defencehealth.com.au/2019/04/17/signaller-silas-the-anzac-artist-and-adventurer-in-gallipoli.
11 DVA, 'Gallipoli Diary and Sketches by Signaller Ellis Silas', *DVA Anzac Portal*, anzacportal.dva.gov.au/wars-and-missions/ww1/where-australians-served/gallipoli/landing-anzac-cove/ellis-silas-diary-extracts#2.
12 Ibid.
13 'The Post and Telegraph Department at War', New Zealand History, nzhistory.govt.nz/war/first-world-war-postal-service/gallipoli.
14 'Cyril Bassett Wins VC on Chunuk Bair', New Zealand History, nzhistory.govt.nz/media/sound/cyril-bassett-and-chunuk-bair.
15 DVA, 'First Australian Imperial Force in World War I', *DVA Anzac Portal*, anzacportal.dva.gov.au/wars-and-missions/ww1/military-organisation/australian-imperial-force.
16 Ibid.
17 'Battle of the Somme Summary', *Encyclopaedia Brittanica*, britannica.com/summary/First-Battle-of-the-Somme.
18 John Garth, *Tolkien and the Great War: The Threshold of Middle Earth*, London: HarperCollins Publishers, 2003, pp.165–166.
19 Ibid, p.166.
20 Lambley, *op. cit.*, p.110.
21 Ibid, p.99.
22 Paul Gannon, 'WWI: First World War Communications and the Tele-net of Things', *Engineering and Technology*, eandt.theiet.org/content/articles/2014/06/ww1-first-world-war-communications-and-the-tele-net-of-things.
23 Ibid.
24 Ibid.
25 Charlotte Dubenskij, 'World War One: How Radio Crackled into Life in Conflict', BBC News, bbc.com/news/uk-wales-27894944.
26 'Wireless Telegraphy: First World War', Spartacus Educational, spartacus-educational.com/FWWairwireless.htm.
27 'Hamel: The Textbook Victory', Australian War Memorial, awm.gov.au/visit/exhibitions/1918/battles/hamel.
28 'Battle of Beersheba: Signals Intelligence, 1st Australian Light Horse', ABC, abc.net.au/ww1-anzac/beersheba/dioramas.
29 Ibid.
30 Lambley, *op. cit.*, p.40.
31 Richard Arundel, 'Communications at the Outbreak of World War I and Their Evolution', in Andrew Forbes (ed.), *The War at Sea, 1914–18: Proceedings of the King Hall Navy Conference 2013*, Canberra: Sea Power Centre Australia, 2015, p.156, navy.gov.au/sites/default/files/documents/The_War_at_Sea_1914-18.pdf.

32 Australia began the war with 16 surface ships, 2 submarines and 3,800 personnel. By the end of the war in November 1918, the make-up of the RAN had grown to 37 ships and 5,000 personnel (anzacportal.dva.gov.au/wars-and-missions/ww1/military-organisation/royal-australian-navy); John Perryman, 'Visual Signalling in the Royal Australian Navy', navy.gov.au/history/feature-histories/visual-signalling-royal-australian-navy.
33 'World War I', in Bruce B. Pratt (editor in chief), *Australian Encyclopaedia*, 3rd edition, Sydney: Grolier, 1977.
34 Perryman, 'Visual Signalling in the Royal Australian Navy'.

5. Fireside comfort

1 Harold Williams, *Argonauts Row*, National Film and Sound Archive of Australia, nfsa.gov.au/collection/curated/argonauts-row-harold-williams-1941.
2 Murray Goot, 'Fisk, Sir Ernest Thomas (1886–1965)', *Australian Dictionary of Biography*, adb.anu.edu.au/biography/fisk-sir-ernest-thomas-6177.
3 Marina Koestler Ruben, 'Radio Activity: The 100th Anniversary of Public Broadcasting', *Smithsonian*, 26 January 2010, smithsonianmag.com/history/radio-activity-the-100th-anniversary-of-public-broadcasting-6555594/.
4 Ibid.
5 Michael Osborne, 'Radio Comes of Age in Australia—Broadcasting 1922–1930', Museums Victoria, collections.museumsvictoria.com.au/articles/12666.
6 Ibid.
7 Franklin D. Roosevelt, 'Inaugural Address Online by Gerhard Peters and John T. Woolley', *The American Presidency Project*, presidency.ucsb.edu/node/208712.
8 'Franklin D. Roosevelt Second Fireside Chat', 7 May 1933, American Presidency Project, presidency.ucsb.edu/documents/second-fireside-chat.
9 'Prime Minister Joe Lyons' New Year Address during the Great Depression', National Archives of Australia, naa.gov.au/learn/learning-resources/learning-resource-themes/society-and-culture/great-depression/prime-minister-joseph-lyons-new-year-address-during-great-depression.
10 'Menzies Speech: Declaration of War', National Film and Sound Archive of Australia, nfsa.gov.au/collection/curated/menzies-speech-declaration-war.
11 'ABC History', ABC, about.abc.net.au/abc-history.
12 'Celebrating the History of Australian Radio Drama with Peter Philp', ABC Radio National, Overnights, interview with Peter Philp (author of *Drama in Silent Rooms: The History of Australian Radio Drama*, Eureka Media, 2016), broadcast 9 January 2017, abc.net.au/radio/programs/overnights/peter-philp-radio-drama/8169502.
13 Christopher H. Stirling, 'Radio: A New Art Form', *Encyclopaedia Britannica*, britannica.com/topic/radio/A-new-art-form.
14 'The Golden Age of Radio', ABC Radio National, broadcast 30 August 2007, transcript: abc.net.au/radionational/programs/archived/mediareport-1999/the-golden-age-of-radio/3211582.
15 'Australian Radio Series (1930s to 1970s): A Guide to Holdings', National Film and Sound Archive of Australia, nfsa.gov.au/collection/curated/nfsa-radio-series-collection-amended.
16 ABC Radio National, 'Celebrating the History of Australian Radio Drama ...', *op. cit.*
17 'Caltex Theatre', Times Past: Old Time Radio, otrarchive.blogspot.com/2009/11/caltex-theater-au.html.
18 ABC Radio National, 'Celebrating the History of Australian Radio Drama ...', *op. cit.*
19 ABC, 'ABC History', *op. cit.*
20 J. Korff, 'Aboriginal Radio Stations', Creative Spirits, creativespirits.info/resources/tv-radio/aboriginal-radio-stations.
21 'World Radio Day—Celebrating Our Indigenous Broadcasters', indigenous.gov.au/news-and-media/stories/world-radio-day-—celebrating-our-indigenous-broadcasters.

22 'Radio; The Kriesler Radio Company; 1946–1947; 32851', eHive, ehive.com/collections/5051/objects/397676/radio.
23 Advertisement in *The Northern Star* (Lismore), 1876–1954, 10 December 1947.
24 Gadigal Information Service Aboriginal Corporation, kooriradio.com.
25 'Redfern—The Untold Story of 1970s Aboriginal Activism and Resurgence', AIATSIS, aiatsis.gov.au/whats-new/news/redfern-untold-story-1970s-aboriginal-activism-and-resurgence.
26 'Our History', Gadigal Information Service Aboriginal Corporation, kooriradio.com/history.
27 'World Radio Day—Celebrating Indigenous Broadcasting in Australia', National Indigenous Australians Agency, niaa.gov.au/news-centre/indigenous-affairs/world-radio-day-celebrating-indigenous-broadcasting-australia.
28 'The History of Australian Radio', Radio Adelaide, media.adelaide.edu.au/radio/intro/history_OZ-radio.pdf.
29 The National Ethnic and Multicultural Broadcasters Council, 'Ethnic Community Broadcasting', Treasury, treasury.gov.au/sites/default/files/2019-03/360985-National-Ethnic-and-Multicultural-Broadcasters-Council.pdf.
30 Ibid.
31 George Zangalis, *From 3ZZ to 3ZZZ: A Short History of Ethnic Broadcasting in Australia*, Fitzroy (Vic.): Ethnic Public Broadcasting Association of Victoria, 2001, p.29.
32 Ibid, p.37.
33 The National Ethnic and Multicultural Broadcasters Council, *op. cit.*
34 'Somali Language Show', 3CR 855AM, 3cr.org.au/somali.
35 Kelly Burke, *The Stamp of Australia: The Story of Our Mail—From Second Fleet to Twenty-first Century*, Sydney: Allen & Unwin, 2009, p.99.
36 Ibid, p.102.
37 Peter Stanley, 'Wizard of the Air: Maurice Guillaux', *The National Library of Australia Magazine*, September 2014, nla.gov.au/sites/default/files/september-2014-magazine_0.pdf.
38 Alisdair McGregor, 'Flying Far: The Largely Forgotten 1919 England to Australia Air Race', *Australian Geographic*, australiangeographic.com.au/topics/history-culture/2019/12/flying-far-the-largely-forgotten-1919-england-to-australia-air-race.
39 'The 1919 Great Air Race', History Trust of South Australia, epicflightcentenary.com.au/the-1919-air-race.
40 Burke, *The Stamp of Australia*, p.117
41 Ibid, p.111.
42 Ibid.
43 Ibid, p.117.
44 Tom Joyner, 'The Great Australian Flying Outback Mail Service', ABC News, abc.net.au/news/2018-05-06/great-australian-flying-outback-mail-service/9701182.

6. War in the Pacific

1 'The Golden Age of Radio in the US', Digital Public Library of America, dp.la/exhibitions/radio-golden-age/radio-frontlines/radio-codes.
2 Ted Ling, 'Commonwealth Government Records about the Northern Territory', National Archives of Australia, naa.gov.au/sites/default/files/2020-02/research-guide-government-records-nt.pdf.
3 Lawrence Durrant, *The Seawatchers: The Story of Australia's Coast Radio Service*, North Ryde: Angus & Robertson, 1986, pp.82–83.
4 Ibid.
5 Ibid, pp.101–102.
6 Roland Perry, *Pacific 360: Australia's Battle for Survival in World War II*, Sydney: Hachette Australia, 2012, p.122.
7 Ibid, pp.122–23.
8 Ibid, p.123.
9 Ibid, p.144.

10 Ibid, p.135.
11 'Defining Moments: Curtin Brings Home Troops', National Museum of Australia, nma.gov.au/defining-moments/resources/curtin-brings-home-troops.
12 Michael McKernan, *The Strength of a Nation*, Sydney: Allen & Unwin, 2006, p.226
13 Winston S. Churchill, *The Hinge of Fate*, New York: Rosetta Books (electronic edition), 2002, p.165. Originally published in 1950 by Houghton Mifflin Co., Boston.
14 Perry, *op. cit.*, p.187.
15 A.B. Feuer, *Coast Watching in World War II: Operations Against the Japanese in the Solomon Islands, 1941–43*, Mechanicsburg, Pa: Stackpole Books, 2006, p.31.
16 'Battle of the Coral Sea, 4–8 May 1942', Australian War Memorial, awm.gov.au/articles/encyclopedia/coral_sea/doc.
17 'Warrant Officer Class 2 Kevin Leonard Winton 'Wint' Healey', Australian War Memorial, awm.gov.au/collection/P21962.
18 'Building a Radio in a POW Camp—Part Two', WW2 People's War, BBC, bbc.co.uk/history/ww2peopleswar/stories/89/a4127889.shtml.
19 Jerry Proc, 'Naval Radio Operations during World War Two', jproc.ca/rrp/nro_ww2.html.
20 Ibid.
21 Allan A. Murray, *Get the Oars Out: When I-24 Sank the Iron Chieftain*, self-published, 2022.
22 Peter Dunn, 'HMAS *Coonawarra* (VHM), W/T Station and D/F Station, Darwin Area during World War II', Australia at War, ozatwar.com/sigint/hmascoonawarra.htm.
23 Australian Navy, 'HMAS Voyager (1)', navy.gov.au/hmas-voyager-i.
24 Peter Dunn, *op. cit.*
25 Ian Connellan, 'Defending Darwin: Australia's WWII Front Line', *Australian Geographic*, 11 May 2011, australiangeographic.com.au/topics/history-culture/2011/05/defending-darwin-australias-wwii-front-line.
26 Petar Djokovic, 'The Coastwatchers and Ferdinand the Bull', *Semaphore*, navy.gov.au/media-room/publications/semaphore-coastwatchers-and-ferdinand-bull.
27 Ibid.
28 Owen Edwards, 'Remembering PT-109: A Carved Walking Stick Evokes Ship Commander John F. Kennedy's Dramatic Rescue at Sea', *Smithsonian Magazine*, November 2010, smithsonianmag.com/history/remembering-pt-109–63427209/.
29 Ibid.
30 Extract from an interview conducted in 1979 by Louise Lansley and Islay Wybenga of the Sydney High Old Girls' Union, quoted in Catherine Freyne's article, 'McKenzie, Violet', The Dictionary of Sydney, dictionaryofsydney.org/entry/mckenzie_violet.

7. Post World War II: TV and the space race

1 Neil McMahon, 'Looking Back on 60 Years of Australian Television', *The Sydney Morning Herald*, 14 September 2016, smh.com.au/entertainment/m17cover-20160901-gr6tag.html.
2 Ibid.
3 Vanessa Berry, 'The Artarmon Triangle', *Mirror Sydney*, mirrorsydney.wordpress.com/2013/11/29/the-artarmon-triangle.
4 Elma Farnsworth interview, Television Academy Foundation, interviewed by Jeff Kisseloff, interviews.televisionacademy.com/interviews/elma-farnsworth.
5 John M. Logsdon, 'History of Space Exploration', *Encyclopaedia Britannica*, britannica.com/science/space-exploration/History-of-space-exploration#ref237028.
6 Kerrie Dougherty, *Australia in Space*, Adelaide: ATF Press, 2017.
7 'Crowds Fill Offices, Stores and Pubs', *The Canberra Times*, 22 July 1969, nla.gov.au/nla.news-article136945257.
8 'Apollo 13 @ 50—Parkes Observatory's Support of NASA's Finest Hour', youtube.com/watch?v=zK6EoIkpZwA.
9 'Parkes to Sydney', Honeysuckle Creek Tracking Station, honeysucklecreek.net/Apollo_11/Parkes_to_Sydney.html; Hamish Lindsay; 'Apollo 13: "Houston, We've Had a Problem

Here"', Honeysuckle Creek Tracking Station, honeysucklecreek.net/msfn_missions/Apollo_13_mission/hl_apollo13.html.
10 NASA, 'History of Tracking Stations in Australia', *NASA*, cdscc.nasa.gov/Pages/other_history.html.
11 Tracey Stewart, 'How the Apollo 11 Moon Landing Was Achieved with the Vital Help of Carnarvon Tracking Station, ABC News, 16 July 2019, abc.net.au/news/2019–07–14/the-vital-role-played-by-carnarvon-in-the-apollo-11-moon-landing/11261800.
12 Clara Heeroma, 'Carnarvon's Role in Putting Man on the Moon', ABC News, 7 April 2010, abc.net.au/news/2010-04-07/carnarvons-role-in-putting-man-on-the-moon/2602332.
13 Stewart, *op. cit.*
14 David Flannery, 'Why Isn't Australia in Deep Space?', *The Conversation*, theconversation.com/why-isnt-australia-in-deep-space-119533.
15 John Sarkissian and Ed Kruzins, 'From the Edge of the Solar System, Voyager Probes Are Still Talking to Australia after 40 Years', ABC News/The Conversation, 22 August 2017, abc.net.au/news/science/2017–08–22/from-edge-of-solar-system-voyagers-still-talking-to-australia/8827606.
23 Kyra Haas, 'Scottsdale Motorola Workers Made Devices That Transmitted Famous Words and Images from the Moon', *azcentral*, 17 July 2019. azcentral.com/story/news/local/scottsdale-history/2019/07/17/moon-landing-anniversary-motorola-scottsdale-made-broadcast-possible/1739639001/.

8. Search, rescue, respond

1 *Asiatic Mirror* (Calcutta), 'Narrative of the Shipwreck of Captain Hamilton and the Crew of the Sydney Cove', in F.M. Bladen (ed.), *Historical Records of NSW*, Sydney: NSW Government Printer, 1895, gutenberg.net.au/ebooks13/1300541h.html.
2 Ibid.
3 Rob Mundle, *Flinders: The Man Who Mapped Australia*, Sydney: Hachette Australia, 2012, p.149.
4 Ibid, p.150.
5 State Library of New South Wales, 'The French in Australia: The Fate of La Perouse', sl.nsw.gov.au/stories/french-australia/fate-la-perouse.
6 'Titanic, Marconi and the Wireless Telegraph', Science Museum (UK), sciencemuseum.org.uk/objects-and-stories/titanic-marconi-and-wireless-telegraph.
7 Ibid.
8 Ibid.
9 L.J. Lind, *HMAS Parramatta*, Garden Island: The Naval Historical Society of Australia, 1974, p.73.
10 Ibid.
11 Frederick Howard, 'Kingsford Smith, Sir Charles Edward (1897–1935)', *Australian Dictionary of Biography*, adb.anu.edu.au/biography/kingsford-smith-sir-charles-edward-6964.
12 Beau Sheil, 'The World's Greatest Airman', *Sun* (Sydney), 23 May 1937, nla.gov.au/nla.news-article229397757.
13 'Keith Anderson Memorial', mosman1914–1918.net/project/blog/keith-anderson-memorial.
14 'Solo Yachtsman Saved by Personal Locator Beacon on Life Jacket', AMSA Media Hub, media.amsa.gov.au/media-release/solo-yachtsman-saved-personal-locator-beacon-life-jacket; 'Yachtie Blown Overboard Rescued off NT', *The Senior*, 5 January 2021, thesenior.com.au/story/7075889/yachtie-blown-overboard-rescued-off-nt/.
15 John Roberson, 'Bullimore: Surviving Inside', *Sailing World*, web.archive.org/web/20060509091532/http://old.cruisingworld.com/vendmisc.htm.
16 Brett Mitchell, 'Search and Rescue: A Miracle in the South', *Semaphore*, navy.gov.au/media-room/publications/semaphore-search-and-rescue-miracle-south.
17 Ibid.
18 Cristescu, Burns and McDonald, 'Cultural Burning Is Safer for Koalas and Better for People

Too', The Conversation, 16 March 2023, theconversation.com/cultural-burning-is-safer-for-koalas-and-better-for-people-too-200997.
19 'History of Australian Bushfires: Interactive', *The Guardian*, 1 December 2013, theguardian.com/news/datablog/interactive/2013/dec/01/history-bushfires-australia-interactive.
20 *The Empire* (Sydney), 20 February 1851.
21 'History of Australian Bushfires: Interactive', *op. cit.*
22 Anna Henderson and Georgia Hitch, 'Bushfire Royal Commission Recommends National State of Emergency, Aerial Firefighting Fleet', ABC News, 30 October 2020, abc.net.au/news/2020–10–30/bushfire-royal-commission-final-report-recommendations/12815204.
23 Bucknall, G., 'Flynn, John (1880–1951)', *Australian Dictionary of Biography*, adb.anu.edu.au/biography/flynn-john-6200; 'Australian Inland Mission', National Library of Australia, nla.gov.au/collections/guide-selected-collections/australian-inland-mission.
24 'History', Royal Flying Doctor Service, flyingdoctor.org.au/about-the-rfds/history/.
25 'About', Royal Flying Doctor Service, flyingdoctor.org.au/about-the-rfds/.
26 'A Conversation, Not a Broadcast: How Indigenous Radio Stations Are Responding to the Coronavirus Crisis', Social Ventures Australia, socialventures.com.au/blog/indigenous-radio-stations/.
27 Ibid.
28 Ibid.
29 'Our Story', Wangki Yupurnanupurru Radio, wangki.org.au/our-story.
30 B. Backhaus and K. Foxwell-Norton, 'At Fitzroy Crossing and Around Australia, Community Radio Empowers Local Responses to Climate Impacts', *The Conversation*, theconversation.com/at-fitzroy-crossing-and-around-australia-community-radio-empowers-local-responses-to-climate-impacts-197679.
31 Facebook post, Wangki Yupurnanupurru Radio, 16 January 2023.
32 Facebook post, Wangki Yupurnanupurru Radio, 14 January 2023.

9. The daily news

1 Peter Wilby, 'How Newspapers Have Failed Us', *New Statesman*, 12 February 2014, newstatesman.com/2014/02/how-newspapers-have-failed-us.
2 Ibid.
3 Will Slauter, 'The Rise of the Newspaper', in Richard R. John and Jonathan Silberstein-Loeb (eds), *Making News: The Political Economy of Journalism in Britain and America from the Glorious Revolution to the Internet*, Oxford: Oxford University Press, 2015.
4 Ibid, p.21.
5 'Hughes, George', *Australian Dictionary of Biography*, adb.anu.edu.au/biography/hughes-george-2208.
6 J.V. Byrnes, 'Howe, George (1769–1821)', *Australian Dictionary of Biography*, adb.anu.edu.au/biography/howe-george-1600.
7 Ibid.
8 'Myall Creek Massacre', Trove, trove.nla.gov.au/list/79912.
9 Ibid.
10 'The Lords of the Soil', *The Colonist*, 12 December 1838, nla.gov.au/nla.news-article31722188.
11 'A Newspaper about the History of Newspapers—The Melbourne Sirius', ABC, Radio National, 27 February 2014.
12 'SA Newspapers: Non-English Language Newspapers', State Library of South Australia, samemory.sa.gov.au/site/page.cfm?u=1475.
13 Diamadis, P., 'Greeks', Dictionary of Sydney, dictionaryofsydney.org/entry/greeks.
14 '*Il Giornale Italiano*', Trove, trove.nla.gov.au/newspaper/title/279.
15 Vantomme, F. and Le Boursicot, Bernard, 'Message from the Owners of *Le Courrier Australien*', *Le Courrier Australien* Friends, lecourrieraustralienfriends.org/stories/message-from-the-owners-of-le-courrier-australien.
16 'About *La Fiamma*', *La Fiamma*, lafiamma.com.au/en/about-la-fiamma/.

17 'Newspapers', in Bruce Pratt (editor in chief), *Australian Encyclopaedia*, 3rd edition, Sydney: Grolier, 1977.
18 Caitlynn Gribbin and Marian Faa, 'Regional Australia Laments Loss of News Print as News Corp Titles Go Digital', ABC News, abc.net.au/news/2020–05–28/news-corp-makes-regional-papers-digital-only/12295408.

10. Screen time

1 Science Museum, 'From ARPANET to the Internet', sciencemuseum.org.uk/objects-and-stories/arpanet-internet#:~:text=The%20first%20message%20was%20sent,Processors'%20or%20'IMPs'.
2 J.C. Herz, 'Funky Internet to Rule the Roost', *The Canberra Times*, 11 October 1993, nla.gov.au/nla.news-article127510710.
3 Jack Schofield, 'Congress Hearing Kicks off Today', *The Canberra Times*, 26 July 1993, nla.gov.au/nla.news-article13968829.
4 Roger Clarke, 'Morning Dew on the Web in Australia: 1992–1995', rogerclarke.com/II/OzWH.html, published in *Journal of Information Technology 29 (2013)*, pp.93–110.
5 Ibid.
6 'CSIRO's WLAN Patent', IP Australia, ipaustralia.gov.au/tools-resources/case-studies/csiro-wlan-patent.
7 Lauren Day, 'NBN's Tasmanian Rollout Problems Continue', ABC News, 13 May 2014, mobile.abc.net.au/news/2014–05–13/nbn27s-tasmanian-rollout-problems-continue/5450418.
8 James Fernyhough, 'It's the End of the Beginning for the NBN', *Australian Financial Review*, 13 June 2020, afr.com/companies/telecommunications/it-s-the-end-of-the-beginning-for-the-nbn-20200610-p5519n.
9 'Timeline of the Mobile Phone', Telstra, connect.telstrawholesale.com/timelinevoice
10 Ibid.
11 J. Thompson, 'Union Hits Plan for Mobile Phone Networks', *The Canberra Times*, 10 April 1990.
12 'Total Number of Mobile Connections in Australia from 2015 to 2022', *Statista*, statista.com/statistics/680482/australia-number-of-mobile-subscriptions/.
13 Mike Murphy, 'From Dial-up to 5G: A Complete Guide to Logging on to the Internet', *Quartz*, qz.com/1705375/a-complete-guide-to-the-evolution-of-the-internet.

11. An uncertain future

1 Zaryn Dentzel, 'How the Internet Has Changed Everyday Life', BBVA OpenMind, bbvaopenmind.com/en/articles/internet-changed-everyday-life.
2 Ben Egliston and Marcus Carter, 'Ray-Ban Stories Let You Wear Facebook on Your Face. But Why Would You Want to?', *The Conversation*, 13 September 2021, theconversation.com/ray-ban-stories-let-you-wear-facebook-on-your-face-but-why-would-you-want-to-167708.
3 Andrew Probyn and Stephen Dziedzic, 'Cyber Attacks on Australia Blurring the Lines Between Peace and War, Defence Minister Says', ABC News, 4 September 2020, abc.net.au/news/2020–09–04/cyber-attacks-on-australia-peace-war-defence-minister/12626396.

Opposite page: Carnarvon tracking station in about 1972.

MEN
WORKING ON
ANTENNA

List of illustrations

Covers, Front and Back Matter

front cover *Mr Wallace, Wireless Operator on the Ship La Perouse, New South Wales*, 1929, nla.cat-vn6296510, courtesy Fairfax Syndication; **back cover** CSIRO, *Radio Telescope at Parkes*, 1961, nla.cat-vn3627079; George Baxter, *Australia, News from Home*, 1840s, nla.cat-vn1753207; *AWA Television Receiver*, 1956, Museum of Applied Arts & Sciences, B2015; **front endpaper** Frank Hurley, *The Inland Section, Sorters Engaged in Sorting Letters*, Sydney, c.1940s, nla.cat-vn91770; **back endpaper** *General Post Office Employees Sorting Christmas Parcels, Sydney*, 1929, nla.cat-vn6329056, courtesy Fairfax Syndication; **265** *Research—Astronomy and Space—Australian Tracking Station Important NASA Link, Carnarvon*, National Archives of Australia, 11896267; **270–271** *Men Creating Newspaper Blocks in the Composing Room at the Herald Office, Sydney*, c.1930, nla. cat-vn6343082, courtesy Fairfax Syndication..

Introduction

ii *Telegraph Boy Holding up a Roll of Telegraph Messages from the General Post Office, Sydney*, 1932, nla.cat-vn6301519, courtesy Fairfax Syndication; **vii** *Three Wireless Telephone Operators at a Wwitchboard, Sydney*, c.1930, nla.cat-vn6334178, courtesy Fairfax Syndication.

1. The Ships Sail Tomorrow

2–3 John Allcot, *The First Fleet in Sydney Cove, January 27, 1788*, 1937, nla.cat-vn624123; **4** Edward Dayes, *View of the Settlement of Sydney Cove, Port Jackson, 20th August 1788*, courtesy Dixson Library, State Library of New South Wales; **6–7** Francis Fowkes, *Sketch & Description of the Settlement at Sydney Cove Port Jackson Taken by a Transported Convict on the 16th April, 1788*, 1789, nla.cat-vn1084748; **11** Letter from Arthur Phillip to the Marquis of Lansdowne, 1788, State Library of New South Wales, SAFE/MLMSS 7241 (Safe 1/234); **13** Edward Dayes, *Western View of Sydney Cove*, 1797, nla.cat-vn2250288; **14** *The First Parliament of Botany Bay in High Debate*, 1786, nla.cat-vn1140381; **17** Edward Collier, *A Letter Rack*, 1695, Yale Center for British Art, B2018.6; **20** Jan Ekels, *A Writer Trimming His Pen*, 1784, Rijksmuseum, SK-A-690; **21** George Cruikshank, *Death of a Convict on the Hulk Justitia*, 1830s, nla.cat-vn1562141; **23** Joseph Lycett, *Parramatta, New South Wales*, 1824, nla.cat-vn8031944; **25** [Settlers hut], c.1820, nla.cat-vn858222; **27 top** *Arrest of Governor Bligh, January 26, 1808*, 1900s, nla.cat-vn536378; **27 bottom** Copy of letter from William Bligh to William Wellesley-Pole, 1808, State Library of New South Wales, SAFE/ Banks Papers/Series 40.90; **28–29** John Lewin, *View of Sydney from the North Shore*, 1812, nla.cat-vn914183; **30** *Milestones in Australian History: Australia's First Postmaster*, 1959, nla.cat-vn6578035; **33** Robert Russell, *Dawes' Battery, Dawes' Point, Sydney*, 1836, nla.cat-vn7382620; **35** *The Sydney Gazette and New South Wales Advertiser*, 20 January 1816, page 1, trove.nla.gov.au/newspaper/page/492966; **37** George Baxter, *News from Australia*, 1840s, nla.cat-vn230763; **39** Joseph Fowles (artist), F. Mansell (engraver), *The Post Office, Sydney*, 1849, nla.cat-vn1184703; **41** John Skinner Prout, *Interior of Settler's Hut in Australia*, 1849, nla. cat-vn3408520; **43** Thomas Balcombe, *Mr. E.H. Hargraves, the Gold Discoverer of Australia*, 1851, nla.cat-vn2851735; **45** John Skinner Prout (artist), Thomas Gilks (engraver), *Off for the Diggings at Bathurst; Ascending a Pass in the Blue Mountains*, 1851, nla.cat-vn337434; **47** George Lacy, *Nothing Like Opposition*, c.1855, nla.cat-vn2582641; **49** Nicholas Chevalier (artist), Frederick Grosse (engraver), *Emigrants Landing at the Queen's Wharf, Melbourne*, 1860s, nla.cat-vn422154; **51 top** George Baxter, *Australia, News from Home*, 1840s, nla. cat-vn1753207; **51 bottom** Thomas Carrington, *Arrival of the Mail, Myers Flat Diggings*, c.1873, nla.cat-vn2833847; **53** Axel Poignant, *Two Women Collect Their Supplies on the Upper Reaches of the Hawkesbury River, New South Wales*, c.1952, nla.cat-vn4403993.

2. Connecting to the World

54–55 Emrik & Binger, *The Australian Mail Steamer Orient*, 1880s, nla.cat-vn732597; **55 top** John Allcot, *The Race for News in the Fifties*, 1931, State Library of Western Australia, W324a; **57** *Morse Electric System Telegraph Set, 1857*, Museums Victoria, Item ST 7096; **58–59** Nathaniel Whittock and Goodman Teale (artists), *The City of Melbourne*, 1855, State Library of Victoria, H34147; **60** *Cable*

Sample of Submarine Telegraph, Atlantic, 1865, Museums Victoria, Item ST 5685.3; **61** George French Angas (artist), John Greenaway (engraver), *Planting the Flag on the Shores of the Indian Ocean*, 1865, nla.cat-vn333300; **63** Samuel White Sweet, *Overland Telegraph Party, J.A.G. Little, Robert Patterson, Charles Todd, Alexander James Mitchell*, c.1873, nla.cat-vn1780539; **64–65** Samuel Thomas Gill, *Waterplace, Depot Creek*, c.1846, nla.cat-vn1981038; **67** Samuel Calvert, *Construction of the Overland Telegraph to Port Darwin*, c.1870, nla.cat-vn293424; **68–69** Samuel Sweet White, *Workers on the Overland Telegraph Line, Southport, Port Darwin*, c.1870, nla.cat-vn6381048; **72–73** Robert Morse Withycombe, *Post and Telegraph Office, New South Wales*, 1890s, nla.cat-vn922639; **73 bottom** *Experimental Telephone Receiver Used by Alexander Graham Bell, 1876*, Museums Victoria, Item ST 35633; **75** Front cover and pages of *Melbourne Telephone Exchange*, c.1882, nla.cat-vn560107; **77** Alexander Lorimer Kennedy, *Interior View of the Telegraph Station, Eucla, Western Australia*, 1914, nla.cat-vn6977094; **78** Laplante, *Andreas Cunaeus Discovering the Leyden Jar*, commons.wikimedia.org/wiki/File:Andreas_Cunaeus_discovering_the_Leyden_jar.png, reproduced under CC BY-SA 4.0 creativecommons.org/licenses/by-sa/4.0/deed.en.

3. Seeking Awarua Station

81 Charles Sandell, *Wireless Engine Hut, Macquarie Island*, between 1911 and 1914, nla.cat-vn3158410; **83** Frank Hurley, *W.H. Hannam Wireless Operator, Cape Denison, Australasian Antarctic Expedition*, between 1911 and 1914, nla.cat-vn3123146; **84–85** Andrew D. Watson, *Guiding Sledge over a Gully, Australasian Antarctic Expedition*, between 1911 and 1914, nla.cat-vn3125227; **87** Frank Hurley, *A Winter Evening at the Hut*, c.1911, nla.cat-vn2938503; **89–90** F.J. Gillies, *Group of Members of the Land Parties Relieved in 1913, Australasian Antarctic Expedition*, 1913, nla.cat-vn2402460; **92** Martin Walch, *Communications at Mawson*, courtesy Australian Antarctic Division TBC; **95** Frank Hurley, *Thirteen Men on Elephant Island Wave Farewell to Sir Ernest Shackleton and Party as They Leave for South Georgia*, 1916, nla.cat-vn1614852; **96–97** Frank Hurley, *Steaming through Light Pack-ice, Australasian Antarctic Expedition*, between 1911 and 1914, nla.cat-vn3255263; **99** Frank Hurley, *At Night We Drew Our Boats up on to an Ice-raft and Kindled a Blubber Fire to Warm Our Frozen Bodies*, 1916, nla.cat-vn1613009; **100** *Telefunken Morse Key Used with Radio Spark Transmitter, between 1910 and 1920*, Museums Victoria, Item ST 15474; **102** *Captain Roald Amundsen on Board the 'Fram' at Hobart*, 1912, nla.cat-vn316500; **103** Gary Houston, *Bust of Roald Amundsen Originally Sculpted by Victor Lewis in 1921*, 2017, commons.wikimedia.org/wiki/File:Roald_Amundsen_bust_20171117-004.jpg, reproduced under CC BY-SA 4.0 creativecommons.org/licenses/by-sa/4.0/deed.en.

4. Running the Line

106 *Bitapaka, New Britain. One of the Wireless Telegraph Masts Demolished by the German Force as It Moved out When the Australian Forces Were Attacking*, between 1914 and 1918, Australian War Memorial, H17201; **108** *Laying a Telephone Line*, 1910s, nla.cat-vn3890980; **109** Adolfobrigido, *Fullerphone*, 2016, commons.wikimedia.org/wiki/File:Aparato_Fullerphone_Mod._1917.jpg, reproduced under CC BY-SA 4.0 creativecommons.org/licenses/by-sa/4.0/deed.en; **111 left** *Two Members of 1st Divisional Signals, AIF, Laying Cable along a Trench at Anzac Cove*, 1915, Australian War Memorial, H05440; **111 right** *Two Australian Signallers, Sgt Johnson and Sgt James at an Australian Signal Station Located in a Trench, Gallipoli*, 1915, Australian War Memorial, P02952.005; **114** *Royal Australian Artillery, Entrance to Signallers' Dugout, Laviéville, France*, 1918, nla.cat-vn 6422956; **116–117** *Signal Engineers, with a Reel of Cable, Leaving a Signal Office on Westhoek Ridge, in the Ypres Sector, to Lay a Surface Telephone Line to a Forward Unit*, 1917, Australian War Memorial, E00798; **119** Frank Hurley, *A Linesman of the Australian Corps Signal Company Working on the Telegraph Line on the Bray-Corbie Road, France*, 1918, nla.cat-vn5981334; **120** *Shortwave Mark 3 Radio Tuner*, Museums Victoria, Item ST 24861; **121** *Soldiers Using Heliographs to Signal Distant Comrades, Huj, Gaza, Palestine*, c.1917, State Library of Queensland, Image number: 30590-0001-0026.

5. Fireside Comfort

126 *The First Direct Wireless Messages from England to Australia*, 1918, nla.cat-vn 3421834; **127** Arthur G. Foster, *2KY Radio Station, Kings Cross Sydney*, between 1920 and 1945, nla.cat-vn3064009; **129 top** Healingram Vauchuse advertisement, in *Electric Industries: Trade Catalogues Ephemera Collected by the National Library of Australia*, nla.cat-vn4667573; **129 bottom** *AWA Radiola Broadcast Receiver, Model C39, 1927*, Museums Victoria, Item ST 29060; **131** Harris & Ewing, *FDR Radio Broadcast*, between 1933 and 1940, Library of Congress, LC-H21- C-2219; **133 top** *Prime Minister Joseph Lyons Using a Radio Microphone, Sydney*, c.1931, nla.cat-vn6297082, courtesy Fairfax Syndication; **133 bottom** *The Rt. Hon. R.G. Menzies Broadcasting to the Nation the News of the Outbreak of War*, 1939, nla.cat-vn1457047; **135** Russian *Orchestra at 2CH, Sydney*, 1936, nla.cat-vn7827903; **136** *Dave, Mabel, Mum and Dad, Main Characters of Dad and Dave Radio Program*, 1937–1953, nla.cat-vn6449060; **137** M. Michaelis, *Portrait of Lyndall Barbour*, c.1940, nla.cat-vn2625978; **139** *Mantle Model Radio Made by Kriesler in Australia*, Powerhouse Collection, 259627, gift of P. Mulligan, photo. Ordre; **140** *Koori Radio Poster, Gadigal Information Services, 1998–1999*, Powerhouse Collection, 2000/61/1, gift of Steve Miller, photographed by Danica Micallef; **141** Alex Ozolins, *Producer-announcer Vic Kennedy Records a Learn Italian Program for 3ZZ Melbourne with Anna Maria Sabbione and Laura Bregu*, Australian National University Archives, AU ANUA 226-606; **143** Algernon Darge, *Maurice Guillaux in His Bleriot XI Monoplane Holding Aerial Mail Bag at the Agricultural Society's Show Grounds before Flying to Sydney on First Air Mail Delivery, Melbourne*, 1914, nla.cat-vn4941748; **144–145** *Front View of Vickers Vimy Biplane G-EAOU on the Ground with Engines Running*, 1919, nla.cat-vn3722834; **146** *Young Man Holding an Air Mail Bag, Sydney*, 1931, nla.cat-vn6301121, courtesy Fairfax Syndication.

6. War in the Pacific

149 *Look after Your Radio, so Our Boys Can Have These*, c.1943, nla.cat-vn7819260; **151** Howard Burke, *Rabaul, Key to Japan's Offense and Defense in Pacific*, 1942, nla.cat-vn6451653; **152–153** Rand McNally & Co., *International Radio News Map*, 1941, nla.cat-vn5156958; **155** Vernon Jones, *A Spitfire at Darwin*, 1943, State Library of Victoria, H2007.115/37; **156** *Radar Point in Darwin Area*, 1943, National Archives of Australia, MP535/9: NN/55: 32694384; **159** *Oil Storage Tanks Burning after Being Hit during the First Japanese Air Raid on Darwin*, 1942, nla.cat-vn5126064; **161** Ternes, *Your Country Needs You! Join the A.I.F. Now!*, 1940s, nla.cat-vn4702420; **163** *The Japanese Aircraft Carrier Shokaku under Attack by American Aircraft during the Battle of the Coral Sea*, 1942, Australian War Memorial, 148953; **164** *Stalag XX A Prisoners of War Camp, Peeling Vegetables*, 1940, University of Melbourne Library, 2016.0081.00052; **167** *Telegraphist W.G. McCartney, HMAS Vendetta, Contacting Rabaul by Radio*, 1945, Australian War Memorial, 095700; **169** *Transmitter Unit*, 1944, Library & Archives NT, PH0839/0004; **170** *Communications Staff*, 1940, Library & Archives NT, PH0411/0013; **171** *AWA Teleradio 3B2 Transmitter Type IJ50062*, Museum of Applied Arts & Sciences, K409-3/2; **173** *Diploma of Electrical Engineering Awarded to Miss Florence Violet Wallace, 1923*, Museum of Applied Arts & Sciences, K50.

7. TV and the Space Race

175 *AWA Television Receiver, 1956*, Powerhouse Collection, B2015, gift of Mr & Mrs E.A. & V.I. Crome, photographed by Marinco Kojdanovski; **177** Wolfgang Sievers, *Television Assembly at Richardson Television, Victoria*, 1958, nla.cat-vn3311769; **179** *The War of the Worlds*, 1953, commons.wikimedia.org/wiki/File:The_War_of_the_Worlds_(1953_film_poster).jpg, reproduced under CC BY-SA 4.0 creativecommons.org/licenses/by-sa/4.0/deed.en; **180** Музей Космонавтики, *Exploded view of Sputnik, Memorial Museum of Cosmonautics*, 2017, commons.wikimedia.org/wiki/File:Sputnik_1_Exploded_View_3F9A6199_(36924864550)_modified.png, reproduced under CC BY-SA 4.0 creativecommons.org/licenses/by-sa/4.0/deed.en; **181** NASA, *Astronaut Alan B. Shepard Jr. inside Freedom 7 Spacecraft Awaiting Launch*, 1961, commons.wikimedia.org/wiki/File:Alan_Shepard_seen_inside_Freedom_7.jpg, reproduced under CC BY-SA 4.0 creativecommons.org/licenses/by-sa/4.0/deed.en; **183** *Honeysuckle Creek Tracking Station*, 1969, National Archives of Australia, A1500: K20421: 11896250; **184–185** NASA, *Aldrin Looks Back at Tranquility Base*, 1969, www.nasa.gov/multimedia/imagegallery/image_feature_616.html; **187** CSIRO, *Radio Telescope at Parkes*, 1961, nla.cat-vn3627079; **190** *Woomera Rocket Range*, c.1949, State Library of Victoria, H2002.199/3616; **192** NASA, *Voyager 2 Launch*, 1977, NASA Image and Video Library, PIA21744; **193** NASA, *Mission Control Center*, 1969, NASA Image and Video Library, S69-39815.

8. Search, Rescue, Respond

195 *Wreck of the Antelope Packet on a Reef of Rocks, near the Pelew Islands*, 1800s, nla.cat-vn1601778; **197** *The Morning after the Wreck*, 1881, State Library of Victoria, A/

S04/06/81/189; **199** Edward Thomson, *Bluff near Tenterfield, New South Wales*, c.1848, nla.cat-vn638373; **200–201** A. St Aulaire (lithographer), Louis Auguste de Sainson (artist), *La Corvette l'Astrolabe en Perdition sur des Récifs, Tonga-Tabou*, 1833, nla.cat-vn2689376; **202** *Marconi Multiple Radio Tuner, c.1908*, Museums Victoria, Item ST 15459; **203** Graeme Andrews, *HMAS Parramatta*, 1911, City of Sydney Archives, A-00086755; **206** *Ross Smith and Keith Smith in Vickers Vimy Biplane G-EAOU, Calcutta, India*, 1919, nla.cat-vn4926221; **208–209** Broughton Ward & Chaseling, *The Southern Cross on its Arrival in Sydney from the Flight across the Pacific*, 1928, nla.cat-vn2432515; **210** *Tools, Equipment and Supplies next to de Havilland DH61 Giant Moth Biplane Airliner G-AUHW 'Canberra' 6 Miles from Wyndham, Western Australia*, 1929, nla.cat-vn4970359; **211** Mdarcangelo, *Personal Locator Beacon*, 2021, commons.wikimedia.org/wiki/File:Personal_Locator_Beacon.jpg, reproduced under CC BY-SA 4.0: creativecommons.org/licenses/by-sa/4.0/deed.en; **212–213** Tony McDonough, *British Yachtsman, Tony Bullimore Emerging from His Upturned Yacht while Crew Members from HMAS Adelaide Knock on the Opposite Side of the Hull*, 1997, Fairfax Media, FXT37096; **212–217** William Strutt, *Black Thursday, February 6th. 1851*, 1864, State Library of Victoria, H28049; **217 bottom** *Mr and Mrs D. Guard of Sorell Watch the Blazing Remnants of Their Home, Tasmania*, 1967, nla.cat-vn3674562; **219** John Flynn, *Unidentified Woman with Pedal Powered Transceiver and Morse Typewriter*, 1926, nla.cat-vn2401357; **220** Ian Sam James, *Natalie Davey (left) and Bullen Rogers, Hosts of Danggujarra—Good Language, Wangki Yupurnanupurru Radio's Breakfast Show, with Guest Host Carolyn Davey*, courtesy Wangki Yupurnanupurru Radio.

9. The Daily News

223 *The London Gazette*, 14–17 May 1705, page 1, commons.wikimedia.org/wiki/File:London_Gazette(1705).jpg, reproduced under CC BY-SA 4.0 creativecommons.org/licenses/by-sa/4.0/deed.en; **224** *At the Theatre, Sydney on July 30, 1796 Will Be Performed Jane Shore*, 1796, nla.cat-vn4200235; **226** *The Sydney Gazette and New South Wales Advertiser*, 5 March 1803, page 1, trove.nla.gov.au/newspaper/page/5653; **227** S.T. Gill, *Ease without Opulence*, 1860s, nla.cat-vn2930004; **230** Edward William Searle, *Boy Wearing a Bowler Hat beside a Cart Filled with Newspapers and Magazines, Melbourne*, c.1902, nla.cat-vn4654392; **231** *Geelong Advertiser*, 27 April 1915, page 3, trove.nla.gov.au/newspaper/page/13390608; **232** Jim Fitzpatrick, *Drouin Newsagency, Victoria*, c.1944, nla.cat-vn2200601; **236** *Interior of Newspaper Office, Showing Linotype Machine, Singleton, NSW*, 1905, State Library of New South Wales, At Work and Play—05345, **237** Trish Ainslie and Roger Garwood, *Delivering the Newspaper*, 1998, nla.cat-vn1600836, courtesy Trish Ainslie; **237** John Immig, *Worker Sorting Loose Copies*, Chullora, 2000, nla.cat-vn3086595.

10. Screen Time

239 Ern McQuillan, *GIO Computer Centre, Botany, New South Wales*, 1965, nla.cat-vn5978503; **241** Carol Porter, *Anyone Can Use the Internet*, 1996, State Library of Victoria, H2003.90/73; **243** Greg Power, *Margaret Phillips Examines the PANDORA Website with Amy Bartlett*, 2006, nla.cat-vn3891982; **244** *Computer Chip Plot of the First 802.11a PHY Chip (RM11a), c.2000*, Museum of Applied Arts & Sciences, 2020/1/1; **246 top** Sean Davey, *Jessica Berliner, 18, Talks on Her Mobile Phone while 'Texting' on a Friend's Phone*, 2004, nla.cat-vn3354931; **246 bottom** *Telecom Walkabout Mobile Phone*, Powerhouse Collection, 2009/70/1, gift of Jan Batten, photographed by Marinco Kojdanovski; **247** *Unknown Library*, City of Sydney Archives, A-00028605.

11. An Uncertain Future

251 XH4D, *Working in Metaverse*, 2022, iStock image 1383384109.

Following pages: The all-male team works on creating blocks for the next edition of the paper in the composing room of the *Sydney Morning Herald* in about 1930.

Index

Page numbers in **bold** indicate illustrations.

W

Y

SELL IT FOR LESS